COOK
JAPANESE
AT HOME

COOK
JAPANESE
AT HOME

FROM SOBA AND RAMEN TO TERIYAKI AND HOT POTS, 200 EVERYDAY RECIPES USING SIMPLE TECHNIQUES

KIMIKO BARBER

PHOTOGRAPHY BY EMMA LEE

KYLE BOOKS

I dedicate this book for memories of Ratan Engineer and Tom Read

Published in 2017 by Kyle Books
www.kylebooks.com

Distributed by National Book Network
4501 Forbes Blvd, Suite 200,
Lanham, MD 20706
Phone: (800) 462-6420
Fax: (800) 338-4550
customercare@nbnbooks.com

First published in Great Britain in 2016 by
Kyle Books, an imprint of Kyle Cathie Ltd

10 9 8 7 6 5 4 3 2 1

ISBN 978-1-909487-63-5

Text © 2016 Kimiko Barber
Design © 2016 Kyle Books
Photographs © 2016 Emma Lee

Editor: Judith Hannam
Editorial Assisant: Hannah Coughlin
Editorial Adaptation: Lee Faber
Designer: Miranda Harvey
Photographer: Emma Lee
Food Stylist: Aya Nishimura
Prop Stylist: Lucy Attwater
Production: Nic Jones and Gemma John

Library of Congress Control Number: 2016956329

Color reproduction by F1 colour
Printed and bound in China by C&C Offset
Printing Co., Ltd.

CONTENTS

AN INVITATION TO JAPANESE FOOD AND COOKING

Over the past decade or so, Japanese cuisine has gained phenomenal international popularity. When I first arrived in England in the 1970s, there were only a handful of Japanese restaurants, which seemed to exist largely for the benefit of Japanese tourists and lonely businessmen longing for a taste of home. Today, there are over two hundred in central London alone, many of which require booking days, if not weeks, in advance, and boxes of sushi are sold next to sandwiches in supermarkets. How things have changed!

Despite its recognition as a healthy choice—Japan has one of the highest life expectancies in the world—the cuisine is often still perceived as difficult. My aim with this cookbook is to dispel any fears you may have, and to show you just how easy it is to cook Japanese food at home. After all, millions of ordinary Japanese do it every day. As you'll discover, the culinary methods are not so very different, and if you have a reasonably well-equipped kitchen, you won't need any new equipment. Japanese ingredients have also become much easier to find in supermarkets. To begin with, my suggestion is to make just one Japanese dish to serve with your usual meals, perhaps a bowl of miso soup as a starter, plain boiled rice instead of potatoes, or a green salad with a Japanese dressing, and then, as you gain more confidence, to gradually expand your repertoire.

WASHOKU JAPANESE FOOD

What is it that makes a food or a dish Japanese? In 2013, the cuisine was added to the United Nation's cultural heritage list, only the second, after France's, to have been so honored. According to UNESCO's definition, washoku is based on skills, knowledge, practice, and traditions related to the production, processing, preparation, and consumption of food, and is associated with a respect for nature that is closely related to the sustainable use of natural resources.

Written in two Chinese characters, the first, 和, *wa*, refers to all things Japanese, and the second, 食 *shoku*, means food. Coined at the time of the 1868 Meiji Restoration when Japan emerged from over 200 years of self-imposed isolation, and embraced all things Western, washoku is inextricably linked to Japan's natural conditions, geography, and climate as well as its history.

The Japanese archipelago stretches over 1,864 miles, north to south, along the eastern coast of the Asian continent, and is composed of four large islands—*Hokkaido, Honshū, Shikoku,* and *Kyūshū*—plus another three thousand or so smaller islands. The climate ranges from semi-tropical in the south, to cool temperate in the north. The land is 70 percent mountainous or forested, and the population of 127 million is crammed into an area only slightly bigger than the American state of Montana. To make it even more crowded, over 40 percent of the population is squeezed into just three major coastal cities—Tokyo, Nagoya, and Osaka—while only 12 percent of land is agricultural.

Adapting to challenging living conditions, maintaining psychological personal space, rather than physical distance from each other, and following carefully prescribed rules of behavior, have been traditionally accepted ways of dealing with life in a land where overcrowding, and devastating earthquakes, typhoons, volcanic eruptions, and landslides are common. In such an environment, permanence is a difficult quality to achieve, and is, indeed, seldom sought. Instead, Japanese people have learned to adjust to, and esteem, the fleeting moment of being in balance with nature.

It is no coincidence that as well as representing all things Japanese, *wa* also means peace, harmony, balance, mildness, to blend, or to join together. The multiple meanings provide a good clue as to what Japanese food is all about. Japanese cooks are praised for drawing out natural tastes and flavors, rather than adding or imposing man-made ones; also for presenting ingredients in ways that reflect nature.

One of the most striking aspects of Japanese cuisine is the emphasis on seasonality. Every food has 旬, *shun*, a point in time when a particular food is at its best. *Shun* can last for several weeks, even months, or it can be as fleeting as a few hours or days. Eating food that is in season, not only ensures that Japanese tastes are in harmony with natural rhythms, but also that they enjoy the freshest and most plentiful seasonal ingredients. Japan enjoys four distinct seasons, and the land and surrounding seas and ocean currents bring an abundance of vegetables, fruits, and fish. The emphasis on seasonality is not limited to selecting and cooking fresh seasonal ingredients, but also extends to the presentation, with food served in appropriate tableware—pale pastel colored dishes in spring, cool glass bowls in summer, rustic bamboo baskets in autumn, and earthy pottery in winter. There is a Japanese phrase *me de taberu*, literally "eat with your eyes."

The diversity of Japan's climate results in regional cuisines as varied as the land itself. *Hokkaido* is the island that is the least Japan-like. Its wide, open spaces with lakes and mountains is unsuitable for rice cultivation, and so the land is used for growing corn and potatoes, and dairy farming. Its specialties include crabs, scallops, and salmon, as well as *konbu* seaweed, which is the essential ingredient of dashi. There is a huge food divide between the residents of the *Kantō* region (centered around Tokyo and Yokohama) and the *Kansai* region (Kyoto, Osaka, and Kobe). In *Kansai*, seasoning is milder both in color and taste, whereas the Kyoto cuisine prides itself on its delicate sophistication, stemming from its position as the site of the ancient Imperial court. There is an unspoken feeling in western Japan, that in *Kantō* they are heavy-handed with the soy sauce and salt, and a little lacking in refinement. Nagoya, the third largest city, located halfway between Tokyo and Osaka, is known for its flat *kishimen* udon noodles, chickens, and pure soybean *hattchō-miso*. Pilgrims visiting the eighty-eight sacred places around *Shikoku* are offered the island's famous *Sanuki* udon noodles, fresh mackerel bonito, and sweet mandarin oranges. *Kyūshū* is renowned for its tea, fruits, sweet potatoes, and for the Chinese and Western influences that developed from Nagasaki's role

as Japan's only trading center with the outside world during the isolation period. On the islands of *Okinawa*, septuagenarians are considered mere youngsters, and its cuisine features pork, bitter melon called *gōyā*, and tropical fruits and vegetables.

What also distinguishes Japanese food (*washoku*) from Western food (*yōshoku*), is that it is designed to be eaten with chopsticks. These were introduced by the Chinese around the sixth century. Initially, they were used only by the ruling aristocrats who did so to avoid being thought of as "barbaric" by the Chinese for eating with their hands, but by the twelfth century, they had been adopted by most of the population. Other Asian countries—China, Korea, Taiwan, and Vietnam—use chopsticks too, but Japan is unique in not also using spoons. Chopsticks require a level of manual dexterity, and for the food to be cut into small morsels, another reason why, in Japan, food preparation is equally, if not more important, than the actual cooking.

THE EVOLUTION OF JAPANESE CUISINE

Condensing more than 2,000 years of Japanese culinary history into just a few paragraphs is almost impossible, but a few key historical events stand out. The first, and perhaps most important, was the introduction of rice cultivation, believed to have come from China in about 500 B.C. Until the mid nineteenth century, rice was not just a staple, but an alternative currency, and form of taxation. Many would argue that it is the soul of Japan, inextricably bound up with the country's history, politics, and culture; even its national characteristics of being hard working and diligent. Rice cultivation is labor-intensive and time-consuming—the character for rice, 米, incorporates a figure of 88, 八八, as a rice plant needs to be tended to eighty-eight times before producing a single grain. Rice growing also requires community effort; at each key stage, villagers form a production line and help each other. The social unity and cohesion that is essential for its cultivation, is a highly respected virtue, even in today's modern industrialized society. Between 500 B.C. and the third century A.D., rice cultivation became widespread, though differences in soil quality, land management, and skills led to disparities in wealth and power, and resulted in the formation of numerous small countries. By the beginning of the seventh century, central Japan unified under the most able rice farming clan, who became the Imperial Family.

The second most important event was the introduction of Buddhism from China at the beginning of the sixth century. Buddhists are forbidden to kill animals and birds for food, and in 676 A.D. the Emperor banned the slaughter of cows, oxen, and horses used for farming and transport, birds that signaled daybreak, dogs that kept watch during the night, and monkeys that had a sense of closeness to humans. Several more such orders followed, so it is doubtful whether the ban was initially successful, but as Buddhism became more widespread, meat disappeared, and fish and beans became the main sources of protein.

In 794 A.D., the capital moved from Nara to *Heian-kyō* (present day Kyoto). During the *Heian* period (794 to 1192), as China went into a decline, Japan moved away from Chinese influences. Toward the end of the period, power struggles among the ruling *Fujiwara* led to the rise of the martial element, personified by the samurai. Once employed by the aristocracy as lowly palace guards, they now emerged as the new ruling class. In 1192, *Minamoto Yoritomo* was granted Imperial permission to set up a military government in Kamakura (40 miles south-west of Tokyo). It was during this period that eating three meals a day became popular. The *Kamakura* period lasted just over one hundred years, and was then followed by more than two hundred years of political upheaval until, in 1603, *Tokugawa Ieyasu* unified the country, and established a military government in Edo (present-day Tokyo). In the late twelfth century, austere Zen sects arrived from China, bringing with them *shōjin ryōri*, a strict Buddhist vegan cuisine, but also *ten jin*—little snacks eaten between meals—a new cooking method of deep-frying with oil, and, most notably, the reintroduction of tea. Zen Buddhism became popular among the ruling samurai class (although the more pragmatic of them continued to eat meat), with the result that Zen influence was far-reaching, and its emphasis on certain tastes, colors, cooking techniques, and presentations lives on today.

Tea was first introduced to Japan from China in the sixth century, but was popular only with the aristocracy, who drank it for medicinal purposes. It was reintroduced by the Zen monk *Eizai*, founder of the *Rinzai* sect, in 1191,

who brought seeds, and by the fourteenth century, it had become the most important non-alcoholic drink. Another Zen monk, *Murata Junkō*, established the Tea Ceremony, incorporating the Zen philosophy of *wabi* (serenity) and *sabi* (rustic simplicity). Around the second half of the sixteenth century, *Sen-no-Rikyū* instituted rules governing every aspect, elevating the act of making a cup of tea into high art. It is impossible to overstate the influence of the Tea Ceremony on almost all aspects of Japanese culture, The Way of Tea also led to two important aspects of Japanese cuisine: *cha kaiseki*, Japanese haute cuisine designed to be served as a light meal before a tea ceremony, and *wagashi*, traditional confectionary that is served with tea.

In 1543 A.D., a Chinese boat with Portuguese passengers was shipwrecked off the coast of *Kyūshū*, prompting nearly a century of trading with Europe, until, in 1633, Japan again closed its doors. To Japanese eyes, Europeans were large, clumsy, and hairy, but trading with them brought new foods and drinks, including cane sugar, potato, sweet potato, kabocha squash, bread, sponge cake, wine, and the most famous culinary import of all, tempura, arguably the best example of how Japanese cuisine adopts something from abroad and transforms it into a Japanese dish.

The Japanese cuisine as we know it today was established during the *Edo* Period in the seventeenth century. A strict caste system was imposed to restore political stability, with samurai at the top, followed first by farmers (almost 90 percent of the population), and then craftsmen, leaving merchants and traders, who posed a potential economic threat, at the bottom. Although socially the second tier, farmers, were prohibited, except on a few special occasions, from eating rice. This led to the rise of noodles, especially *soba* noodles, as *soba* (buckwheat) is not only fast-growing (seventy-five days from sowing to harvest), but can also be grown almost anywhere.

The self-imposed isolation also reinforced the Buddhist vegetarian diet. The nation looked inward, and enjoyed a period of stability and prosperity. Farmers grew more rice, which not only meant more food, but also more sake and rice vinegar. The latter transformed the sushi-making process from weeks or months of long, slow, natural fermentation, to a few hours. *Hako-zushi*, box sushi, was the most popular, and used wooden molds

to press vinegar-flavored rice into shapes. Equally popular in Edo was *nigiri-zushi*, hand-formed sushi, thought to have been invented by a chef called *Yōhei* (family names were allowed only for the samurai class) in the 1820s to 1830s. Many sushi chefs in Edo copied it, calling it *Edomae-zushi* (meaning in front of *Edo*, referring to the Bay of Tokyo). Elsewhere, regional specialties were popular, including *battera*, an Osaka specialty of cured mackerel pressed sushi, and *funa-zushi*, slow fermented carp from the Lake *Biwa*, which is believed to be similar to the earliest form of sushi.

The arrival of Commodore Perry and four American battleships in 1853, resulted in the beginning of the *Meiji* Period (1868 to 1912), and a desire to modernize. The reopening of foreign trade brought a wave of new foods, including cabbages, onions, tomatoes, peaches, apples, coffee, milk, and beer. More significantly, it heralded the end of starvation as the main cause of death—contrary to popular belief, Japan didn't grow enough rice until the 1960s, when demand fell, due to the popularity of a more Westernized diet. Initially, the speed and ferocity of modernization was astonishing. Fortunately, as the nation became better informed and gained more confidence, the new arrivals settled into a place. Dishes such as *karei-raisu*, curry and rice, *korokke*, croquettes, *tonkatsu*, breaded pork cutlets, *omu-raisu*, omelet wrapped rice, and *ebi-furai* (deep-fried shrimp), were typical homestyle cooking of the *Meiji* era, and they remain family favorites today.

In the boom and bust years that followed the Second World War, many predicted the decline of Japanese food culture, citing the electric rice cooker, instant cup noodles, instant miso soup, and takeout fast food as the cause. Yet the numerous cooking programs on television, and the huge number of cookbooks, confirm that modern Japanese are still very interested in the preparation of good food at home. The desire to adapt outside influences to local tastes has never waned, and has produced such unique fusions of East and West as green tea ice cream, seaweed-flavored potato chips, and cod-roe spaghetti. Having relinquished its proud second position in the world economic ranking to China, Japan's confidence has taken a knock, but it has made the nation more humble and led to a reassessment of traditional values, including the way we cook and eat. Simple home cooked food is once again rising.

APPETIZERS

HIJIKI AND DEEP-FRIED TOFU IN SOY
HIJIKI TO AGE NO NIMONO

Hijiki, a dark edible seaweed, is popular and highly nutritious. It contains twice as much calcium as *konbu*, kelp, and is also rich in iron and magnesium. It is high in fiber, aiding healthy digestion, and helping to reduce blood pressure. Outside Japan, it is sold dried, and needs to be soaked and softened before cooking.

SERVES 4

1¾ ounces dried *hijiki*, preferably softer
  me-hijiki variety
2 *aburaage*, deep-fried tofu
½ tablespoon vegetable oil
1 medium carrot, pared, and cut into julienne strips
½ tablespoon sugar
scant 1 cup Dashi (see page 29)
2 to 3 tablespoons soy sauce
1 tablespoon toasted white sesame seeds

Rinse the *hijiki* in plenty of water, then soak in a bowl of warm water for 20 minutes, and drain.

Place the deep-fried tofu in a strainer, pour over boiling water to degrease, then pat dry, and cut into small strips.

Heat the oil in a large deep-sided skillet or wok over medium heat, add the *hijiki*, and sauté for 2 to 3 minutes before adding the tofu and carrot. Cook for an additional 1 to 2 minutes, then add the sugar and cook for 4 to 5 minutes before adding the dashi and soy sauce. Reduce the heat to very low, and place a drop-lid (see page 134), or an improvised cover with cooking foil, on the pan and simmer for 20 to 30 minutes or until the cooking juice is reduced by a third. Remove from the heat, add the sesame seeds, and let it cool in the pan with the lid in place. It is during this cooling down period that the flavors develop.

This dish is typically served at room temperature, but if you prefer it hot, reheat briefly just before serving. It will keep, covered and refrigerated, for up to 5 days.

CHILLED TOFU
HIYAYAKKO

Tofu is soybean curd. Soybeans are soaked in water, crushed, boiled, and strained to make soymilk, then coagulated with traditional *nigari*, bittern, which mostly consists of magnesium chloride of traditionally made sea salt (see note on tofu, page 156). Tofu is rich in well-balanced soy protein, but low in calories and carbohydrates, it's completely fat free, and an ideal health food. In Japan, tofu is used fresh, usually on the day it is made. In the West, however, tofu can be kept for a few days in fresh water and chilled in the fridge. Chilled tofu, with a dash of soy sauce and various choice toppings, is one of the classics.

SERVES 4
about 3½ ounces soft silken tofu per person

FOR THE TOPPINGS
chopped scallions
grated fresh ginger
thinly sliced *shiso*, perilla leaves
katsuo-bushi, dried bonito flakes
umeboshi, pickled plum
chirimenjako, dried small young sardines or
  anchovies diced tomato with basil leaves
crispy bacon bits
scrambled egg and peppercress
chopped olives

Remove the tofu from its packaging and drain by letting it stand on an angled cutting board for 10 to 15 minutes. Then cut into four equal-size blocks, and garnish with toppings of your choice.

Instead of presenting the tofu into blocks, you may also roughly crumble it, and serve in small cups with teaspoons.

SAVORY EGG TOFU
TAMAGO-DŌFU

A deliciously light, savory egg custard, delicate and smooth, that is usually served chilled. Although this dish is named "tofu", due to its soft, smooth texture, tofu is not an ingredient in this dish. The one simple rule to follow if adjusting this recipe to serve any number, is to use equal amounts of dashi to the volume of beaten eggs. In Japan, it is usually served with the edible garnish of *shiso* (perilla) flowers, which are sadly difficult to find outside the country. Cherry tomatoes, and basil are useful substitutes.

SERVES 4

6 eggs, beaten (about 1¼ cups)
1¼ cups Dashi or Vegetarian Dashi
  (see pages 29 to 31)
½ tablespoon salt
1½ tablespoons mirin (fermented sweet rice wine)
3 tablespoons light soy sauce

TO GARNISH
2 baby cherry tomatoes, halved
4 basil leaves

Line an 8-inch square baking pan (a chocolate brownie pan is ideal because of its clean edges) with aluminum foil, so that the foil extends over two opposite sides of the pan by 2 inches at each end. Make sure the foil is not wrinkled at the bottom, and do not oil or butter.

Beat the eggs thoroughly, then pour through a fine mesh strainer into a large bowl. In another larger bowl, mix the dashi, salt, mirin, and soy sauce until the salt is dissolved completely. Stir the eggs into the dashi mixture until evenly mixed. Pour the mixture through a fine mesh strainer again back into the bowl, ensuring it is thoroughly combined.

Gently pour the egg mixture into the prepared pan and spoon off any tiny bubbles on the surface. Place the pan in a bain marie, resting it on chopsticks or a folded towel, so that the bottom of the pan is insulated from the base of the bain marie. Insulate further by placing more folded towels around the sides of the pan. Cover the pan by gently placing a single sheet of crinkled foil over the top like a tent. All those protective measures are to ensure that the tofu is only cooked by an even, mild heat to give a soft and smooth texture. Fill the bain marie with hot water halfway up the sides of the pan.

Put the pan and bain marie in a steamer, and steam over high heat for 3 minutes. Reduce the heat to low, and continue steaming for an additional 25 minutes. Or, if you don't have a large steamer, place the arrangement in a large baking tray filled with hot water up to just below the depth of the arrangement, and place in a preheated 425°F oven for 30 minutes. The tofu is done when a toothpick inserted into the center comes out clean. Do not worry about any clear broth seeping out of the hole made by the toothpick—this will reseal. The custard should not be dry or firm, but wobble a little if you tap the side. Carefully lift the pan out of the steamer or the oven, and let it cool down a little before refrigerating overnight.

To serve, lift out the custard by picking up the two ends of the foil, and transferring to a cutting board, still resting on the foil. Cut into four blocks. Place each block in an individual dish. Garnish with one half a cherry tomato and one basil leaf in the center of each block and serve.

BROILED EGGPLANT WITH SEASONED MISO
NASU-DENGAKU

The rather bland, spongy flesh of eggplant is another ideal canvas for the robust dengaku miso. As eggplants found in the West tend to be much bigger than their Japanese counterparts, I allow half per person.

SERVES 4

2 eggplants
2 tablespoons vegetable oil
½ recipe *dengaku* miso of your choice (see page 24)
2 teaspoons poppy seeds, to garnish

Preheat the broiler to high. Leave the stems on the eggplants, as they look attractive, and cut in half lengthwise. Prick the eggplants all over, and score the cut surface in a criss-cross pattern (this will help them soak up the miso topping). Heat the oil in a large skillet over medium heat, and cook the eggplant, cut-side down, for 8 to 10 minutes, or until tender. Spread the miso topping on the cut side, sprinkle with the poppy seeds, and place under the broiler for 2 to 3 minutes, until lightly browned.

SPINACH AND TOFU JELLY

This is a very pretty, delicious and healthy starter that you can prepare in advance. *Kanten* (agar-agar) is the Japanese equivalent of gelatin, but is made from a seaweed called Ceylon moss, and hence vegetarian. It is also ten times more coagulant and completely fat and calorie-free. Because it is rich in calcium, iron and edible fiber, it's an ideal food if you're looking for something on the lighter side.

SERVES 4

9 ounces spinach
3½ ounces soft silken tofu
1⅛ cups Dashi (see page 29)
1 teaspoon *kanten*, agar-agar powder
1 tablespoon sugar
2 teaspoons sake
½ teaspoon salt
drizzle of tamari soy sauce, to serve

Cook the spinach in salted boiling water for 30 seconds, and drain very well. With a food mixer or food processor, blitz the cooked spinach into a thick paste. Roughly break up the tofu with your hands.

Put the dashi and *kanten* in a saucepan and dissolve over medium heat. Bring to a boil for 2 minutes. Add the tofu, sugar, sake, and salt. When the tofu begins to float to the surface, turn off the heat. Add the spinach and stir once or twice, to mix through, then pour the mixture into a mold (6 × 8 × 1½ inches) to set at room temperature, before transferring to the fridge to chill until ready to serve.

Cut into thick slices, and serve with a drizzle of tamari soy sauce.

NOTE ON TAMARI

Tamari is a type of soy sauce, but unlike dark or light soy sauce, it is made of pure soybeans, with no addition of wheat. It is dark, thick, and slightly sweet in taste, and used for dipping sashimi and sushi.

DASHI-SOAKED SPINACH
HŌRENSŌ NO OHITASHI

Ohitashi is a popular and classic way to serve vegetables such as spinach, cabbage, or bean sprouts. They are soaked in a dashi-based broth to enhance their natural flavors, as well as allowing them to soak up the subtle flavor of the broth. This dish is normally served with garnishes such as toasted sesame seeds, *katsuobshi*, or *chirimenjako*.

SERVES 4

FOR THE SOAKING BROTH
scant 1 cup Dashi or Vegetarian Dashi
  (see pages 29 to 31)
pinch of salt
1 teaspoon mirin
2 teaspoons soy sauce

FOR THE SPINACH
14 ounces spinach
1 teaspoon salt

OPTIONAL GARNISHES
white sesame seeds, freshly dry-toasted
katsuobushi, dried bonito flakes
chirimenjako, dried small young sardines or anchovies

Put the dashi in a saucepan, and briefly bring to a boil, then add the rest of the broth ingredients. Remove from the heat, transfer to a metal bowl, then force-cool by placing the metal bowl in a larger bowl filled with ice water. Swirl it around, then set aside to cool.

While the broth is cooling down, blanch the spinach in salted water for 2 to 3 minutes. Drain and rinse under cold running water until cold, then drain well by gently wringing with your hands. Cut the spinach into 2-inch lengths. Add the spinach to the cooled broth and mix. You may prepare to this point and keep refrigerated for up to 6 hours.

To serve, take the spinach out of the broth, lightly drain, then divide between 4 individual dishes. Drizzle some broth over the spinach, and garnish with sesame seeds, *katsuobushi*, or *chirimenjako*.

COOK'S TIP
Try the same technique with other vegetables instead of the spinach, such as cabbage, Napa cabbage, green beans, asparagus, or bean sprouts, adjusting the cooking time accordingly.

Sesame seeds are sold either ready-toasted or raw. To dry-toast raw ones which are flat in appearance, put the seeds in a nonstick skillet over medium heat, while gently shaking the pan, until the seeds begin to jump, and a nutty aroma rises.

CUCUMBER AND WAKAME WITH VINEGAR
SUNO-MONO

Suno-mono, literally "vinegar flavored things," is often found on Japanese menus where seasoned rice vinegar is matched with fresh seasonal ingredients, which are often raw, or briefly prepared.

SERVES 4

FOR THE SANBAI-ZU
scant ½ cup rice vinegar
1½ tablespoons sugar
1 teaspoon light soy sauce
½ teaspoon salt

FOR THE SALAD
2 tablespoons dried wakame seaweed
2 teaspoons salt
2 Japanese *or* hothouse cucumbers
2 tablespoons white crabmeat
2 teaspoons red pickled ginger, or pink sushi ginger

Mix the *sanbai-zu* ingredients in a glass jar, and set aside.

Put the wakame seaweed in a small glass bowl, and cover with cold water to soak for about 10 minutes.

In another bowl, mix the salt with 2¼ cups cold water until dissolved. Thinly slice the cucumbers, and put them in the mild salt water for about 5 to 7 minutes—this refreshes the cucumber, and makes them tender yet crispy, as well as brightening the green color.

Drain the wakame by squeezing by hand, and roughly cut into manageable lengths. Drain the cucumber slices well, and pat them dry with paper towels.

Put all the salad ingredients in a large glass bowl, and add the *sanbai-zu* and toss lightly—do not overdo this, as it will make the finished dish watery. Divide between four, preferably glass dishes, and serve immediately.

CUCUMBER AND TUNA WITH SPICY SANBAI-ZU

Here is a variation on the above recipe with a bit of kick.

SERVES 4
4 Japanese or hothouse cucumbers
1 teaspoon salt
5 ounce can tuna in spring water, drained

FOR SPICY SANBAI-ZU
4 tablespoons *sanbai-zu* (see above)
1 teaspoon toasted sesame oil
¼ to ½ teaspoon *shichimi-tōgarashi*,
   seven-spice chili powder

Roughly chop the cucumbers into small bite-size pieces, and put in a glass bowl. Sprinkle the salt over, and with your hand squeeze and mix for a minute or two, then drain the liquid that comes out. Rinse the cucumbers under cold running water, and drain well.

In a large bowl, mix the *sanbai-zu* with the sesame oil and chili powder. Add the cucumbers and the drained tuna into the bowl, and mix and lightly drain before dividing into four portions to serve.

JAPANESE-STYLE SHRIMP COCKTAIL

This is an adaptation of a dish I came across in a small restaurant in Tokyo.

SERVES 4

2 red onions
2 avocados, ripe, but not too soft
2 tablespoons rice vinegar
7 ounces cooked large shrimp,
    without shells and heads
a few sprigs of flat-leaf parsley to garnish

FOR THE WASABI SOY

2 teaspoons wasabi powder
1 teaspoon sugar
2 tablespoons soy sauce

Thinly slice the onions, and soak in ice water for 8 to 10 minutes, then drain.

Cut the avocados in half and remove the pit. Peel the skin, and cut the flesh into bite-size pieces. Put the avocado pieces in a glass, or non-reactive bowl, and sprinkle over the vinegar to stop it discoloring.

Mix the ingredients for the wasabi soy in a small bowl.

Put the onions, avocado, and shrimp in a large mixing bowl, pour the wasabi soy over, then lightly mix to coat.

Divide between four glasses, garnish with parsley leaves, and serve immediately.

SAVORY JAPANESE PANCAKE
OKONOMI-YAKI

Okonomi literally means "choice," and the dish is loosely translated as a savory Japanese pancake. Although it is said that *Sen-no-Rikyū*, the founder of the Tea Ceremony, invented it back in the late sixteenth century, *okonomi-yaki* as we recognize it today, became a popular, cheap snack after the Second World War.

In Japan, there are many regional varieties, and specialty restaurants are equipped with hot plate tables. But you don't need any special equipment to enjoy this highly versatile dish. This is a basic recipe that you can expand, using any filling ingredients of your choice, such as shrimp, squid, scallops, canned tuna, ham, chicken, or ground beef.

SERVES 4

FOR THE BATTER

6 tablespoons all-purpose flour
scant ½ cup Dashi (see page 29), or 2 tablespoons
    soy sauce and 4½ tablespoons water

FOR THE FILLING

2 tablespoons vegetable oil
7 ounces Savoy cabbage, finely shredded
2 eggs, lightly beaten
2 scallions, finely chopped
2 teaspoons grated fresh ginger
4 slices unsmoked bacon, halved lengthwise

FOR THE TOPPING

okonomi sauce (A1 or Worcestershire sauce are
    good substitutes)
aonori, dried nori powder, or crushed nori
a handful of *katsuobushi*, dried bonito flakes

Start by preparing the batter. Put the flour in a bowl, and whisk in half the dashi, or soy and water mixture. Add the remaining liquid, and continue to whisk until the batter is smooth and lump-free. Cover the bowl with plastic wrap, and set aside for 30 minutes. It is important to allow the batter to rest—this will make it taste less powdery, and produce a smooth and light pancake.

Put half the cabbage in a large bowl, add the batter, and mix well. Add the eggs, and the rest of the cabbage with the scallions and ginger, and continue stirring, then divide the mixture into four equal portions.

Heat a large nonstick skillet with ½ tablespoon of oil. With a large serving spoon, spread about two-thirds of one batter portion into the hot skillet and, using the back of the spoon, spread it out to about a 6-inch circle (it will get bigger as it cooks). Add the rest of the batter portion on top, and spread it out. Place one quarter of the bacon to cover the top, and cook the pancake over high heat for 2 to 3 minutes. Use two flat spatulas to turn over the pancake, and continue to cook for an additional 4 to 5 minutes. Remove from the heat and keep warm, while you repeat the process to cook three more pancakes.

Spread the *okonomi* sauce evenly over the pancakes, using the back of a spoon, then sprinkle over the *aonori* and bonito flakes, and serve.

YAKITORI

These delectable little bits of chicken and vegetables broiled on skewers hardly needs any introduction. *Yakitori* is a very popular snack served with drinks, and makes a perfect hot appetizer. The sauce keeps well up to a month, and can be used for barbecue dishes.

SERVES 4

FOR THE YAKITORI SAUCE
9 ounces chicken bones
2½ cups sake
⅔ cup dark soy sauce
1⅛ cups tamari soy sauce
scant ⅔ cup sugar

FOR THE SKEWERS
7 ounces chicken thigh fillets, cut into
    twelve even pieces
2 baby leeks or thick scallions, white part only,
    cut into eight short lengths
8 baby corn, halved
8 asparagus spears, cut into 2-inch length pieces
12 small shiitake mushroom caps
shichimi-tōgarashi, seven-spice chili powder
16 bamboo skewers, soaked in water for
    at least 1 hour

COOK'S TIP
Any leftover sauce will keep in a sterilized jam jars placed in the refrigerator for up to a month.

For the sauce, wash the chicken bones under running water, drain, and pat them dry. Place the bones on a lightly greased baking pan. Preheat the broiler to 400°F and broil for 15 to 20 minutes, turning over once, or until any flesh still left on the bones turns white in color.

Put the sake in a large saucepan, and bring to a boil to burn off the alcohol. Add the broiled bones and the remaining ingredients, and simmer until the liquid has reduced by one-third. Skim off any scum, strain, and let it cool to room temperature before transferring into a sterilized glass container.

Reduce the broiler to 350°F, and drain the skewers.

To make the chicken skewers, thread three pieces of chicken and two pieces of leek onto each of four skewers, starting with a piece of chicken, and alternating with leek. Brush each skewer with the *yakitori* sauce, and set them aside.

To make baby corn skewers, thread four pieces onto each of four skewers, brush them with the *yakitori* sauce, and set them aside.

To make asparagus skewers, allow four pieces for each skewer, brush them with the *yakitori* sauce, and set them aside.

To make shiitake mushroom skewers, thread three caps onto each of four skewers, brush them with the *yakitori* sauce, and set them aside.

Place all the skewers under the hot broiler for 2 to 3 minutes, turn over, brush them with the sauce, then cook for an additional 1 to 2 minutes. Remove all the skewers from the broiler, except the chicken, and baste them with the sauce. Keep them warm. Continue to cook the chicken skewers for another 2 to 3 minutes.

Arrange the skewers on a large plate, brush on both sides with more sauce, sprinkle with chili powder, and serve.

BROILED TOFU WITH SEASONED MISO
TOFU-DENGAKU

The term *dengaku* derives from the ancient agricultural ritual music of the same name, where the musicians dressed in white, and danced to pray for a good rice harvest. The traditional method requires specially designed flat bamboo skewers and careful handling of delicate tofu, which is rather tricky, so I have adapted the recipe using a broiler without skewers to suit Western home kitchens.

SERVES 4

FOR THE DENGAKU MISO TOPPINGS *(pick white or red)*

FOR THE WHITE MISO
heaping ¾ cup white or light-colored miso
2 egg yolks
2 tablespoons sake
2 tablespoons mirin
2 tablespoons sugar
7 tablespoons Water Dashi or Vegetarian Dashi
   (see page 31)

FOR THE RED MISO
⅔ cup red or dark-colored miso
3 tablespoons white miso
2 egg yolks
2 tablespoons sake
2 tablespoons mirin
2 tablespoons sugar
7 tablespoons Water or Vegetarian Dashi
   (see page 31)

FRAGRANT SEASONINGS *(choose one of the below)*
ground toasted white or black sesame seeds,
   for a nutty flavor
grated rind of *yuzu*, lemon, or lime,
   for a refreshing taste
grated fresh ginger, for mild heat

FOR THE TOFU
7 ounces firm tofu
poppy seeds, toasted
white or black sesame seeds, to garnish

As it is almost impossible to make *dengaku* miso toppings in small quantities, and as they keep well refrigerated for a few weeks, prepare them in advance and use as needed.

The method is the same for the white or red miso topping: combine the miso in a double boiler with the egg yolks, sake, mirin, and sugar. Put the pot over hot water, and heat gently to keep the water simmering. Gradually add the dashi, and stir until the mixture thickens and turns glossy, then turn off the heat. Just before turning off the heat, add one of the fragrant seasonings of your choice, varying the quantity according to taste, and mix well.

Cut the tofu block into four blocks and then slice each block in half to make 8 pieces. Place the pieces on a cutting board lined with paper towels. Put a chopstick under one end of the board to prop it up at an angle, so that the liquid can run down, cover the tofu pieces with more paper towels, and place a baking pan on top of the tofu as a weight. Leave the tofu to drain for 10 to 15 minutes. The tofu pieces should feel quite firm to handle.

Preheat the broiler to high. Broil the tofu for about 3 minutes on each side, or until the surface is speckled brown, and the tofu is heated through. Remove from the broiler, and spread one side of each piece of tofu with the miso topping, about 1/16 to 1/8-inch thick, sprinkle with your chosen garnish, and return to the broiler for 1 to 2 minutes. Serve two pieces per person.

SOUPS, SASHIMI, AND SALADS

SOUPS SHIRU-MONO

In Japanese the entire category of soups is known as *shiru-mono*, literally "liquid things," that includes both consommé-type clear, and thick soups, with the latter being by far the largest group. Soups occupy an important and prominent position in Japanese cuisine—the most basic format of a Japanese meal is "*ichi-jū i-ssai*," one soup and one side dish to accompany the main rice. While in an elaborate multi-course banquet, soups appear at both the beginning and the end, and sometimes at the midpoint as a palate cleanser, like sorbet. It is often said that such a clear soup is impressive in its purity and restraint, a showpiece for a professional chef, while a simple bowl of miso soup is otherwise known as "mother's taste," which no restaurant chefs can match.

Although I believe in a minimalist approach to kitchen equipment, and encourage use of what you already have, maybe with a little improvisation, in order to maximize the pleasure of Japanese soups, especially clear types, lidded lacquer bowls are a great investment. With a lidded bowl, one gets to enjoy a clear soup three times—first in keen anticipation diners remove the cover, second, a cloud of exquisite fragrant steam rises, and finally in the middle of the clear broth floats an elegant arrangement, perhaps a bite-size slice of young bamboo shoot sitting among wakame seaweed with a tiny fragrant sprig of *sansho* pepper leaves called *kinome,* or a pink curl of shrimp nestled next to a beautifully shaped slice of winter melon, and a sliver of citrus rind set at a jaunty angle. Soups, especially clear ones, are both simple in their clarity, as well as the ultimate expression of sophistication in their restraint.

Sui-mono, clear soup, is made according to a deceptively simple formula: stock and usually three solid elements that lend texture, flavor, color, and aroma. The first is the main component, often consisting of a bite-size piece of fish, or part of the fish head, with the eye reserved for the guest of honor, shellfish, chicken, egg, tofu, or a cooked vegetable such as bamboo shoot. The second will visually complement the first with vegetables, mushrooms, or seaweed, and there are many prescribed combinations. For example, paper-thin squares of nori go well with bamboo shoot; slices of mushroom with shellfish; julienned strips of boiled burdock with porgy, and so on. But the pairing combination need not be bound by convention, and the cook can create his or her own complementary combinations. The third element is purely for aroma and fragrance, and is often not to be eaten. These garnishes include *mitsuba*, trefoil, *kinome*, tender leaves of Japanese pepper, *yuzu*, or lemon zest.

Alongside elegant clear soups, there is the large category of "thick" soups, which includes miso soups, and other hearty soups full of meat, fish, and vegetables that are more like Western stews. Paraphrasing M.F.K. Fisher, miso is to Japanese cooking what butter is to French cuisine, and olive oil is to Italian cooking. Beneath miso's omnipresence in the Japanese kitchen lies a wealth of common sense—it not only takes just a few minutes to prepare, but a typical serving provides about one-sixth of the adult daily requirement of protein. Furthermore, it is impossible for miso soup to be boring—with almost endless choices of both seasonal and all-year-round ingredients.

A bowl of soup in Japan, whether it's a sophisticated clear soup, or a rustic miso soup, always begins with good dashi.

DASHI—THE INVISIBLE FOUNDATION OF JAPANESE CUISINE

There is a saying in Japan that food is to be eaten with the eye—meaning that it should not only taste good, but also be a feast for the eye. But there is one element that is not apparent to the eye called "dashi," the stock that forms the foundation of, and invisibly penetrates, much of Japanese cuisine.

Dashi, unlike Western stock where simple ingredients are simmered for a long time, is instead a selection of carefully prepared ingredients that are briefly soaked in water, or heated so as to extract nothing other than the very essence of the ingredients' flavor. Indeed, the correct term of making dashi is "to draw" it.

Dashi most commonly uses a combination of *konbu*, kelp, and *katsuobushi* (dried bonito flakes), but other ingredients such as dried shiitake mushrooms, or *niboshi* (small dried fish) are also used. In general, there are two types—*ichiban* (primary) dashi and *niban* (secondary) dashi.

In Japanese cuisine, dashi provides a subtle undertone to almost all foods. It is not an overstatement to say that dashi is at the heart of Japanese cuisine, not because of the prominence of its own flavor, but because of the way it enhances and harmonizes the flavors of other ingredients. The quintessence of Japanese cooking is not to change, nor to impose, but to enhance and harmonize the taste and flavor of natural ingredients.

Before the age of instant seasonings, almost every Japanese meal began with making fresh dashi from scratch. Today, most Japanese home cooks rely on instant dashi, packaged granules that dissolve in hot water, generically called *dashi-no-moto*, and you probably will turn to this instant method also. Although some are excellent, nothing compares with the subtle flavor and delicate aroma of freshly-made dashi. I believe it is important that you understand the traditional method, especially when it is neither difficult nor time consuming.

PRIMARY DASHI
ICHIBAN DASHI

Ichiban dashi is delicate-tasting with an exquisite aroma. It is mainly used in clear consommé-type soups for its fragrance, and as a stock base for simmered and steamed dishes. Well-made *ichiban* dashi is so delicious and fragrant, it is good enough to drink on its own. *Ichiban* dashi does not keep well as the aroma fades if left to stand, so make it just before it is needed, and use it immediately. It takes less than 15 minutes.

MAKES 4¼ CUPS

1 postcard-size piece of dried kelp
4¼ cups soft mineral water or filtered water, left to stand overnight, or boiled, then cooled to disperse any chlorine smell
1 ounce *katsuobushi*, dried bonito flakes

Place the kelp and water in a saucepan. Gently heat, uncovered, to just below boiling point where tiny bubbles begin to appear—this should take about 10 to 12 minutes. Don't allow the water to reach a full boil, and if necessary, add ¼ cup of water to keep the temperature steady. Kelp emits a strong odor, and will discolor the water if boiled, so remove it immediately when the bubbles start to appear, and set aside. Bring the water to a rapid boil briefly, add ¼ cup cold water, and turn off the heat. Add the bonito flakes, but do not stir, and allow the flakes to settle naturally on the bottom of the pan. Skim off any scum that has risen to the surface. Strain the dashi through a cheesecloth-lined strainer and use immediately. Reserve the bonito flakes and kelp for Secondary Dashi (see page 30).

NOTE

In this book where dashi is listed as an ingredient, it refers to primary dashi unless otherwise stated.

SECONDARY DASHI NIBAN-DASHI

While primary dashi holds the namesake prime position because of its fragrance, subtle flavor, and clarity, secondary dashi is versatile as a basic seasoning for many dishes including soups, noodle broths, cooking stock for vegetables, dipping sauces, and salad dressing.

MAKES ABOUT 4¼ CUPS

katsuobushi, bonito flakes, and kelp, reserved from Primary Dashi (see page 29 or tip below)

6¼ cups soft mineral or tap water, left to stand overnight, or boiled then cooled, to disperse any chloric smell

½ ounce *katsuobushi,* dried bonito flakes

Put the reserved bonito flakes and kelp in a large saucepan with the water and heat gently, uncovered, until just below boiling point when tiny bubbles begin to appear. Reduce the heat, and simmer gently for 15 to 20 minutes, until the liquid has reduced by about one-third. Add the dried bonito flakes, and immediately remove from the heat. Allow a few minutes for the flakes to settle at the bottom of the pan, then strain through a cheesecloth-lined strainer, and wring thoroughly to squeeze out every drop.

Unlike its older brother, secondary dashi can be stored in the fridge for 2 days, or frozen for up to 3 months in an airtight container.

TIP

If you just want to make secondary dashi alone from fresh, put a postcard-size piece of dried kelp, 1 ounce of bonito flakes and 6¼ cups of cold water in a saucepan, and heat gently over medium heat. Reduce the heat when small bubbles begin to appear, and try to maintain the water temperature at a steady simmer for 4 to 5 minutes (add ¼ cup of cold water if necessary to keep the temperature steady). Strain through a cheesecloth-lined strainer, and the dashi is ready for use.

WATER DASHI
MIZU-DASHI

Since the flavor and nutrients of kelp infuse water, it is actually not necessary to heat it to make dashi. Soaking for around 8 hours yields a delicious dashi. Because of the simplicity of the method, it is of paramount importance to choose the best quality kelp possible—look out for thick, wide (no less than six inches across) leaves, in dark, rich amber, with whitish powder encrusting the surface. Also the quality of water is important—if possible use soft mineral water, such as Polish Spring water or Volvic. Do not leave the kelp soaking for more than eight hours, as in addition to the glutamate which gives the most umami, other unwanted substances like alginic acid and minerals also seep out and discolor the water, and the water becomes glutinous. Good quality kelp can be reused up to three times for this method.

MAKES 4¼ CUPS

1 postcard-size piece of dried kelp
4¼ cups soft mineral or tap water, left to stand overnight, or boiled then cooled, to disperse any chloric smell

Wipe the kelp lightly with a clean damp cloth. Fill a large glass bowl with the water, and add the kelp. Let it stand to soak at room temperature for 8 hours.

VEGETARIAN DASHI
SHŌJIN-DASHI

Shōjin-dashi is a fish-free stock suitable for any vegetarian dishes, and features widely in the *Shōjin* cuisine—Buddhist vegetarian cooking. It can be made with many varieties of dried vegetables, such as dried gourd (calabash) strips, dried soybeans, and *kiriboshi daikon* (dried *daikon*), but the most popular combination is dried shiitake mushrooms and kelp. While water dashi is delicate and delicious, for some it lacks in depth, but with an addition of dried shiitake mushrooms, this vegetarian dashi has fuller flavor.

MAKES 5 CUPS

3 to 4 dried shiitake mushrooms
scant 1 cup boiling water
1 postcard-size piece of dried kelp
4¼ cups cold soft mineral water

Place the mushrooms in a bowl, pour the boiling water over, and leave for 10 to 15 minutes to soak.

Meanwhile, put the kelp in a saucepan with the cold water, and heat over gentle heat, until tiny bubbles begin to appear; this should take about 10 to 15 minutes. Remove the seaweed immediately, then turn off the heat.

Strain the shiitake soaking water through a fine mesh strainer, and add to the pan. Combine. Strain the dashi through a strainer lined with paper towels, and it is ready to use. This keeps for 2 to 3 days refrigerated.

MACKEREL CLEAR SOUP
SABA NO SENBA-JIRU

This hearty soup was a specialty of *Senba* (in Osaka). The key to its success lies in removing the strong fishy smell of mackerel by prior salting. If you can't fillet a fish, ask your fish market to do it, and get them to give you the head and backbone for use in the stock.

SERVES 4

1 mackerel, filleted, head and backbone reserved
3 tablespoons sake
1 postcard-size piece of dried kelp
3 ounces *daikon,* giant white radish or turnip, peeled and cut into bite-size pieces
3 ounces carrot, pared and cut into bite-size pieces
3⅓ cups soft mineral water
2 scallions, roughly chopped on the diagonal
2 to 3 teaspoons light soy sauce
2 teaspoons grated fresh ginger
salt

Roughly chop the head and backbone, then sprinkle with a generous amount of salt and set aside for 1 hour. Cut the fillets into 1¼ to 1½-inch pieces, and salt to stand for 30 minutes. Both the bones and fillets will be covered with beads of moisture. Wipe dry with paper towels. Quickly blanch in a pot of boiling water, then plunge in cold water, and pat dry again.

Put the sake, kelp, backbone, head, fillets, radish, and carrot in a large saucepan with the 3⅓ cups of water, and slowly bring to a boil over medium heat, skimming off any scum that floats to the surface. Remove the kelp just before it reaches a boil, when small bubbles begin to rise. Reduce the heat to low, and simmer for 10 minutes, continuing to skim off any scum.

The soup must be served hot, so warm soup bowls with hot (not boiling) water.

Remove the head and backbone, and add the scallions. Season with soy sauce and salt (if needed). Add the grated fresh ginger, turn off the heat, divide the soup between four soup bowls, and serve immediately.

TIGER SHRIMP CLEAR SOUP
EBI NO SUIMONO

This is another classic clear soup that is relatively easy to prepare at home. I have substituted *mitsuba*, trefoil Japanese wild chervil with cilantro leaves.

SERVES 4

8 tiger shrimp in shells, each weighing ¾ ounce
2 tablespoons cornstarch, for dusting
2½ cups Dashi (see page 29)
1 tablespoon sake
1 tablespoon light soy sauce
4 sprigs of cilantro
finely shredded lemon zest
salt

Shell the shrimp, remove the heads, but leave the tails, and devein. Reserve the shells and heads. Wash and pat dry with paper towels, lightly sprinkle with salt, and dust with cornstarch. Bring a pot of 2½ cups water with 1 teaspoon of salt to a boil, and blanch the shrimp for 2 minutes, drain and keep warm.

Meanwhile, put the reserved shells and heads in a pot with the dashi, and bring to just below a boil over medium heat. Reduce the heat to low, and simmer for 3 to 5 minutes, until the shrimp shells turn bright red, then remove from the dashi and discard, using a slotted spoon. Season the dashi with sake, soy sauce, and salt according to your taste.

The soup must be served hot, so warm soup bowls with hot (not boiling) water.

Arrange 2 shrimp, tails up in each warmed bowl, place a sprig of cilantro and shredded lemon zest in between the shrimps. Carefully ladle in the seasoned dashi around the shrimp so that it does not splash and disturb the arrangement, and serve immediately.

SWIRLING EGG CLEAR SOUP KAKITAMA-JIRU

This is probably one of the most popular clear soups that is made more often at home, rather than in restaurants. It is easy to make, visually pleasing, nourishing, and very tasty.

SERVES 4

2½ cups Dashi (see page 29)
1 tablespoon sake
1 tablespoon light soy sauce
2 tablespoons cornstarch mixed with
  2 tablespoons cold water
2 eggs, lightly beaten
½ teaspoon finely grated lemon zest
2 tablespoons peppercress, to garnish
salt

The soup must be served hot, so warm your soup bowls with hot (not boiling) water.

In a saucepan, bring the dashi to just below a boil, then simmer over low heat. Season to taste with sake, soy sauce, and salt. Add the cornstarch mixture, and stir for 30 seconds to thicken.

Slowly pour in the beaten egg in a spiral over the entire surface of the soup. Resist the urge to stir immediately, but wait for about 30 seconds to allow the eggs to settle, and then stir gently with a wire whisk for about a minute. The eggs should appear as if they are thread-like filaments.

Finally add the lemon zest, and immediately remove from the heat. Ladle the soup into the warmed bowls, garnish with peppercress, and serve immediately.

CLEAR SOUP WITH PORGY TAI NO SUIMONO

This is an adaptation of a classic recipe which uses the head and bones of a porgy, the closest relative to sea bream in the US. *Tai*, sea bream, is arguably the most prized fish in Japan and almost every part of the fish is used.

SERVES 4

4 × 1¾ ounce fillets of porgy
4 asparagus spears, trimmed
2½ cups Dashi (see page 29)
1 tablespoon light soy sauce
salt
a pinch of peppercress, to garnish

The soup must be served hot, so warm your soup bowls with hot (not boiling) water.

Bring a pot of 2½ cups water with a teaspoon of salt to a boil, and blanch the fish fillets for 2 minutes. Drain, and keep the fish warm.

In a separate pot, bring 1¾ cups water with a pinch of salt to a boil, and blanch the asparagus for 2 to 3 minutes. Drain, and pat them dry with paper towels. Cut each spear into three angled pieces and set aside.

Put the dashi in a pot, and heat to just below a boil. Season with soy sauce and salt to your taste — remember not to over-season, as the elegance of the soup is in its restraint.

Arrange the fish, asparagus pieces and peppercress in each bowl, and gently ladle in the dashi. Serve immediately.

MISO

For a Japanese person, a bowl of steaming hot miso soup and freshly cooked rice evokes a taste of home. Miso, fermented soybeans, is packed with easily digestible soy protein, and is the oldest and one of the most important ingredients in Japanese cuisine. Every Japanese person, on average, consumes a few spoonfuls a day in one form or another. Miso can be thinned, and then used to make a dressing, left in its thick state as a pickling and marinating medium, spread on broiled foods as in *dengaku*, or added to simmered dishes. But by far, miso is consumed in great quantities in soups served at breakfast, lunch, and dinner.

Miso is made all over Japan, with regional variations each offering their own aroma, flavor, taste, color, and texture and often named after its region of origin. It is essentially fermented soybean—made from boiled and crushed soybeans with an addition of *kōji* (malt), which is mostly made from rice (around 80 percent) wheat or barley. The soybean mixture is left to mature for six months, or even up to three years. It comes in either smooth or grainy texture, and ranges in color from pale cream to almost steely dark brown. An average household in Japan usually has more than one type of miso, and will choose one according to its use. For example, mild, light-colored miso for marinating, or darker-colored miso for soup served at the end of an evening meal. If you are going to get just one type, buy the versatile smooth-textured, medium-colored miso.

THE MOST POPULAR TYPES INCLUDE:

SHIRO-MISO, a white miso which is creamy soft, smooth textured, and mild flavored. *Saikyō* miso from Kyoto is the most well-known of this type. Good for soups, dressing and marinade (as in the famous "black cod.")

SHINSHŪ-MISO, takes its name from the mountainous central part of the main island, Nagano Prefecture, where it is made. It is smooth-textured, and deep yellow in color, tends to be on the salty side in taste, and is a good all-rounder.

AKA-MISO, red miso, which includes the famous *Sendai miso*, comes in both smooth and grainy textures. It is salty in taste, and, like *shinshū-miso*, is another good all-rounder.

HACCHŌ-MISO, is made purely from soybeans, and is extremely rich and salty, with a hint of bitterness. It is steely dark brown in color, and almost dry and hard in texture. It takes its name after the village of Hacchō outside Nagoya, where a former Samurai, turned miso maker, settled in the middle of the sixteenth century.

BROILED EGGPLANT MISO SOUP
YAKINASU NO MISO-SHIRU

A rich and smoky-flavored soup, which lends well to being served in shallow Western-style soup bowls, perhaps as an appetizer for robust beef or lamb dishes.

SERVES 4
2 eggplants
2½ cups Dashi (see page 29)
3 tablespoons white miso
1 tablespoon dark or red miso
strong mustard, to serve

Preheat the broiler to the highest setting. Prick the eggplants with a fork, and broil until the skin is blackened all over, turning occasionally until cooked through. Remove from the broiler, and allow the eggplants to cool. Peel off the blackened skin, and cut the flesh into large bite-size pieces. Set aside and keep warm.

The soup must be served hot, so warm your soup bowls with hot (not boiling) water.

Pour the dashi into a pan over medium heat, and bring to just below a boil, then reduce the heat to low, and maintain the temperature.

Put the miso pastes in a bowl, and mix to blend, then add a ladleful of hot dashi from the saucepan, and stir to soften the pastes. Add the mixture back into the saucepan, bring to a boil, and immediately turn off the heat.

Arrange the eggplant pieces in the center of the warmed soup bowls. Gently ladle in the soup around the eggplants, put a small dab of mustard on the top, and serve.

JAPANESE ONION SOUP
TAMANEGI NO MOSI-SHIRU

This is the Japanese answer to the famous French onion soup. The slow-cooked onions give an almost sweet flavor to the broth.

SERVES 4
1¾ pounds onions, thinly sliced
2 tablespoons vegetable oil
3⅓ cups soft mineral water
2⅔ tablespoons medium-colored miso
light soy sauce, to taste
2 teaspoons finely chopped flat-leaf parsley, to serve

Put about ¼ cup of the onion slices in a bowl of cold water, and set aside. Put the rest of the onions in a heavy-bottomed saucepan with the vegetable oil. Place a piece of dampened parchment paper directly on top of the onions. Cover tightly with a lid, and cook over very low heat, stirring occasionally, until the onions are tender—this will take 30 to 40 minutes.

Add the 3⅓ cups of water to the pan, and bring to a boil over high heat. Put the miso in a small bowl, add a ladleful of soup liquid, and mix to soften the mixture, then return to the soup. Taste and adjust the seasoning with soy sauce, if necessary, and let the soup return to a boil. Once at a boil, turn off the heat immediately.

The soup must be served hot, so warm four soup bowls with hot (not boiling) water.

Drain the soaked onion slices. Divide the soup between the warmed soup bowls, add the drained onion slices, garnish with the parsley, and serve.

TOFU AND WAKAME MISO SOUP
TOFU TO WAKAME NO MISO-SHIRU

Among countless variations of miso soups, this is an absolute classic, especially for breakfast. You could consider it Japan's equivalent of a peanut butter sandwich.

SERVES 4

¾ ounce dried wakame seaweed

7 ounces tofu (either soft silken or firm)

3⅓ cups Dashi, Water Dashi, or Vegetarian Dashi (see pages 29 to 31)

1 heaping tablespoon light-colored miso

1 heaping tablespoon medium-colored miso

2 scallions, finely chopped on the diagonal

Soak the dried seaweed in 4 tablespoons of water for 10 to 15 minutes and drain. Meanwhile, to drain the tofu, wrap it in paper towels, microwave on high for 2 minutes, and cut into ⅜-inch cubes.

Pour the dashi into a saucepan, and bring to a boil over medium–high heat. Put the miso pastes in a small bowl and mix well, then add a ladleful of warm dashi from the pot to soften.

The soup must be served hot, so warm four soup bowls with hot (not boiling) water.

Add the seaweed, tofu, and miso mixture to the pan, and let the soup return to a boil for a few seconds, then turn off the heat immediately. (Never let the miso soup reach a rapid boil, as it will spoil the flavor.)

Ladle into the warmed bowls, garnish with the scallions, and serve immediately.

ALTERNATIVE FLAVORINGS

Tofu and *aburaage*, deep-fried tofu with chopped scallions

Tofu and shiitake mushrooms with peppercress

Tofu and snow peas

Tofu and broccoli with ground sesame seeds

DAIKON WITH DEEP-FRIED TOFU MISO SOUP
DAIKON TO ABURAAGE NO MISO-SHIRU

Daikon is one of the most commonly used vegetables in Japanese cooking, and there is always a piece to be found in the fridge. *Aburaage* are thin, deep-fried sheets of tofu. They are normally sold frozen outside Japan.

SERVES 4

1 *aburaage*, deep-fried tofu
3½ ounces *daikon*, giant white radish, peeled
3⅓ cups dashi of your choice (see pages 29 to 31)
2⅔ tablespoons medium-colored miso
2 scallions, finely chopped on the diagonal, to garnish
sprinkle of *shichimi-tōgarashi*, seven-spice chili powder (optional)

Pour boiling water over the deep-fried tofu to degrease. Thinly slice the radish and cut it into 1½-inch long oblong strips. Cut the deep-fried tofu in half lengthwise, and cut the pieces into ¼-inch wide oblong strips.

Put the radish, deep-fried tofu, and dashi in a saucepan, and bring to a boil over medium–high heat, skimming off any scum that floats to the surface. Reduce the heat to low, and simmer for an additional 5 to 6 minutes.

Put the miso in a small bowl, and add a ladleful of dashi to soften. Pour the mixture into the soup, and heat to just before boiling, then turn off the heat immediately. Serve in pre-warmed soup bowls garnished with chopped scallions and sprinkled with chili powder, if using. Serve immediately.

ALTERNATIVE FLAVORINGS
Deep-fried tofu and spring cabbage
Deep-fried tofu and Napa cabbage
Deep-fried tofu and cherry tomatoes with basil

THREE MUSHROOM AND SPINACH MISO SOUP
KINOKO TO HŌRENSŌ NO MISO-SHIRU

The beauty of this recipe, apart from its deliciousness of course, is that by using the soaking juices of dried shiitake mushrooms, there is no need to prepare dashi.

SERVES 4

4 dried shiitake mushrooms
3⅓ cups soft mineral water
3½ ounces shimeji mushrooms
3½ ounces enoki mushrooms
1 cup roughly chopped spinach leaves
2⅔ tablespoons medium-colored miso
1 tablespoon toasted sesame seeds, to garnish

Put the dried shiitake mushrooms in a saucepan with 3⅓ cups water and set aside for 10 to 15 minutes while you prepare the other mushrooms. When the shiitake mushrooms become soft in the water, take them out with a slotted spoon, and squeeze to extract as much juice as possible. Cut and discard the stems, and thinly slice the caps, then return to the saucepan.

Both shimeji and enoki mushrooms come jointed at the base. Cut and discard the bases and separate.

Place the saucepan with the shiitake mushrooms over gentle heat, and slowly bring to a boil. Add the shimeji and enoki mushrooms, and increase heat to medium to bring the soup to a boil. Add the spinach leaves.

The soup must be served hot, so warm four soup bowls with hot (not boiling) water.

Put the miso in a small bowl, add a ladleful of soup, and mix to soften. Pour the mixture into the soup, and let the soup return to a boil for a second, then turn off the heat immediately.

Divide between the warmed soup bowls, garnish with the sesame seeds, and serve immediately.

CLAM AND SEA BEAN MISO SOUP ASARI NO MISO-SHIRU

This recipe is more suited to adventurous cooks who go foraging on wild beaches. For me, it brings back fond childhood memories of shellfish gathering, which was a fun and highly rewarding activity in spring just as the sea was beginning to warm up. Nowadays, gladly or regrettably, depending on your point of view, it is possible to buy both clams and sea beans from fish markets without venturing on to a beach.

SERVES 4
14 ounces live clams
3 ounces sea beans, trimmed
2⅔ tablespoons white miso
1 tablespoon red miso

Wash and clean the clams by gently rubbing the shells together. Put the clams in a saucepan with 3⅓ cups water, and bring to a boil over gentle heat, while constantly skimming away any scum that floats to the surface. When the shells begin to open, add the sea beans, turn up the heat to let the soup return to a boil, and cook for 1 to 2 minutes. Discard any unopened clams.

The soup must be served hot, so warm four soup bowls with hot (not boiling) water.

Put the white and red miso paste into a small bowl and add a ladleful of the soup liquid to soften; stir well. Pour the mixture into the soup, and bring back to a boil for a second. Turn off the heat, and serve immediately in warmed bowls.

COOK'S TIP
Shopping and careful selection of ingredients is an important part of good cooking. Choose clams with perfect shells. You can tell whether a clam is alive or not by tapping two together—if it sounds metallic, the clams are most likely still fresh, and they will open up when heated. But if the sound is dull, they are dead and should be discarded before cooking. Before cooking, cover the clams with lightly salted water for a few hours in a cool dark place—this will help them spit out any sand or dirt.

HOKKAIDŌ SALMON MISO SOUP HOKKAIDŌ SAKE MISO-SHIRU

Hokkaidō is renowned for salmon fishing and this soup, served at the annual fishing festival, is its regional specialty. Traditional recipes use *sake-kasu*, the lees that are filtered out when sake is brewed. It is also used for making soup, drinks, and pickles. As it is difficult to find outside Japan, I have used mirin instead.

SERVES 4

14 ounces skinless and boneless salmon fillets, cut into bite-size chunks
1 tablespoon salt
2 average-size waxy potatoes, such as Yukon Gold, peeled and cut into chunks
3½ ounces Savoy cabbage
1 carrot, pared and cut into chunks
1 onion, thinly sliced
1 leek, thickly sliced on the diagonal
3⅓ cups Dashi (see page 29)
2⅔ tablespoons medium-colored miso
4 tablespoons mirin

Sprinkle the salmon with 1 tablespoon of salt and set aside on a plate lined with paper towels.

Soak the potato pieces in a bowl of cold water for about 10 minutes to get rid of the starch and drain. Cut the hard core out of the cabbage leaves, discard, and cut the leaves into large bite-size squares.

Put all the vegetables in a saucepan with the dashi, and bring to a boil over medium heat, skimming off any scum that floats to the surface. When the soup begins to bubble, add the salmon, reduce the heat and simmer for 20 minutes, continuing to skim off any scum.

Put the miso and mirin in a small bowl, and mix well, add a ladleful of the soup liquid to soften, then pour into the soup. Let the soup return to just below a boil, then turn off the heat immediately.

Divide between warmed soup bowls and serve.

RED MISO SOUP OF PORGY TAI NO AKA-DASHI

Aka-miso or *aka-dashi*, dark red miso is generally reserved for soups. Red miso soup is considered rather sophisticated, and is served in expensive restaurants.

SERVES 4

7 ounces boneless porgy fillet
1 postcard-size piece of dried kelp
3⅓ cups Dashi (see page 29)
4 asparagus spears, cut into 1¼ to 1½-inch pieces on the diagonal
2⅔ tablespoons red miso
pinch of peppercress, to garnish
sansho, Japanese pepper, to serve
salt

Cut the porgy into large bite-size pieces, sprinkle with salt, and set aside on a plate lined with paper towels for 10 to 15 minutes.

Put the kelp in a saucepan with the dashi, and slowly bring to just below a boil over low heat. When small bubbles begin to appear, add the asparagus. Place the fish in a small strainer, and blanch for 3 to 4 minutes, or until the fish is just cooked. Remove the fish and asparagus, and keep warm. Let the dashi return to a gentle simmer, then remove the kelp and discard.

The soup must be served hot, so warm your soup bowls with hot (not boiling) water.

Put the miso in a small bowl with a ladleful of dashi, and mix well to soften, then pour into the soup. Let the soup reach just below a boil, and turn off the heat immediately.

Arrange the fish, skin-side up, and the asparagus in the warmed soup bowls, and carefully ladle in the soup. Garnish with the peppercress in the center of each bowl, sprinkle the *sansho* pepper over, and serve.

SASHIMI

Sashimi is raw fish and shellfish eaten at the beginning of a meal and served in various cuts and styles, with decorative edible condiments as well as dipping sauces (usually soy), and wasabi (although grated fresh ginger, garlic, or mustard can also be used). One of the most famous dishes of Japanese cuisine, it is also called *otsukuri*, literally "to make," and is an opportunity for a chef to wield his knife, and demonstrate his presentation skills.

The origin of sashimi is believed to stem from the oldest Japanese dish called "*namasu*," a vinegared dish of raw meat, fish, or vegetables. The cardinal principle of Japanese cuisine is that any seafood that is fresh enough, should be eaten raw. This is because we believe the cook's job is to choose the best seasonal ingredients, and to draw out and present the very essence of their natural flavor, rather than to impose man-made flavors. In Japanese, the word "*sashimi*" implies cutting or slicing flesh. For example, raw oysters are not sashimi, while slices of scallop are.

Preparing sashimi is a job best done by professionals, and in Japan, sashimi for home eating is normally bought ready-prepared by fish markets. Therefore, I have not given a description of how to prepare sashimi at home, but instead list a few helpful tips, plus three achievable slicing methods—for cubes, rectangular slices, and paper-thin slices—using a Western-style kitchen knife (just make sure it is razor sharp).

Everything related to the preparation of sashimi is done with elaborate care, but the first and the foremost important task is to source the freshest fish. So, start with finding and getting to know good fish markets in your local area. To be a good home cook, you first must become a good shopper—to know what to buy, when, and where from. And this is particularly important when one is dealing with Japanese cuisine, where freshness and seasonality of each ingredient is paramount. It is possible to buy almost any food nearly all year around nowadays, but at the cost of a blurred sense of seasons, and with the diminished pleasure of anticipation. There is simple, but unmeasurable pleasure in being in tune with the nature, eating what each season brings.

CHOOSING FISH Freshness is paramount. Ask your fish market what is in season, and the catch of the day that is freshest to eat raw. Choose fish with bright, clear eyes and bright red gills. Fresh fish should have a pleasant smell of the sea, but not be "fishy." Its belly should be firm and resilient to the touch, and should spring back. Its scales should be firm and glistening. Almost all fresh fish and shellfish are suitable for sashimi, except cod, because decomposition begins as soon as it is fished out of water. Hence why cod sashimi is only available on board fishing boats, or dockside restaurants.

FILLETING If your fish filleting skills are not up to very high standards, ask the fish market to fillet the fish and remove the skin, bone and darker flesh from around the spine. If you are not going to slice it into sashimi pieces immediately, keep the fillet refrigerated, and wrapped in a clean (damp but not wet) cloth—wrapping it will prevent the fish from absorbing the smells of other foods in the fridge, as well as stopping it from drying out.

TO PREPARE Run your fingers along the fillet to feel if there are any bones embedded. Trim the thin sides to make the fillet rectangular in shape, and an even thickness.

CUBE CUTTING, *KAKU-ZUKURI* This style of cutting is suitable for fish such as tuna, salmon, and bonito with thick, but tender-fleshed fillets. It is particularly suited to tuna as this is sold in steak form rather than as a fillet. Choose ¾-inch thick steaks, and cut them into ¾-inch wide strips, but do not separate the strips. Rotate the strips 90 degrees, and cut straight down at ¾-inch intervals to form cubes.

TUNA CUBES WITH WASABI AVOCADO DRESSING

Cube-cut is most probably the easiest sashimi cut of all, especially in the West, where tuna is often sold in a steak form.

SERVES 4

1 very ripe avocado
2 tablespoons rice vinegar
1 tablespoon wasabi powder mixed with
   1 tablespoon water to form a paste
1 tablespoon soy sauce
14 ounces tuna steaks cut into ¾-inch cubes
   (see page 44)

Cut the avocado in half and remove the pit. Peel the skin and roughly chop the flesh. Use a fork to mash the avocado into a smooth paste in a large bowl. Add the rice vinegar, wasabi paste, and soy sauce, and mix well. Add the tuna cubes and combine, making sure to coat each cube with the avocado mixture. Serve immediately.

YELLOWTAIL SASHIMI
HAMACHI NO HIRA-ZUKURI

Hirazukuri is a sashimi cut consisting of rectangular (about ⅜-inch thick) slices. It is the most popular cutting technique, and can be used for almost any type of fish.

SERVES 4

2 to 2¾-inch piece of *daikon*, giant white radish, peeled
9 ounces boneless and skinless yellowtail fillet
4 *shiso*, perilla leaves
4 teaspoons wasabi paste
tamari soy sauce, for dipping

With a mandoline, finely shred the radish, and then soak the shreds in ice water for 20 to 30 minutes.

Place the fish fillet lengthwise on a cutting board, former skin-side up, then cut into ⅜-inch thick slices along the grain (you should have about 20 slices). See also below.

Drain the radish, and divide into four portions. Pile each portion on individual serving dishes or plates into a small mound. Place the *shiso* against each radish mound and rest 5 fish slices, like domino pieces, with a small dab of wasabi on the bottom corner. Serve with a small dish of soy sauce on the side.

RECTANGULAR SLICES, HIRA-ZUKURI

Place the fillet, former skin-side up, lengthwise, 1¼ inches away from the bottom edge of the cutting board, thicker side away from you. Place your left hand on the fillet, without applying too much pressure, just enough to hold it in place. Hold the knife so that the tip of the blade is slightly inclined to the left. Use the knife in a sweeping draw motion, starting from the base to the tip, cutting through the fillet gently but without too much force.

Start cutting at the right of the fillet. A ⅜-inch slice is standard thickness. Firm-fleshed fish such as porgy or sea bass may be cut into ¼-inch slices and soft-fleshed fish into ⅝-inch slices.

Wipe the knife clean occasionally with a clean, moist towel. Because of the way the knife is held, each slice will come to rest on the blade near the tip. Slide the knife, with the slice still attached, several fractions of an inch, away to the right, and then lay the slice on its right side. Keep repeating this process until the fillet is finished and you should have a neat row of "domino" slices on the right.

PAPER-THIN SASHIMI OF FLOUNDER
HIRAME NO USU-ZUKURI

Usu-zukuri, paper-thin slices, is most suitable for firm, white-fleshed fish such as porgy, sea bass, or flounder. Think of this as the Japanese equivalent of Italian carpaccio or Peruvian ceviche.

SERVES 4

9 ounces boneless and skinless flounder fillet
3½ ounces *daikon*, giant white radish, peeled
2 dried red chiles, seeded
a few sprigs of chives, finely chopped
scant ½ cup *ponzu*, Citrus Soy Vinegar (see page 51)

Wrap the fish in plastic wrap and place it in the freezer while you prepare *momiji-oroshi (see below)*. You don't want the fish to freeze solid, but it needs to be firm enough to make slicing it easier. At the same time chill four individual serving plates in the fridge.

Meanwhile, make 2 holes in the radish with a chopstick then plug the seeded chiles into them, using the chopstick to push the chiles in. Grate the radish—the result will be rather watery, so lightly drain by either squeezing in your hand or wring in a piece of clean cheesecloth.

Take the fish out of the freezer and unwrap. At the same time, take the serving plates out of the fridge.

Thinly slice the fish and immediately transfer each slice onto a plate (allow 5 to 7 slices each).

Scatter the chopped chives on top of the fish slices. and make a small mound of grated chile radish in the center. Serve with a dish of *ponzu* on the side.

PAPER-THIN SLICES, *USU-ZUKURI*

Wrap the fish in plastic wrap and place in the freezer for about 10 to 15 minutes. You want the flesh to be firm enough to make thin slicing easier, but not for it to become frozen solid.

Put a fillet on a cutting board, former skin-side up, and thicker flesh side facing away from you. Place your left hand on the left end of the fillet, without applying too much pressure, just enough to hold it in place. Hold the knife so that the tip is tilted to the right, and the blade is almost horizontal. Start at the left side of the fillet, positioning the base of the knife about ¼-inch right of where your fingers are placed. Draw the blade from one o'clock to seven o'clock in one smooth controlled movement. You should have a thin slice

resting at the tip of the knife. Carefully transfer each slice immediately to a plate, overlapping the slices slightly to make a rosette. Add garnishes such as a curl of carrot, scattering of finely chopped scallion, or finely grated lemon zest. Serve immediately with *ponzu* sauce (see page 51) or a mixture of soy sauce and lemon juice. This type of sashimi is typically served with *momiji-oroshi*, red chile-infused grated giant white radish.

SALAD

There is no direct equivalent of salads in the traditional Japanese repertory, but *sunomono*, literally "vinegared things," and *aemono*, '"dressed things," can be loosely described as salads. Both *sunomono* and *aemono* are normally served in small portions in dainty bowls or elegant dishes on the side to complement the main dish in taste, color, and texture. However, they never feature as a main dish on the traditional Japanese table. Basic vinegar mixtures and *aemono*-dressings are easy to make and highly adaptable for making into Western-style salads, and to serve as one-course healthy meals.

Although both *sunomono* and *aemono* play a supporting role, the scope for creativity in Japanese-style salads is literally endless. *Sunomono* embrace a wide range of ingredients—almost all vegetables, raw or parboiled, and many fish and shellfish, raw, broiled, steamed, or even fried and then cooled. The ingredients are tossed with, or sprinkled with, a thin vinegar mixture or citrus dressing. *Aemono*, dressed things, also uses all sorts of raw or cooked, then cooled vegetables, fish and shellfish, or poultry. Although in Japanese cookbooks the two categories are usually listed together, because strictly vinegar mixtures are a kind of a dressing, and therefore, the two are alike, but for an easier distinction and for identification purposes, one might say that *aemono* dressings are generally thicker than vinegar-based *sunomono* dressings. In general, *aemono* dressings are based on puréed tofu, toasted then ground sesame seeds, or miso.

Two important points for the success of Japanese-style salads—never use warm ingredients, everything must be cooled to room temperature, or even chilled, especially in the summer. And secondly, all ingredients must be thoroughly dried before being mixed with dressings, otherwise the final result will be watery.

TWO BASIC AEMONO DRESSINGS

WHITE SESAME DRESSING
SHIRO-GOMA AEGOROMO

This tastes like delicately roasted peanuts. Do not be tempted to add too much sugar—it's used to give a rounded taste, rather than to sweeten. Seemingly quite dry and coarse, once mixed it will be just right.

MAKES ABOUT 4 TABLESPOONS

4 tablespoons toasted white sesame seeds
1 teaspoon sugar
1 tablespoon light soy sauce

Put the toasted sesame seeds and sugar in a Japanese mortar, or a mortar and pestle, and grind to a coarse paste—leave some seeds still visible. Add the soy sauce, and mix well.

It's best to prepare as needed, although it will keep for up to a month refrigerated in a zip-lock bag, with as much air pressed out as possible.

TOFU DRESSING   SHIRO AEGOROMO

A delicate, smooth dressing. Firm tofu gives a slightly more pronounced taste and flavor than soft silken tofu. The key to success is to make sure the tofu is well drained (see page 156).

MAKES ABOUT I CUP

3½ ounces tofu
2 tablespoons white sesame paste or tahini
1 tablespoon sugar
1 teaspoon salt
1 teaspoon light soy sauce

Roughly break up the tofu, then wrap it in a cloth and tightly squeeze to drain. Put the tofu and sesame paste, sugar, and salt in a *suribachi*, a Japanese mortar, and blend well. Add the soy sauce, and stir well until it becomes a thick and smooth mixture. This dressing should be prepared just before it is needed.

FOUR BASIC
SUNOMONO VINEGARS

TWO-FLAVOR VINEGAR NIHAI-ZU

A vinegar to use with fish and seafood.

MAKES 1¼ CUPS

scant ½ cup rice vinegar
2 tablespoons soy sauce
⅔ cup water

Mix the ingredients together and transfer to a glass jar. Keeps almost indefinitely refrigerated in a glass jar with a lid.

SWEET VINEGAR AMA-ZU

This is sweet and mild, and can be used to dress vegetables such as cabbage (see page 60). The amount of sugar may be varied according to personal taste.

MAKES 1¼ CUPS

⅓ cup mirin
2 to 3 tablespoons sugar
⅓ cup rice vinegar
⅓ cup soy sauce

Put the mirin and sugar in a small saucepan, and bring to a boil over medium heat. Simmer for 1 to 2 minutes to burn off the alcohol, and dissolve the sugar. Remove from the heat, and let it cool down before adding the vinegar and soy sauce. Keeps almost indefinitely refrigerated in a glass jar with a lid.

THREE-FLAVOR VINEGAR SANBAI-ZU

This is arguably the most versatile vinegar mix that can be used for almost any food.

MAKES 1⅓ CUPS

⅓ cup mirin
⅓ cup rice vinegar
2 tablespoons soy sauce
⅓ cup water

Put all the ingredients in a saucepan, and bring to a boil over medium heat. Simmer for 1 to 2 minutes. Remove from the heat, and cool to room temperature. Keeps almost indefinitely refrigerated in a glass jar with a lid.

CITRUS SOY VINEGAR PONZU

This is another highly versatile vinegar mix.

MAKES 1⅓ CUPS

½ cup lemon, lime, tangerine, or yuzu juice, or a mixture
½ cup soy sauce
⅓ cup rice vinegar
⅓ ounce *katsuobushi*, dried bonito flakes
2-inch square piece of dried kelp

Put all the ingredients in a large glass bowl and let stand for 24 hours to infuse. Strain through cheesecloth, and transfer to a glass jar. Although this keeps almost indefinitely refrigerated, it is best to use within 2 to 3 months.

TWO FLAVORED VINEGAR VARIATIONS

SESAME VINEGAR GOMA-SU

This is thicker and more highly aromatic than other vinegars—the nutty flavor of sesame seeds comes alive when they are toasted and ground.

MAKES A SCANT I CUP

¾ cup toasted white sesame seeds
1 tablespoon sugar
⅓ cup Two-flavor Vinegar or Three-flavor Vinegar (see page 51)

Put the toasted sesame seeds and sugar in a *suribachi*, a Japanese mortar, or a normal Western style mortar and grind well until it becomes a smooth paste, and oil from the seeds begins to seep out. Stir in the vinegar, and mix well. This is best prepared as needed, because the characteristic sesame aroma is lost quickly.

WASABI VINEGAR WASABI-ZU

A highly refreshing vinegar mix for wasabi fans.

MAKES A SCANT ¼ CUP

2 teaspoons wasabi powder
2 teaspoons mirin
⅓ cup Two-flavor Vinegar or Three-flavor Vinegar (see page 51)

Mix the wasabi powder with mirin, then add the vinegar. As wasabi quickly loses its aroma, prepare this just before it is needed.

FIVE COLORS IN VINEGAR
GOSHIKI NAMASU

Namasu is one of the oldest dishes in Japanese cooking. Raw meat, fish, or fruits and vegetables are cut into thin strips, and mixed with vinegar-based dressings. Dried persimmons are a winter delicacy in Japan, but you can use almost any dried fruit instead, such as apricots, figs, or prunes.

SERVES 4

2 dried persimmons or dried apricots, figs, or prunes
3½ ounces *daikon*, giant white radish, peeled
1 medium-size carrot, pared
3½ ounces fine green beans, trimmed
4 shiitake mushrooms
⅓ cup Three-flavor Vinegar (see page 51)
salt

Cut the dried persimmons into julienne strips. Cut the radish and carrot into julienne strips about 1½ inches long.

Put the beans on a cutting board, and sprinkle over some salt. Using flattened hands, roll the beans around a few times—this will help to tenderize them, as well as retain the fresh green color when cooked.

Blanch each vegetable separately in lightly salted water—green beans for 3 minutes, radish and carrot for 2 minutes. Then rinse in cold water, drain thoroughly, and pat dry with paper towels. Set aside.

Preheat the broiler to high. Cut and discard the stalks of the shiitake mushrooms, and broil the caps for 1 minute each side. Slice thinly and set aside.

Put the dried fruit and vegetables together in a mixing bowl, then pour the vinegar over and toss.

To serve, divide the mixture into four equal portions, and lightly squeeze each portion before arranging neatly into mounds in small individual serving dishes.

MUSHROOM IN SESAME MISO DRESSING
KINOKO NO GOMA MISO AE

I am delighted that some exotic Oriental mushrooms have become easier to find in the supermarket recently.

SERVES 4

4 to 6 shiitake mushrooms, stems discarded
2 ounces shimeji mushrooms
2 ounces enoki mushrooms
⅔ cup soy sauce
2 tablespoons toasted white sesame seeds, plus 2 teaspoons, to garnish
1 tablespoon sugar
4 tablespoons white or light-colored miso

Cut the caps of the shiitake mushrooms into thin slices. Both shimeji and enoki mushrooms come jointed at the base—cut off and discard the bases, and separate the stems by hand.

In a saucepan, bring 2¼ cups of water to a boil, add ½ cup of the soy sauce and all the mushrooms, then parboil for 1 minute. Drain thoroughly, and leave to stand in a strainer to continue draining.

Put the 2 tablespoons toasted sesame seeds and the sugar in *a suribachi*, a Japanese mortar, and grind until most of the seeds are crushed. Add the miso, and the remaining soy sauce and mix. You may need to add more soy sauce to soften the mixture to a double cream consistency.

Press down on the mushrooms with your hand to drain any excess liquid, then add to the dressing and mix.

Divide the mushroom mixture into four equal portions to serve in neat mounds in individual serving dishes, sprinkle with the remaining toasted white sesame seeds, and serve.

VINEGARED CUCUMBER
KYŪRI NO SUNOMONO

Here is a quick and easy, and above all, very healthy dish—it can be served as a vegetarian appetizer, or as a side for meaty dishes.

SERVES 4

2 tablespoons dried wakame seaweed
4 Lebanese cucumbers or standard cucumbers
thumb-size piece of fresh ginger, peeled and thinly sliced
1 to 2 tablespoons salt
½ cup Three-flavor Vinegar (see page 51)
2 teaspoons toasted white sesame seeds, for garnish

Put four individual serving dishes in the fridge to chill.

Soften the seaweed by covering with plenty of water in a bowl for 10 minutes. Drain.

Thinly slice the cucumbers (if using standard cucumbers, peel and slice lengthwise, and scoop out the central seeds). Put the cucumber slices and the ginger in a medium-size non-metallic mixing bowl, sprinkle with salt, then squeeze with your hands for about 1 minute. A fair amount of water will come out—the aim is to squeeze and drain off as much liquid as possible.

Add the wakame and 1 tablespoon of the vinegar to the cucumber, then lightly mix. Squeeze and drain away any excess liquid. Add 4 tablespoons of the vinegar, mix, and drain again. Finally, pour in the remaining vinegar, and mix lightly. The reason for staging the vinegar addition is to avoid the finished dish becoming watery.

Divide into four equal portions, and gently squeeze and drain any excess liquid before arranging in small mounds in the chilled dishes. Sprinkle over the sesame seeds and serve.

VINEGARED CRAB
KANISU

This is another classic sunomono favorite with a touch of elegance. Although crabs are available all year round, they are the best in winter.

SERVES 4

7 ounces freshly boiled or steamed white crabmeat
2 teaspoons salt, plus 2 tablespoons extra
1 tablespoon rice vinegar
2 Lebanese cucumbers
½ cup Three-flavor Vinegar (see page 51)
2 teaspoons grated fresh ginger juice

Put four individual serving dishes in the fridge to chill.

Pick over the crabmeat, discard the cartilage, and finely shred into a bowl. Sprinkle over the rice vinegar, lightly mix, then set aside. (Applying vinegar or other seasonings such as salt or soy sauce beforehand gives crabmeat a subtle undertone—what the Japanese call *shita-aji*, literally "under taste.")

Place the cucumbers on a cutting board, sprinkle over 2 teaspoons of salt, and using the palms of your hands, roll them around for a few times—this tenderizes the cucumbers as well as freshens the color. In a large bowl combine 2 tablespoons of salt with 4½ cups of cold water. Thinly slice the cucumbers, and soak in the salted water for 10 minutes. Drain well, and pat dry with paper towels.

Mix the vinegar with the ginger juice in a small bowl. Put the crabmeat and cucumber slices in a separate bowl, spoon on the ginger mixture, and stir thoroughly. Divide the crabmeat mixture between the chilled dishes, and lightly squeeze each portion of cucumber before placing in the dishes to ensure there is no excess moisture. Serve immediately.

COOK'S TIP

This dish or any other *sunomono* should not be prepared ahead and left to stand, because it will become watery.

VARIATION

Try using thinly sliced cooked octopus, or flaked, cooked, white-fleshed fish, such as sea bass or flounder instead of the crab.

GREEN BEANS AND CARROT IN WHITE SESAME DRESSING
INGEN TO NINJIN NO SHIRO-GOMA AE

Sesame dressing is a quick and easy way to transform otherwise rather ordinary vegetables.

SERVES 4

3½ ounces fine green beans
1 medium-size carrot, pared
2 tablespoons light soy sauce
4 tablespoons White Sesame Dressing
  (see page 50)
salt

Trim the beans and cut into half lengths. Thinly slice the carrot into 1¼-inch long julienne strips. Parboil the vegetables separately in lightly salted water for 2 minutes each, then rinse in cold water and drain thoroughly. Pat them dry with paper towels.

Put the vegetables in a bowl, then add the soy sauce. Use your hands to mix and lightly squeeze them—this adds a subtle soy flavor to the vegetables.

Transfer the vegetable mix to another bowl, add the white sesame dressing, and toss. Divide the mixture into four equal portions, and serve in neat mounds in small individual dishes.

HIJIKI IN TOFU DRESSING   HIJIKI NO SHIRO AE

This is a quick and easy recipe that is light in texture and full of high-quality protein from tofu and rich in calcium, iron, and magnesium from *hijiki* (a sea vegetable).

SERVES 4

8 tablespoons dried *hijiki*
1 medium-sized carrot, pared and julienned
1 *aburaage*, deep-fried tofu
2 tablespoons toasted white sesame seeds
1 tablespoon sugar
2 tablespoons light soy sauce
4 tablespoons Tofu Dressing (see page 50)
salt

Put the *hijiki* in a bowl, pour over enough water to cover, and stand for 10 to 15 minutes. Pour through a strainer, and press down on the *hijiki* with a rubber spatula, then stand to drain further while you prepare the other ingredients.

Parboil the carrot strips in salted water for 1 minute and drain. Set aside.

Put the deep-fried tofu in a strainer and pour boiling water on both sides to remove excess oil, and pat dry with paper towels. Slice in half lengthwise, and cut into thin strips.

Put the sesame seeds and sugar in a *suribachi*, a Japanese mortar, and grind until about half of the seeds are still visible. Transfer to a mixing bowl. Add the soy sauce and the tofu dressing, and mix well. Add the drained *hijiki*, carrot, and deep-fried tofu strips, and use a rubber spatula to lightly mix.

Divide between four individual dishes and serve.

SERVING SUGGESTION

To add a contemporary touch, I often serve this classic dish in little gem lettuce leaves, or scooped-out tomatoes. Cucumber cups or celery sticks also make attractive edible serving vessels.

GREEN BEANS IN BLACK SESAME DRESSING
INGEN NO KURO-GOMA AE

Compared to white sesame seeds, black ones have a stronger flavor, and therefore, dark or normal soy sauce can be used.

SERVES 4

3½ ounces fine green beans
2 tablespoons dark soy sauce

FOR THE BLACK SESAME DRESSING

4 tablespoons toasted black sesame seeds
1 teaspoon sugar
1 tablespoon dark soy sauce

Cut the beans into 1¼ to 1½-inch lengths. Blanch them in plenty of lightly salted boiling water for 2 to 3 minutes. Rinse in cold water, drain, and pat dry with paper towels.

Put the beans in a bowl, then add the soy sauce, and, with your hands, mix and lightly squeeze.

To make the dressing, put the toasted sesame seeds and sugar in a Japanese mortar, *suribachi*, and grind to form a coarse paste—do not over grind them—leave some seeds still visible. Add the soy sauce and mix well.

Transfer the beans to a separate bowl, then add the black sesame dressing, and mix well to coat each bean. Divide into four equal portions, and serve in neat mounds in small individual dishes.

TOFU AND WATERCRESS SALAD WITH HOT OIL

I first learned this technique of pouring hot sesame oil over salad ingredients from a Chinese friend. It is surprisingly light, and not at all oily. The key to success is to ensure the oil is almost smoking hot.

SERVES 4

14 ounces soft silken tofu
1 red onion
1 bunch watercress (weighing about 4 to 5 ounces)
3½ ounces spinach leaves
2 celery stalks
thumb-sized piece fresh ginger, peeled
4 tablespoons *ponzu*, Citrus Soy Vinegar (see page 51)
2 tablespoons soy sauce
2 tablespoons sesame oil

Cut the tofu into 1¼ to 1½-inch cubes, and leave to drain for 10 to 15 minutes on a plate lined with paper towels.

Thinly slice the red onion, then soak in a bowl of cold water for 10 to 12 minutes. Drain.

Trim the watercress into manageable lengths, and put on a large serving platter with the spinach. Thinly slice the celery on the diagonal, and add to the watercress bed. Thinly slice or julienne the ginger, then scatter it over the watercress bed. Add the drained tofu cubes and onion slices on top.

Mix the Citrus Soy Vinegar and soy sauce, then pour over the salad mix.

Heat the sesame oil in a small pan over medium heat until almost smoking hot, then drizzle over the salad—it will make a dramatic sizzling sound. Quickly toss, and serve immediately.

VINEGAR-SQUEEZED SPRING CABBAGE
KYABETSU NO SUMOMIAE

This dish combines two traditional techniques—*momi*, squeezing, and *su-ae*, vinegar-dressed.

SERVES 4

18 ounces pointed spring cabbage (sweetheart lettage), or Savoy cabbage

1 carrot, pared

small thumb-sized piece fresh ginger, peeled

2 teaspoons salt

6 tablespoons *amazu*, Sweet Vinegar (see page 51)

Cut the cabbage into ¾ to 1¼-inch squares, and discard the thick cores. Cut the carrot and ginger into 1¼-inch long matchsticks.

Put the cabbage, carrot, and ginger in a large ziplock plastic bag, and sprinkle over the salt, then seal, and with your hands, squeeze the bag for 2 to 3 minutes as if you are massaging it. A great deal of liquid will come out as the cabbage begins to wilt. Drain the liquid.

Add 4 tablespoons of sweet vinegar, reseal, then squeeze again for another 2 to 3 minutes. Drain as much liquid as possible.

Divide the cabbage mix between 4 individual serving bowls, and drizzle ½ tablespoon of sweet vinegar over each and serve.

TOFU, AVOCADO, AND CRABMEAT SALAD WITH WASABI DRESSING

Both tofu and avocado lend themselves very well to wasabi.

SERVES 4

14 ounces soft silken tofu

1 red onion

2 ripe avocados

2 tablespoons lemon juice

3½ ounces white crabmeat

2 tablespoons roughly chopped flat-leaf parsley

FOR THE WASABI DRESSING

4 tablespoons Wasabi Vinegar (see page 52)

2 tablespoons extra virgin olive oil

Cut the tofu into ⅜-inch thick 1¼ to 1½-inch square pieces, and set aside on a plate lined with paper towels for 10 to 15 minutes to drain.

Thinly slice the red onion, and soak in a bowl of cold water for 10 to12 minutes. Drain.

Halve the avocados, peel, and remove the pit, then cut the flesh into ⅜-inch thick slices. Drizzle over the lemon juice to prevent the avocados from discoloring.

Put the wasabi vinegar and the oil for the dressing in a lidded jam jar, and shake vigorously to mix.

On a large serving platter, arrange the tofu pieces like fallen dominos. Put the avocado and onion on top, and scatter over the crabmeat. Pour the wasabi dressing over, and garnish with the parsley to serve.

WARM SPRING VEGETABLE SALAD

Here is a one-course salad using seasonal vegetables. I suggest you serve it in a big salad bowl, and let your guests help themselves.

SERVES 4

4 waxy potatoes such as Fingerling, Yukon Gold or red, scrubbed
2 carrots, pared
14 ounces pointed spring cabbage (sweetheart lettage), or Savoy cabbage
4 baby leeks, trimmed
3½ ounces broccolini
salt

FOR THE SESAME MISO DRESSING

4 tablespoons white toasted sesame seeds
4 tablespoons medium-colored miso such as *sendai* or *shinshū* miso paste
2 tablespoons sugar
1 teaspoon grated fresh ginger
6 tablespoons rice vinegar

Cut the potatoes into ⅔-inch thick slices and soak in a bowl of water for 10 minutes. This will wash off the starch, and stop discoloration while you prepare the other vegetables.

Cut the carrots into ⅔-inch thick slices on the diagonal. Cut the cabbage into large bite-size chunks.

Drain the potatoes, and put them at the bottom of a large steaming basket with all the other vegetables on top. Sprinkle over some salt, then steam over medium heat for 6 to 8 minutes, or until they are cooked through. Turn off the heat, and transfer to a large platter.

While the vegetables are being steamed, prepare the dressing. Put the sesame seeds in a *suribachi*, Japanese mortar, and grind until most of the seeds are crushed. Add the remaining dressing ingredients except the vinegar, and grind to mix. Gradually add the vinegar while continuing to mix—you may need to add more or less—until the mixture becomes like light cream in consistency.

Drizzle the sesame miso dressing over the warm vegetables, and serve immediately.

BROILED SUMMER VEGETABLES WITH SPICY SOY DRESSING

This salad is a perfect accompaniment for a barbecue on hot summer days.

SERVES 4

1 eggplant

12 okra pods

2 green zucchini

2 yellow zucchini

2 red bell peppers

2 yellow bell peppers

3 to 4 tablespoons vegetable oil

salt

FOR THE SPICY SOY DRESSING

2 tablespoons rice vinegar

3 tablespoons light soy sauce

2 teaspoons sugar

1 teaspoon grated garlic

½ teaspoon chili powder

Preheat the broiler to high, or heat a large iron griddle.

Remove the eggplant stem and discard. Cut the eggplant into ⅔-inch slices, soak in a bowl of water for 10 minutes to get rid of any bitterness, then drain. Place the okra on a cutting board, sprinkle some salt on top, then use the palms of your hands to roll the pods around—this removes the fluffy hair. Cut the zucchini into roughly ⅔-inch thick slices on an angle. Quarter the red and yellow peppers, seed, and remove the white pith.

Put all the vegetables in a large mixing bowl, drizzle the vegetable oil over, and toss to coat each piece. Lay the vegetables in a roasting pan and place under the broiler for 4 to 5 minutes on one side, then turn them over to broil for an additional 4 to 5 minutes. If using a griddle, cook in small batches, pressing down on each piece to make char marks on both sides.

Meanwhile, put all the ingredients for the dressing in a glass jar with a lid, and shake vigorously to mix.

Wipe the mixing bowl clean, and add the broiled vegetables. Pour the dressing over, and toss to coat the vegetables. Transfer to a large serving dish, and serve at room temperature.

PAN-SEARED AUTUMN VEGETABLES WITH MISO MAYONNAISE

Here, a combination of miso paste and Western mayonnaise works surprisingly well.

SERVES 4

14 ounces skinless, boneless chicken thigh fillets

14 ounces pumpkin or winter squash

7 ounces cauliflower

7 ounces broccoli

8 shiitake mushrooms

2 to 3 tablespoons vegetable oil

FOR THE MISO MAYONNAISE

4 tablespoons medium-colored miso such as *sendai* or *shinshū* miso paste

2 tablespoons rice vinegar

4 tablespoons ready-made mayonnaise

Cut the chicken into 1¼ to 1½–inch squares. Peel the pumpkin, remove the seeds and fibrous center, then cut into slices about 2 inches long and ⅔-inch thick. Cut the cauliflower and broccoli into bite-size chunks. Cut and discard the stems of the shiitake mushrooms, and halve the caps.

Heat the oil in a large skillet over high heat until almost smoking hot. Add the chicken pieces, and brown on one side for 4 to 5 minutes, and turn to cook on the other side for an additional 3 to 4 minutes. Remove from the pan, and place on a layer of paper towels to soak up any excess oil. Set aside to cool to room temperature while you cook the vegetables.

Put the pumpkin slices into the pan to fry for 2 to 3 minutes on one side, then turn over to cook the other side for an additional 1 to 2 minutes. Transfer onto a plate, and let it cool to room temperature. Cook the rest of the vegetables in the same way in batches (you may need to add more oil), transferring onto another plate to cool.

In a large mixing bowl, stir the miso and vinegar together, then add the mayonnaise, and mix well with a small whisk.

Put the chicken and all the vegetables into the bowl with the miso mayonnaise, and combine well. Transfer to a large serving dish to serve.

WARM WINTER VEGETABLES AND SALMON SALAD WITH YUZU DRESSING

Yuzu is a Japanese citrus fruit, which looks like a tangerine in shape and has a lemon-yellow skin. It is not eaten like a fresh fruit, but instead, the refreshing juice and skin is widely used in Japanese cooking. Outside the country, its juice is available in bottles and the skin in dried form.

You will need a large, deep saucepan, and a large steaming basket for this recipe, as all the vegetables and the salmon are steamed together.

SERVES 4

2 tablespoons sake
14 ounces skinless salmon fillet, cut into bite-size
    pieces
4 small turnips
14 ounces Savoy cabbage
2 leeks
3½ ounces shimeji mushrooms
salt

FOR THE YUZU DRESSING

1 tablespoon *yuzu* juice
2 tablespoons mirin
4 tablespoons light soy sauce

Sprinkle a pinch of salt and drizzle the sake over the salmon, then leave to stand while you prepare the vegetables.

Peel and cut each turnip into 4 wedges, then lay them on the bottom of a large steaming basket placed inside a large lidded saucepan filled halfway with water. Thinly slice the cabbage, then scatter on top of the turnips. Thinly slice the leeks diagonally, and spread evenly on top of the cabbage layer. Place the salmon on top of the leeks. Cut and discard the base of shimeji mushrooms, and with your hands, separate the clump into 2 to 3 stem chunks and put on top of the salmon.

Put the lid on the pan, cover the lid with a dishtowel, and secure the ends with a rubber band. Place over medium–high heat, and bring to a boil to steam for 10 to 12 minutes, or until all the vegetables and the fish are cooked.

Warm a large serving dish.

While the vegetables and fish are steaming, put all the ingredients for the dressing in a glass jar with a lid, and shake vigorously to mix.

Transfer the vegetables and salmon to the warmed dish, pour the dressing over, then toss well. Serve warm.

NIHON NIÇOISE

This is a Japanese take on the famous Salad Niçoise.

4 tuna steaks, 3½ to 4-ounces each
14 ounces waxy baby new potatoes, scrubbed
3½ ounces fine green beans, trimmed and halved
7 ounces fresh or frozen edemame
12 baby cherry tomatoes, halved
12 pitted black olives
2 scallions, finely chopped
a handful of *mitsuba* or flat-leaf parsley, roughly torn
1 tablespoon vegetable oil
salt

FOR THE DRESSING
¼ cup soy sauce
¼ cup rice vinegar
2 teaspoons wasabi powder or paste
1 teaspoon grated garlic
½ cup extra virgin olive oil
1 teaspoon toasted sesame oil

Season both sides of the tuna with salt and set aside for 10 to 15 minutes.

Cut the potatoes into ⅜-inch thick slices. Bring a saucepan of water to a boil over high heat, add the potatoes, and boil for 6 to 8 minutes, or until cooked through. Drain, rinse under cold running water, and drain again.

Place the halved beans on a cutting board, sprinkle with a pinch of salt, and with the palm of your hand roll them around—this helps the beans to keep their color when cooked. Bring a saucepan of water to a boil, add the beans, and cook for 1 to 2 minutes, then add the edamame, and cook for an additional 2 to 3 minutes. Drain, and refresh in cold water, then drain again.

Meanwhile, put all the ingredients for the dressing in a glass jar with a lid, then shake well to combine.

Put the potatoes, both beans, tomatoes, olives, scallions, and *mitsuba* in a large mixing bowl or salad bowl, add all but 2 tablespoons of the dressing, and toss lightly.

Heat the vegetable oil in a large heavy-bottomed skillet over medium–high heat. Pat the tuna dry with paper towels, and sear for 1 to 2 minutes on each side, or until cooked to your liking—ideally the inside should be rare and pink. Cut the tuna steaks into ¼ to ⅜-inch thick slices.

To serve, divide the salad between four plates, put the tuna on top, and drizzle over the reserved dressing.

SEARED BEEF SALAD WITH GRATED DAIKON DRESSING

This salad is a perfect way to ensure beef lovers get plenty of fresh vegetables. The richness of the beef is counterbalanced perfectly with the refreshing *daikon* dressing.

SERVES 4

1 white onion
1 fennel bulb
3½ ounces watercress
14 ounces beef rump, sirloin, or fillet
a few drops of sesame oil
1 teaspoon salt
2 tablespoons rice vinegar

FOR THE DRESSING
scant 1 cup grated *daikon*, giant white radish
3 tablespoons soy sauce
3 tablespoons mirin
1 tablespoon grated fresh ginger

Start by thinly slicing the onion and soak in a bowl of cold water for 10 to 15 minutes to refresh and tone down the strong onion smell.

Cut the fennel into quarters, remove and discard the core, and cut into thin slices. Trim the watercress into manageable length pieces.

Drain the grated radish by putting it through a strainer, and reduce to about half the amount by pressing down with a spoon. Mix with the rest of the dressing ingredients.

Heat a heavy-bottomed skillet or iron griddle over high heat. Rub the beef with a few drops of the sesame oil, and sprinkle over 1 teaspoon of salt just before placing in the pan. Sear on one side for 2 minutes, turn over, and cook the other side for 1 minute. Transfer onto a cutting board, pour the vinegar over, and press and rub the vinegar in. Leave to rest for 5 minutes.

Drain the onion, and mix with the fennel slices. Divide and arrange the vegetables between four individual serving plates. Cut the beef into ¼-inch thick slices and divide into four portions. Arrange the meat slices neatly over the vegetables, pour the dressing on top, and serve.

BOWL FOOD

NOODLES, RICE, AND SUSHI

NOODLES MENRUI

Although more often eaten as lunch, or an evening snack, than as part of a formal meal, more noodles are consumed daily than any other dish in Japan. They are the original Japanese fast food, as they are quick and easy to make, equally easy to eat fast, and cheap.

The many varieties available can broadly be divided into three types. Soba, or buckwheat noodles, are generally associated with northeast Japan. Udon, thick, wheat flour noodles, are more familiar in warmer southwestern regions. Chūka-soba, more popularly known as rāmen, are wheat flour and egg-based Chinese-style noodles.

SOBA are thin, brownish grey in color and are the oldest of all the noodles eaten in Japan. When eaten as a separate course, they are served in a hot broth, arranged on a bamboo lattice with a dipping sauce, or in a shallow bowl with toppings and a sauce to pour over. *Cha-soba* has an attractive green appearance, and subtle tea flavor from the addition of green tea powder. In Japan, soba are available fresh, but elsewhere, you are more likely to find dried.

UDON are thick, round or flat, wheat flour, white noodles. They are often served in hot broth, with a dipping sauce or in hot pot dishes. Outside of Japan they are sold dried, or semi-fresh in vacuum packs.

KISHIMEN are wide, thick and flat white flour noodles popular in and around Nagoya. Sold dried.

HIYAMUGI A fine white flour noodle used especially in cold dishes. Sold dried.

SŌMEN are very fine white noodles, made from hard durum wheat, moistened with cottonseed or sesame oil. Traditionally eaten cold, but occasionally served in hot, clear soups. Almost always sold dried in neat bundles, they come in three colorful variations: *cha-sōmen* (green from the addition of green tea powder), *tamago-sōmen* (yellow with egg yolk) and *ume-sōmen* (pink from the addition of plum).

RĀMEN Chinese-style flour and egg noodle with a creamy yellow color. Available either straight or curly.

The history of soba precedes that of other wheat flour noodles. Buckwheat was originally introduced from China in the late prehistoric Jōmon period, and the earliest written record shows that after a rice crop failure in 727, soba was grown to avert devastating nationwide famines. Soba is a fast-growing hardy annual plant that grows even on relatively poor soil. It takes only seventy-five days from sowing to harvest. Originally, soba was eaten like porridge, then began to be formed into noodle shape in the early seventeeth century, and became very popular among residents of Edo (the old name of Tokyo). There were more soba stands than sushi stalls in the old capital.

Soba is rich in protein, the essential amino acid lysine, which is lacking in most cereal grains, lipids, minerals such as iron, phosphorus, and copper, vitamins B1 and B2, and rutin (4 to 6 percent), an essential nutrient that strengthens capillaries, and so helps people suffering from arteriosclerosis and high blood pressure. Recent research shows that 30mg of rutin per day meets the body's requirements, amply provided by an average serving of soba, which contains about 100mg. Soba proteins also prevent body fat accumulation. Choline, another important micronutrient found in soba, plays a valuable role in metabolism, especially regulating blood pressure and liver function.

Soba also works as a social lubricant. The word soba is a homonym of the word meaning "near." There used to be an endearing old custom to go around neighbors with a gift of soba noodles in hand to introduce oneself when he/she moved into a new home—saying "I moved in near/soba you."

Traditionally, soba noodles in hot broth is the last thing eaten when families gather to see in the New Year. New Year's Eve in Japan is similar to Christmas Eve in the West, and is one of the busiest days in the Japanese calendar. Homes have to be cleaned and decorated, and special New Year food cooked, as stores close for several days. Slurping up a bowl of soba late at night, as the temple bell tolls on New Year's Eve, is one of the most evocative memories of my childhood.

Serving temperature is an important element for almost all Japanese food, and is particularly relevant for noodles. In winter, noodles should be served piping hot to warm both body and soul, while in the humid Japanese summer, chilled noodles stimulate appetite and encourage recovery from summer fatigue. Speed is also of the essence. In Japan, it is considered rude to linger over a bowl of noodles, and one is expected to eat it quickly once served. This involves noisy slurping, as it is impossible to eat noodles quietly, so one just has to discard conventional Western dining etiquette.

HOW TO COOK NOODLES

Outside of Japan you are most likely to come across noodles in the dried form, but the method of preparing noodles whether fresh or dried, is the same—it just takes slightly longer with dried noodles, and when cooked they double in weight. To cook 3½ ounces (a typical portion) of dried noodles bring about 2 quarts of water to a rolling boil in a large saucepan. The saucepan must be big enough so that the noodles are not crowded, and for the boiling water to circulate— just like cooking pasta. Add the noodles gradually into the boiling water, so that the water temperature does not suddenly drop. Stir gently to stop the noodles from sticking to the bottom of the pan. Let the water return to a full boil, and when it froths up to the top and is about to spill over, add a cup of cold water—this is called "*bikkuri-mizu*," surprise water, and the purpose of this is to ensure even cooking. You may need to repeat this two or three times depending on the dryness of the noodles. To test, remove one strand of noodle and bite into it—the noodle should be the same color throughout, and cooked to the center with no hard core, yet still quite firm. Test frequently to avoid overcooking. Drain the noodles in a strainer, and rinse under cold running water, rubbing vigorously with your hands to wash off surface starch, and drain again. To reheat the cooked noodles, simply place in a strainer or a colander, and plunge into a pot of boiling water for 10 seconds or so. Separate the strands by shaking the strainer in the water, then drain.

ALL-PURPOSE NOODLE SAUCE

There are many ready-made noodle sauces available. Although they're a useful standby and many Japanese home cooks have them (including myself, I confess) homemade is much better, and more economical. This keeps for up to 4 weeks refrigerated, and can be used for simmered dishes and broths too.

MAKES ABOUT 6 CUPS

2 postcard-size pieces of dried kelp
3 to 4 dried shiitake mushrooms
scant 1 cup mirin
scant 1 cup sake
1½ teaspoons sea salt
1 ounce *katsuobushi*, dried bonito flakes
3½ tablespoons light soy sauce

Put the kelp, shiitake, and 4½ cups of water in a large glass bowl, and let it stand in a fridge overnight.

Put the mirin and sake in a large saucepan, and bring to a boil for 2 minutes to burn off the alcohol. Add the kelp, mushrooms, and soaking water to the pan, and bring to a boil, then add the salt and bonito flakes. Bring it back to a boil again, then reduce the heat to simmer for 5 to 6 minutes, skimming off any scum that floats to the top, then add the soy sauce.

Remove from the heat, and strain through a cheesecloth-lined strainer. Set aside to cool to room temperature.

Transfer the sauce into a sterilized glass jar with a lid. Store refrigerated for up to 4 weeks.

HOW TO USE

The above recipe gives a concentrated sauce and needs to be diluted according to different uses:

noodle soup broth: 1 part sauce and 1 part water

noodle pouring sauce: 3 parts sauce and 2 parts water

noodle dipping sauce: 2 parts sauce and 1 part water

The above dilution proportions are a rough guide and you may adjust the seasoning to suit your taste.

SOBA WITH DUCK IN HOT BROTH
KAMO NAMBAN

This is one of the most popular classic soba dishes, I have made a slight change to it by substituting Japanese white scallions (which are difficult to find outside of Japan) with young leeks.

SERVES 2

1 duck breast, skin on
1 tender young leek, trimmed
7 ounces dried soba noodles
2½ cups soup broth (1¼ cups All-purpose Noodle Sauce, page 77, mixed with 1¼ cups water)
shichimi-tōgarashi, seven-spice chili powder, optional

Trim the duck breast of excess fat, and prick the skin with a fork. Heat a saucepan over medium heat, and wipe the inside base with a clean cold damp cloth (this stops the meat from sticking). Place the duck breast skin-side down, and cook for 3 to 5 minutes, then turn over and cook for an additional 3 minutes. Remove from the heat, and rinse under running hot water to wash off any remaining fat. Put the breast on a cutting board to rest.

Wipe the saucepan clean with paper towels.

Halve the leek lengthwise, and cut diagonally into thin slices.

Cut the duck into 1¼ to 1¾-inch thick slices. Put the duck and leek in the cleaned saucepan with the soup broth, and bring to a boil while skimming off any scum that floats to the surface, and simmer for 5 to 6 minutes.

Meanwhile cook the noodles as on page 77. Divide the noodles between two warmed bowls. Ladle in the hot broth mixture, arrange the duck slices on top, sprinkle with chili powder (if using), and serve immediately.

CHILLED SOBA IN A BASKET
ZARU SOBA

The Japanese summer is relentlessly hot and punishingly humid, and many people lose their appetite except for these chilled noodles. *Zaru soba* literally means "noodles in basket" and they are served on basketwork or bamboo boxes with slatted bottoms, accompanied by cold dipping sauce. It is a simple and refreshing summer favorite.

SERVES 2

7 ounces dried soba noodles
2 tablespoons finely shredded toasted nori
¾ cup dipping sauce (½ cup All-purpose Noodle Sauce, page 77 mixed with ¼ cup water)

FOR THE SPICY CONDIMENTS

2 teaspoons wasabi paste
2 tablespoons finely chopped scallions
2 tablespoons grated *daikon*, giant white radish, lightly drained

Cook the noodles as on page 77, but do not reheat. Divide them between two baskets (or ordinary plates, as long as the noodles are well drained).

To serve, sprinkle the nori shreds over each serving of noodles. Serve the dipping sauce in individual cups or small bowls alongside. Place the spicy condiments in small dishes, and let each diner help themselves.

To eat, mix a dab of wasabi and some scallion with grated radish in the dipping sauce. Pick up some noodles, and dip into the sauce mixture.

MUSHROOM SOBA KINOKO SOBA

Mushrooms are loved by Japanese people for their flavor, aroma, and texture. In this dish, dashi broth is lightly thickened with cornstarch to match the mushrooms' silky texture. You can use any mushrooms of your choice.

SERVES 2

4 shiitake mushrooms
2 ounces shimeji mushrooms
2 ounces enoki mushrooms
2½ cups soup broth (1¼ cups All-purpose Noodle Sauce, page 77, mixed with 1¼ cups water)
2 tablespoons cornstarch, mixed with 2 tablespoons water
7 ounces dried soba noodles
1 scallion, finely chopped on the diagonal, to serve

Cut and discard the stems of the shiitake mushrooms. Both shimeji and enoki mushrooms are joined at the base, so cut and discard the bases, and separate the clumps into bite-size clusters with your hands. Put the mushrooms and the broth in a saucepan, and heat to just below a boil, then stir in the cornstarch to thicken.

Meanwhile, cook the noodles as on page 77, and portion between two warmed bowls. Ladle in the hot broth, and arrange the mushrooms attractively, then scatter over the chopped scallion, and serve immediately.

CHILLED SOBA WITH SPINACH AND WAKAME WITH SESAME DIPPING SAUCE

I came up with this idea when I faced with a small mountain of home-grown spinach. The addition of spinach and wakame seaweed makes this dish very healthy, and sesame dipping sauce gives it a satisfying depth.

SERVES 2

1½ ounces dried wakame seaweed
7 ounces spinach
7 ounces dried soba noodles

FOR THE SESAME DIPPING SAUCE
5⅔ tablespoons toasted sesame seeds
scant ½ cup All-purpose Noodle Sauce (see page 77)
2 tablespoons finely chopped scallion
shichimi-tōgarashi, seven-spice chili powder, optional

Put the seaweed in a bowl, cover with water, leave to soak for 10 minutes, then drain. Cut the spinach into 4-inch long pieces, removing any thick, tough stalks.

Cook the noodles as on page 77, but just before adding a cup of cold water, add the spinach, and then the water, and let it return to a boil. Remove from the heat and drain, then plunge into cold water, and rinse well. Drain thoroughly, and divide between two baskets (or ordinary plates as long as the noodle mix is well drained).

To prepare the sesame dipping sauce, put the sesame seeds in a mortar, and grind until it becomes a coarse paste. Gradually add the noodle sauce, and adjust the taste by adding 2 to 3 tablespoons of water, then divide between two small cups.

Serve the noodles sprinkled with finely chopped scallion, chili powder (if using), and the cups of dipping sauce on the side.

AVOCADO AND SHRIMP ON SOBA WITH WASABI SAUCE

This is an adaptation of the rather retro dish, shrimp in avocado.

SERVES 2

7 ounces dried soba noodles

½ white or red onion

1 ripe avocado

10 to 12 cooked shrimp

4 tablespoons peppercress

FOR THE WASABI POURING SAUCE

2 to 3 teaspoons wasabi paste

1 cup noodle pouring sauce (scant ⅔ cup All-purpose Noodle Sauce, page 77, mixed with a generous ⅓ cup water)

Cook the noodles as on page 77, drain and portion between two dishes.

Peel and finely slice the onion, then soak in a bowl of cold water for 10 minutes—this helps to remove the strong onion odor.

Mix the wasabi paste and the noodle pouring sauce, then divide between two small bowls.

Slice the avocado in half and remove the pit. Peel, then cut the flesh into bite-size pieces.

Drain the onion slices, and place on top of the noodles. Arrange the avocado and shrimp on top of the onion layer, then garnish with cress. Serve with the wasabi noodle sauce on the side.

TUNA AND ARUGULA ON SOBA

This tasty noodle salad couldn't be easier to make—the only cooking involved is preparing the noodles. The rest is just a simple assembly job. The all-purpose noodle sauce doubles up as a salad dressing and noodle sauce.

SERVES 2

7 ounces dried soba noodles

3½ ounces arugula

9-ounce can tuna, in spring water, drained

shichimi-tōgarashi, seven-spice chili powder, to serve (optional)

FOR THE POURING SAUCE

1 cup noodle pouring sauce (scant ⅔ cup All-purpose Noodle Sauce, page 77, mixed with a generous ⅓ cup water)

2 teaspoons soy sauce

1 teaspoon sesame oil

1 teaspoon grated fresh ginger

1 teaspoon toasted sesame seeds

Cook the noodles as on page 77, drain and portion between two dishes.

Put all the ingredients for the pouring sauce in a glass jar with a lid, and shake well to mix.

Place the arugula on top of the soba, then place the drained tuna on top.

Pour the sauce over the noodle arrangement. Sprinkle with chili powder, if using, and serve.

MOON UDON TSUKIMI UDON

Tsukimi literally means "moon viewing" in Japanese, which is a genteel pastime in autumn when the air is clear, and the moon is full. Here, the whole yellow egg yolk in the center is depicted as the full moon surrounded by semi-cooked egg white, and noodles as clouds. Choose the freshest eggs you can find.

SERVES 2

7 ounces dried udon noodles
1¼ cups All-purpose Noodle Sauce (see page 77)
2 tablespoons mirin
4 slices of *kamaboko*, fish paste cake (optional)
2 eggs
1 scallion, finely chopped, to garnish
shichimi-tōgarashi, seven-spice chili powder (optional)

Cook the noodles as on page 77 and portion between two warmed bowls. Keep warm. Pre-heating the bowls is particularly important for this recipe, as you need all the retained heat to semi-cook the eggs.

Meanwhile, heat the noodle sauce and mirin in a saucepan with 1¾ cups of cold water to just below boiling. Pour half a ladleful of hot broth over each noodle mound, and keep the rest on a simmer.

If including *kamaboko*, arrange 2 slices at the side of the noodles. With the back of a ladle, make a hollowed nest in the center of the noodles. Crack an egg and gently place the whole egg in the nest and ladle the remaining broth around it, then immediately cover each bowl with plastic wrap to "poach" the egg for 1 minute. The egg white should turn opaque white from the heat of the broth, but if you prefer the egg more cooked, microwave on high for 10 to 12 seconds. Remove the plastic wrap, garnish with the chopped scallion and a sprinkle of chili powder, if liked, and serve immediately.

BEEF UDON NIKU UDON

Beef gives extra meaty depth to otherwise simple plain-tasting noodle dishes. Japanese beef is butchered differently from Western beef, and in general, meat is sold thinly sliced.

SERVES 2

6 ounces minute steak or rump steak
1 young leek, white part only
2 teaspoons vegetable oil
1¼ cups All-purpose Noodle Sauce (see page 77)
7 ounces dried udon noodles
sansho pepper, to taste

Slice the beef into thin 1½ to 2-inch long pieces. Cut the leek into ⅜-inch thick slices on the diagonal. Heat the oil in a saucepan over medium heat, and just before adding the beef, place the bottom on a cool damp cloth—this stops the meat sticking to the base, then add the beef, and cook for 1 minute. Pour in 1¾ cups water, and bring to a boil, skimming off any scum that floats to the surface. Add the leek and noodle sauce, and reduce the heat to a gentle simmer while you cook the noodles.

Cook the noodles as on page 77, drain and portion between two warmed bowls.

Ladle in the soup broth, and sprinkle over *sansho* pepper to taste. Serve immediately.

RĀMEN
CHINESE-STYLE NOODLES

Chinese-style noodles better known as *rāmen* were originally brought back from China by returning soldiers and their families after the end of the Second World War. Typically, these straight or curly noodles are served in a hot soup with slices of roasted pork, bean sprouts, and chopped scallion, but there are countless combinations, ranging from a more Japanese flavor of soy- or miso-based stock, to those with a very rich pig's trotter stock and added chili oil. As well as ingredients, *rāmen* may be named after a region where they are popular. For example, in Sapporo in Hokkaido, where *miso-rāmen* originated in 1955, there is an entire street devoted to serving the noodles, and *Sapporo-rāmen* and *miso-rāmen* have become synonymous. Another example of the strong association between an ingredient and a region is *tonkotsu-rāmen*, made of a rich pig's trotter stock, which is particularly popular in Hakata in *Kyūshū*, and the noodles are often called *Hakata-rāmen*.

One major difference between *rāmen* and native Japanese noodles such as soba and udon, is that while the texture of soba and udon is the key element, *rāmen* are identified by the soup stock they are served with. *Rāmen* stores try to distinguish themselves from others by their own stock—the importance of stock-making was humorously illustrated in a foodie film called *Tampopo*. Whether using chicken bones or pig's trotters, *rāmen* stock making is time consuming, and is not normally undertaken by average Japanese home cooks—they either eat out, or use ready-made stock powder. But here are two relatively quick and easy recipes for you to enjoy at home.

SOY RĀMEN
SHŌYU RĀMEN

In this dish, understated dashi broth is transformed into punchy noodle soup with the addition of ginger and garlic.

SERVES 2

2 teaspoons toasted sesame oil
½ onion, finely sliced
1½ tablespoons grated fresh ginger
2 tablespoons grated garlic
3⅓ cups dashi of your choice (see pages 29 to 31)
4 tablespoons soy sauce
2 tablespoons dried wakame seaweed
7 ounces dried or semi-fresh Chinese-style noodles
2 scallions, finely chopped, to garnish
1 teaspoon toasted sesame seeds, to garnish

Heat the oil in a wok, and cook the onion, ginger, and garlic over medium heat until the onions are softened, then add the dashi. Do not let it boil as this will make the broth cloudy, so reduce the heat to low and simmer for 5 to 8 minutes while skimming off any scum that floats to the surface. Season the broth with soy sauce, and adjust the taste with more soy sauce if needed.

Meanwhile, put the seaweed in a bowl, cover with water, and leave to soak for 10 minutes to soften, then drain.

Cook the dried noodles as shown on page 77 and drain. Or if you are using semi-fresh noodles, heat and refresh in boiling water for a few minutes, while separating the strands, then drain.

Divide the noodles between two warmed bowls. Ladle in the soup, place the wakame in the center, top with scallions, sprinkle with sesame seeds, and serve immediately.

SAPPORO MISO RĀMEN
SAPPORO RĀMEN

This is a hearty robust noodle dish that is guaranteed to warm your body and soul.

SERVES 2

1 onion, roughly chopped

1 carrot, roughly chopped

2 garlic cloves

½ teaspoon chili oil

1 teaspoon sesame oil

1 tablespoon sake

2 teaspoons sugar

4 tablespoons soy sauce

4 to 6 tablespoons medium-colored miso

1¾ pints chicken stock (preferably homemade, or use a stock cube)

4 slices unsmoked bacon, cut into 2 to 2½-inch long pieces

7 ounces dried or semi-fresh Chinese-style noodles

1¾ cups bean sprouts

FOR THE TOPPINGS

4 tablespoons cooked corn kernels (fresh or canned)

4 scallions, finely chopped on the diagonal

2 teaspoons toasted sesame seeds

To make the base for the miso, put the onion, carrot, and garlic in a food processor, and whiz until puréed.

Heat the chili and sesame oils in a wok, and lightly stir-fry the vegetable purée over medium heat. Add the sake, sugar, soy sauce, and miso, and stir until well mixed. Pour in the chicken stock, and bring to just below a boil, add the bacon, then reduce the heat to low, and simmer while you prepare the noodles.

Bring a saucepan of water to a boil, and cook the noodles for 3 to 4 minutes (2 to 3 minutes if using the semi-fresh variety). Just a minute before the noodles are ready, add the bean sprouts to the pan, and blanch for the last minute. Drain, and divide the noodles and bean sprouts between two warmed bowls.

Ladle in the soup, arrange the toppings over, and serve immediately.

CHILLED CHINESE-STYLE NOODLE SALAD
HIYASHI-CHŪKA

This is another example of Japanese adaptation of foreign imports. Although this big and colorful noodle salad uses Chinese-style noodles, the origin is not found in China, but is a Japanese invention.

SERVES 2

FOR THE CHICKEN LEG

1 chicken leg
1 tablespoon sake
1 scallion, 4-inch piece of green part only
a few slices of fresh ginger

FOR THE SHIITAKE MUSHROOMS

2 dried shiitake mushrooms
2 teaspoons sugar
2 teaspoons mirin
2 teaspoons sake
2 teaspoons soy sauce

FOR THE OMELETS

1 egg, beaten
½ teaspoon sugar
a pinch of salt
½ teaspoon vegetable oil

FOR THE SOY VINAIGRETTE

2 tablespoons soy sauce
3 tablespoons rice vinegar
1 tablespoon sugar
2 teaspoons toasted sesame oil

FOR THE NOODLES AND SALAD

7 ounces dried or semi-fresh Chinese-style noodles
1 Lebanese cucumber, quartered lengthwise, seeded, and finely sliced
3 cherry vine tomatoes, halved
1 tablespoon toasted sesame seeds

Prick the chicken leg all over with a fork and put in a saucepan with about ½ cup water (just enough to cover), the sake, scallion, and ginger. Cover with a lid, bring to a boil, then reduce the heat to low, and cook for an additional 12 to 15 minutes. Remove the pan from the heat, uncover, and set aside until the chicken is cool enough to handle. Reserve the cooking broth for the vinaigrette later. Remove and discard the skin and bone, and shred the meat with a fork. Set aside.

Soak the shiitake mushrooms in warm water for 5 to 8 minutes. Lightly squeeze the mushrooms (reserve the soaking juice) discard the stems, thinly slice the caps, then put in a small saucepan with the reserved mushroom soaking juice mixed with sugar, mirin, sake, and soy sauce. Cook over gentle heat for 8 to 10 minutes, turn off the heat, and set aside.

Mix all the omelet ingredients, except the vegetable oil, in a bowl, then strain through a strainer to make the mixture smooth. Heat the vegetable oil in a nonstick skillet, about 6 inches in diameter, over medium heat, and thinly spread with half of the egg mixture. Cook for 2 to 3 minutes on each side. Repeat the process with the rest of the egg mixture. Transfer the omelets to a cutting board, fold, and cut into thin strips.

Make the vinaigrette by putting all the ingredients plus 1 tablespoon of the reserved chicken broth in a small lidded jam jar, and shake vigorously.

Cook the dried noodles as on page 77 and drain. If you are using semi-fresh noodles, heat and refresh in boiling water for a few minutes, while separating the strands, then drain. Rinse the noodles under cold running water and drain well. Divide between two individual serving plates.

To assemble, divide the chicken, mushrooms, omelet, and cucumber into two portions, place each topping on the noodle beds, making four colored quarters. Place three tomato halves in the center, sprinkle the sesame seeds over, pour the vinaigrette around the noodles, and serve.

RICE KOME

Rice takes the center stage in Japanese food and culture. Not only is it Japan's staple, it is an essential ingredient in many other foods, including sake (the national drink), mirin, which is an important seasoning ingredient, and vinegar, another key ingredient to many dishes, most famously for sushi. Rice bran is also used to make countless varieties of pickles.

The history of rice parallels that of the nation as a whole. From early times, families who grew more rice became more powerful, seizing agricultural, political, and economic supremacy over other clans, and eventually ruling the whole country. During the medieval period, rice was an alternative currency. Each feudal lord's wealth was counted in terms of a rice volume unit called *koku*, 石 (one *koku* is roughly 5 bushels, about 330 pounds in weight), and samurai were paid their stipends in *koku* of rice. The rice farmers themselves, however, rarely ate the grain, because they were excluded from the currency system, and had to save rice to pay heavy taxes. Rice crops often failed, and there was always the fear of famine. This long, lingering, relative scarcity helped shape the respectful Japanese attitude to rice.

By the 1960s, the rising tide of Westernization meant that the Japanese were eating less rice than previous generations, but it has never lost its special position in people's hearts or stomachs. Regardless of how many other dishes are served, Japanese people feel they have not eaten properly unless there is rice. In fact, the word for cooked rice 御飯 *gohan*, is the same as a meal.

The short-grain rice that is grown and eaten in Japan is *japonica*; a subspecies of *oryza sativa*. It may be non-glutinous *uruchimai* or glutinous *mochigome*. Japanese people generally prefer to eat polished non-glutinous white rice, but recent health trends have led to the wider availability of both unpolished brown rice, and "converted" rice, which is processed so that the nutrients and vitamins lost during the polishing are put back.

Rice is cooked and served in a variety of ways:

PLAIN BOILED RICE 御飯 (*gohan*)

MIXED RICE 混ぜ御飯 (*maze-gohan*) Raw or pre-cooked ingredients are mixed into plain cooked rice during the steaming period, or just before serving.

RICE COOKED WITH THINGS 炊き込みご飯 (*takikomi-gohan*) Various ingredients, raw or pre-cooked, are put in the pot with uncooked rice and cooked all together.

RED RICE おこわ (*okowa*) Originally referred to plain steamed glutinous rice, but today this refers to 赤飯 *sekihan*, red rice, made from glutinous rice steamed with adzuki beans. The dish is prepared for special celebratory occasions.

HOT RICE WITH TOPPINGS 丼 (*donburi*) Hot plain rice is served with various toppings such as fish, meat, egg, or vegetables in a lidded large rice bowl, which is also called *donburi*.

RICE BALLS おにぎり (*onigiri*) Japan's portable food equivalent of Western sandwiches. Cooked rice is shaped usually into triangular, often oval, and occasionally ping-pong ball shapes, with or without tasty morsels such as a pickled plum, or a small piece of broiled salted salmon concealed inside, wrapped in toasted nori seaweed.

TEA-FLAVORED RICE お茶漬け (*ochazuke*) A simple dish or snack where various things such as a piece of salted salmon, shred of nori, or pickled plums, are placed on top of hot or cold cooked rice, and hot tea is poured over it.

RICE PORRIDGE OR GRUEL 雑炊 (*zōsui*) Cooked rice is cooked again with various ingredients such as fish, egg, poultry, or vegetables in dashi.

RICE GRUEL お粥 (*o-kayu*) A Japanese cure-all in which uncooked rice is cooked with a lot of water: the common ratios of rice to water are 1:5, 1:7, 1:10 and 1:15. The thickness of the gruel is determined by the amount of water and the speed of cooking—the more water and faster cooking over higher heat, gives a thinner and more watery consistency.

PLAIN BOILED RICE GOHAN

When I first came to England to attend a boarding school, I had the humiliating experience of not knowing how to cook rice in an ordinary saucepan. Nowadays in Japan, almost every household large or small, even single student lodgings, has an automatic rice cooker, I mumbled in protest. Since then, I relearned the art of cooking rice in a saucepan.

In Japan, rice is measured in the traditional unit of 合, gō, (this is ¾ cup in volume, or about 5¼ ounces dried weight). Allow about 2½ ounces uncooked rice per serving. Short-grain rice expands to roughly double in weight when cooked.

To wash, put rice in a large bowl, cover with cold water, and stir quickly with your hands for about 30 seconds, then drain immediately. Never let the rice stand in this first milky water—the milkiness comes from powdered bran, and starch that should be washed away. Repeat the washing and changing water process until the water runs clear; this should take about 5 minutes. Do not skip this process as poorly washed rice is smelly, and spoils quickly.

Let the rice stand in a colander for 30 minutes to drain. While standing, the rice will absorb moisture, and expand in volume by about 20 percent.

Choose a heavy, round, deep saucepan with a tight-fitting lid. A cast-iron enameled saucepan of an appropriate size is ideal. Cooked in too large a pot, the rice will be dry, or even scorched, while if too small a pot is used, with not enough headroom, the rice becomes gluey.

It is rather difficult to prescribe an exact formula for the amount of water used in cooking rice because there are so many variables—where the rice was grown, in a flooded paddy (Asian origin) or dry field (US or European origin), whether the rice is newly harvested, or it has been sitting on the shelf for some time, etc. As a general, but flexible rule, use enough water to cover the rice by 1 inch.

To cook, place the pan, covered, over medium heat, and bring to just boiling. Turn the heat up to high, and boil vigorously for 2 to 3 minutes: the starchy liquid will bubble up, and steam will escape from under the lid. When the bubbling ceases, and it goes quiet, reduce the heat to very low and cook for an additional 8 to 10 minutes. All this time you must not lift the lid, but learn to listen. Turn off the heat, still keeping the lid on, and stand to steam for 10 to 15 minutes before lifting the lid.

Fluff the rice with a well moistened wooden rice paddle, or a flat spatula in a cut-and-turn motion. If you are not serving it immediately, stretch a dishtowel under the lid, to catch and stop condensation dropping back into the rice.

NOTE ON FOOD SAFETY

I am often asked "Is it safe to reheat rice"? and the answer is "yes," but the important point to prevent food poisoning, rests on how it is cooled and stored, and not with the reheating process itself.

Uncooked rice and other cereal products such as pasta, frequently contain bacteria called *bacillus cereus*. Unfortunately it survives when boiled in water, and if the rice is slowly cooled and stored at room temperature, the bacterium germinate and multiply to produce a poisonous toxin.

Simple tips to safely eat cooked rice:

Cook only the amount of rice needed and serve it immediately.

Either keep cooked rice hot (above 140°F) or cool it as fast as possible, and keep it refrigerated (below 40°F) until needed. Cooked rice cools down quicker if divided into smaller quantities, and placed in clean shallow containers, or in a colander under cold running water.

Rice freezes well, but defrost it quickly, by either using boiling water or microwave directly from frozen, and do not let it stand at room temperature after defrosting or reheating.

CHICKEN AND EGG ON RICE
OYAKO-DONBURI

Oyako, means "a parent and a child" and as the name suggests it is made with chicken and eggs. It is arguably the most representative dish of the *donburi* genre.

SERVES 4

⅓ cup light soy sauce

⅓ cup mirin

1¾ cups Dashi or chicken stock (see page 29)

2 tablespoons sugar

7 ounces chicken breast or mini chicken fillets, thinly sliced

4 scallions, cut diagonally into ¾-inch lengths

4 eggs, lightly beaten

6 cups freshly cooked hot rice (from scant 1½ cups uncooked)

Put the soy sauce, mirin, dashi or stock, and sugar in a saucepan and bring to a gentle boil over medium heat. Add the chicken, and simmer for 8 minutes, then add the scallions, and simmer for an additional minute.

Divide the mixture into four portions, and put one portion in a small pan while keeping the rest warm—this is to make the egg cooking time shorter and easier than handling a larger amount. Gently pour 1 beaten egg, in a steady stream, over the chicken mixture, let the egg spread naturally and do not stir. When the egg starts to bubble at the edges, stir once, and let the mixture just begin to set then turn off the heat. Do not let the mixture set firm.

Put the hot rice into four warmed *donburi*, or deep soup bowls. Slide the egg mixture on top of the rice, and repeat the process with the remaining egg, while keeping the others warm. Serve immediately.

BEEF ON RICE
GYŪDON

This is another popular *donburi* dish, especially among the young. There is a fast-food chain company that boasts an impressive growth record, and is listed on the Tokyo Stock Exchange, serving this single item.

SERVES 4

14 ounces thinly sliced beef steak, such as minute steak

1 tablespoon vegetable oil

2 medium onions, thinly sliced

⅓ cup mirin

⅓ cup soy sauce

2 tablespoons grated fresh ginger

6 cups freshly cooked hot rice (from scant 1½ cups uncooked)

Pound the beef with the back of a knife or rolling pin to flatten, then cut into paper-thin 2-inch length pieces.

Heat the oil in a saucepan over high heat, and stir-fry the onions for a few minutes. Add the beef, and stir-fry until it is just turning brown, then pour in a scant cup of water, the mirin and soy sauce, and bring to a boil. Remove from the heat, and add the grated ginger.

Divide the hot rice between four warmed *donburi*, or deep soup bowls. With a large spoon, scoop one portion of the beef mixture and sauce on top of the rice and serve immediately.

RICE COOKED WITH FRESH PEAS ENDŌ-GOHAN

A bowl of plump green peas among glistening white rice not only looks beautiful, but is also a tasty new-season arrival.

SERVES 4

heaping 1½ cups rice
7 ounces fresh peas in pods
  (or about ⅔ cup podded peas)
1 teaspoon salt
2 teaspoons mirin

Wash the rice and set aside to drain in a colander for 30 minutes.

Shell the peas, rinse under cold running water, and drain. Put the rice, peas, and 1½ to 1¾ cups water in a heavy-bottomed saucepan with the salt and mirin, and stir once. Cook as on page 92. Fluff the rice and serve.

VARIATION

Use frozen edamame beans instead of the peas.

MUSHROOM RICE KINOKO-GOHAN

This is a more economical adaptation of a recipe that usually includes a luxury mushroom called "*matsutake*," literally pine-mushroom. These are highly fragrant and expensive fungi—Japan's equivalent of white truffle.

SERVES 4

heaping 1½ cups rice
3½ ounces shimeji or maitake mushrooms
2 ounces enoki mushrooms
4 shiitake mushrooms
1 tablespoon sake
1 tablespoon light soy sauce
½ teaspoon salt

Wash the rice and set aside to drain in a colander for 30 minutes.

Cut and discard the bases of shimeji and enoki mushrooms, and separate the clumps with your hands. Cut and discard the stems of the shiitake, and slice the caps.

Put the rice with 1¼ to 1½ cups water in a heavy-bottomed saucepan. Add the sake, soy sauce, and salt, and stir. Place the mushrooms on top of the rice, and cover with the lid. Cook the rice as described on page 92. Fluff, and mix the rice when cooked and serve.

TUNA ON RICE
TEKKADON

This is a rather unique dish as the only ingredient which is cooked is the rice.

SERVES 4

14 ounces sashimi-grade tuna

2 ripe avocados

6 tablespoons soy sauce

2 tablespoons sake

2 tablespoons mirin

2 teaspoons wasabi paste

1 tablespoon toasted white sesame seeds

6 cups freshly cooked hot rice (from scant
    1½ cups uncooked)

4 scallions, finely chopped, to garnish

4 small handfuls of shredded nori, to garnish

Cut the tuna into ⅜-inch thick bite-size pieces. Cut the avocados in half, remove the pits, and peel, then cut the flesh into ⅜-inch thick bite-size pieces.

Mix the soy sauce, sake, mirin, wasabi paste, and sesame seeds in a bowl, and add the tuna and avocado. Set aside to marinate for 10 to 12 minutes, turning over a few times.

Put the hot rice in four warmed *donburi* or deep soup bowls. Divide the tuna mix into four portions, and arrange on top of the rice, drizzle over any remaining juice, scatter with chopped scallions and nori, and serve.

RICE MIXED WITH EGG AND TOMATO
TAMAGO-KAKE-GOHAN

Tamago-kake-gohan loosely translates as "egg put on rice" where warm rice is mixed with raw egg, and must be the simplest form of "cooking."

SERVES 4

½ tablespoon vegetable oil

2 tablespoons finely chopped fresh ginger

4 medium-size tomatoes, seeded and cut
    into ⅜-inch dice

2 scallions, finely chopped

2 tablespoons light soy sauce

4 eggs, beaten

4 servings of freshly cooked rice, weighing
    about 5 ounces each

4 small handfuls of shredded nori, to garnish

Heat the oil in a saucepan over medium heat and add the ginger, diced tomatoes, and scallions. Cook for 2 to 3 minutes and add the soy sauce.

Pour in the beaten eggs, quickly stir to mix, and turn off the heat. The residual heat from the pan will semi-cook the egg mixture to a runny consistency. Quickly add the hot rice, and mix in a cut-and-turn motion. Divide between four individual bowls, garnish with nori shreds, and serve.

RED RICE
OKOWA / SEKIHAN

You will need a bamboo steamer for this recipe, and to start the day before you intend serving it.

SERVES 4

scant ½ cup dried adzuki beans
heaping 2¼ cups *mochigome*, glutinous rice
1 teaspoon salt
1 teaspoon toasted black sesame seeds, to garnish
½ teaspoon sea salt

Soak the beans in plenty of water for 3 to 4 hours, then drain. Parboil for 5 minutes in a generous amount of water, drain, change the water and repeat the process.

Put the beans in a saucepan with 1¾ cups of cold water, bring to a boil, uncovered, then simmer for 10 minutes or until the water turns reddish. Drain the beans, reserving the water. Using a ladle held high above another bowl, aerate and cool the water 5 to 6 times to brighten the color.

Wash and rinse the rice (see page 92), put in a pan with the reserved red water, and let stand for 24 hours or overnight; this tints the rice pink. Drain and reserve ⅞ cup of the water. Add 1 teaspoon of salt to the water, and set aside.

Fill a saucepan with plenty of water, and bring to a rapid boil. Mix the rice and beans evenly, and spread out on a damp cloth in a bamboo steamer. Place this over the saucepan, steam over high heat for 20 minutes, then lift off the lid and sprinkle over a tablespoonful of the red salted water, repeat this several times, continuing to steam over high heat for an additional 15 to 20 minutes.

Mix the sesame seeds with the sea salt in a small bowl. If you are not serving immediately, the rice needs to be cooled down quickly (spread it on a large flat surface such as a roasting pan). Serve in individual bowls, sprinkled with sesame salt.

PORGY RICE
TAI-MESHI

This is one of the most celebrated rice dishes of all, which is not surprising, as it combines two of Japan's most popular ingredients—rice and porgy (sea bream in Japan.) Traditionally, a whole handsome fish is cooked in a *donabe*, a lidded clay casserole, and brought to the table. In this version, the fish is broiled separately, and added later for easier eating and serving.

SERVES 4

heaping 1½ cups rice
1¼ cups Primary or Secondary Dashi
   (see pages 29 to 30)
2 tablespoons sake
2 tablespoons light soy sauce
14 ounces porgy fillet, skin on
1 teaspoon salt
1 tablespoon fresh ginger, finely julienned

Wash and drain the rice, then place it in a heavy-bottomed saucepan with the dashi, sake, and soy sauce. Leave to stand for 10 minutes.

Cut the fish into ¼-inch thick bite-size pieces by holding the knife at a 30 degree angle, so that the blade is almost horizontal to the fillet. Transfer onto a flat bamboo basket, or a paper-lined plate, then gently rub the salt on the skin side and set aside for 5 to 8 minutes.

Preheat the broiler to high and broil the fish for 5 minutes on each side.

Cook the rice over medium heat; when it reaches a boil and steam begins to rise, reduce the heat to low, and quickly place the fish, skin-side up, on top of the rice, cover immediately, and continue to cook until the steam stops. Turn off the heat, and quickly scatter over the ginger, cover again, and steam for an additional 10 minutes before serving.

RICE BALLS ONIGIRI

Onigiri is Japan's traditional equivalent of sandwiches. It is highly versatile and portable, and with a bit of practice, can easily be made quickly. Freshly cooked rice is usually shaped into triangular, often oval, and occasionally round pieces, and wrapped in nori or coated with sesame seeds. In the center, there are some concealed tasty morsels such as *umeboshi*, pickled plum, a small piece of broiled salted salmon, *tarako*, cod roe, or soy-seasoned bonito flakes.

It is an ideal picnic food, or party finger food. It can also be served at home for a change from the usual bowl of rice. To make good *onigiri* takes practice. Hot rice is pressed just enough to keep the grains together and keep its shape, but not so hard that all the air pockets are squashed out, making it too solid. It is rather like making *nigiri-zushi*, but *onigiri* is a home food and millions of Japanese people do it without even thinking about it. So here are some helpful tips for you:

Onigiri must be made with freshly cooked hot rice. Cold rice does not easily hold together without a lot of pressing, hence making the balls hard and dry.

An ideal amount of rice is about the size of a normal rice bowl or coffee cup—3½ to 4 ounces in weight.

The way to handle hot rice without scorching your hands is to use a clean damp cloth, and a rice bowl or coffee cup. Put a portion of rice in a rice bowl, and transfer onto a tightly wrung-out cloth held over your hand, then cover the rice with the cloth, and squeeze. Unwrap the rice, and transfer onto well moistened hands (they should be well moistened, but not drenched, with mild salt water to stop the rice from sticking, and to season the rice). Squeeze, and shape into a triangle. Make an indentation in the middle of the rice, and tuck in about a teaspoon of filling (see below) and continue molding to cover the filling with the rice. The key point is to avoid packing the rice too tightly, or too loosely.

Wrap each triangle with a strip of nori, shiny side out.

SUGGESTED FILLINGS: Broiled and flaked salted salmon, broiled salted cod roe (*tarako*), soy-doused bonito flakes (*katsuobushi*), pitted pickled plums (*umeboshi*) or dried salted konbu seaweed (*shio-konbu*).

TEA-FLAVORED RICE OCHAZUKE

A traditional Japanese meal ends with a bowl of rice and pickles, followed by a cup of green tea. Pouring tea over the rice with pickles or crumbled nori started as an informal homely practice, but proved so good, that it developed into a delicious dish of its own right, with a variety of topping ingredients added. It is also a delicious way of using up cold leftover rice. Use any type of tea except matcha, ceremonial powdered green tea (see pages 241 to 242).

SALT-SALMON AND RICE
SAKE-CHAZUKE

Salt-salmon, *shiozake,* is possibly one of my favorite and most used ingredients. There is always a jar of *shiozake* flakes in my fridge, ready to be used for a quick *ochazuke,* rice ball filling, in salads, or with noodles. It is highly versatile, cunningly easy to make, and keeps for a couple of weeks refrigerated, although it always gets eaten before that. When I was a small child, upon seeing a whole salmon or yellowtail hanging under the eaves of my grandparents' house, I used to wonder how cold air and salt could turn the fish even more delicious.

SERVES 4

4 portions of cooked rice, about 5 ounces each, hot or cold
8 heaping tablespoons salt-salmon flakes (see right)
4 tablespoons toasted and ground white sesame seeds
2 teaspoons wasabi paste
4 cups of hot green tea of your choice

Put each portion of rice in a bowl, place 2 tablespoons of salt-salmon flakes over, scatter with 1 tablespoon of sesame seeds, place a dab of wasabi paste on top, pour a cup of hot tea over all and serve.

SALT-SALMON SHIOZAKE

In Japan, salmon is almost always sold ready-salted and it is one of the most popular ingredients—it appears at a traditional breakfast, in lunch boxes, or even at a simple supper table.

1 to 2 tablespoons sea salt
21 ounces salmon fillet, skin on

Rub salt all over both sides of the fillet. Line a plate with a double layer of paper towels and place the fillet skin-side down. Loosely cover the fillet with paper towels, and place in the refrigerator for 5 days, after which time, you will have a rather stiff umami-packed fillet, ready to be portioned and broiled. Salt-salmon can be stored frozen up to 4 weeks.

SALT-SALMON FLAKES

21 ounces salt-salmon (see above)
4 tablespoons sake
2 to 3 teaspoons light soy sauce

Cut the fillet into 2 to 3 portions, so that they fit snugly into a large saucepan, and pour over just enough water to cover. Bring to a boil over medium heat, reduce the heat, and simmer for 10 to 12 minutes. Remove the fish from the pan, and transfer to a cutting board. When cool enough to handle, remove the skin and any bones. Scrape off the brown meat and with your hands, roughly break up the fillets into smaller pieces.

Wipe the bottom of a saucepan with a clean damp cloth (this helps the fish not stick), then add the fish pieces with the sake and soy sauce. Cook over gentle heat until most of the cooking juice has evaporated, stirring constantly. Do not let the flakes become too dry, stopping while they are still moist. Remove from the heat, and spread on a large plate to cool down before storing in sterilized jam jars. The flakes keep for 2 weeks, refrigerated.

RICE PORRIDGE ZŌSUI

Zōsui written 増水 means "increasing water." In the old days when rice was scarce, water or dashi was added to make it go further. Today it is often seen as a delicious dish for rice-loving weight-watchers. You can use almost any ingredients, with either freshly cooked or more often, leftover rice. The key point is to keep the broth clear, so if using freshly cooked rice, it should be slightly undercooked, and leftover rice must be rinsed to get rid of starch. Use about double the amount of water or dashi to the cooked rice, and do not overcook, otherwise it will be gluey. *Zōsui* is a popular and delicious way to round up a casserole—cooked rice is added to whatever is left in the pot at the end. Think of this type of dish as Japan's answer to risotto.

RICE GRUEL O-KAYU

This is the Japanese penicillin-like equivalent to Jewish cure-all chicken soup. When someone is not feeling well, he will be given a bowl of *o-kayu* (honorific kayu) rice gruel. Every Japanese baby is weaned on *o-kayu*, while the sick and old are nursed with it. This most gentle and easily digestible dish is made by cooking rice in a lot of water. The common proportions of water to rice are five times or seven times water to rice, while sometimes ten times, or even twenty times water is used to make very watery versions. The speed of cooking also affects the consistency—the slower the cooking over gentle heat, without stirring, the more smooth and gluey the end result. The main difference between *kayu* and *zōsui* is that *kayu* is made with uncooked rice that is cooked in water from the beginning, while already cooked rice is used for *zōsui*.

CRAB AND BROCCOLI PORRIDGE
KANI-ZŌSUI

Although *zōsui* is often made with leftover rice and whatever off-cuts can be found in the fridge to make an economical meal, this one has a touch of luxury.

SERVES 4

4¾ cups cooked rice
5 cups dashi of your choice (see pages 29 to 31)
4 tablespoons sake
2 tablespoons light soy sauce
1 tablespoon salt
1¼ cups Napa cabbage, roughly chopped
1½ cups broccolini, cut into 1¼ to 2-inch long pieces
7 ounces white crabmeat

If you are using leftover rice, put it in a large strainer, and rinse under hot running water to wash off the starch, and drain. Put the dashi with the sake, light soy sauce, and salt in a saucepan, and bring to a boil over medium heat. Add the vegetables, and simmer for 5 to 7 minutes, or until they are cooked through.

Add the rice and crabmeat, and continue to simmer for an additional 5 minutes. Adjust the seasoning if necessary, remove from the heat, divide between four warmed bowls, and serve immediately.

EGG AND CHIVE PORRIDGE
NIRATAMA-ZŌSUI

My mother used to make me this comforting and tasty dish whenever I was beginning to come down with a cold. It is warming and reviving, yet easy to digest. Chinese chives are deep green and flat leaved, and sold in Asian grocery stores.

SERVES 4

4¾ cups cooked rice
5 cups dashi of your choice (see pages 29 to 31)
4 tablespoons sake
4 tablespoons light soy sauce
2 to 3 teaspoons salt
3½ ounces Chinese chives, cut into
    1¼ to 1½-inch lengths
4 eggs, beaten

If you are using leftover rice, put it in a large strainer, rinse under hot running water to wash off the starch, and drain. Put the dashi, sake, soy sauce, and salt in a saucepan, and bring to a boil over medium heat. Add the chives, then reduce the heat, and simmer for 5 to 7 minutes.

Add the rice, and return to a simmer over medium heat. Then drizzle the beaten egg over the rice; do not stir, but immediately cover, and remove from the heat. The eggs will cook in the residual heat of the pot, but still be soft and runny. Divide between four warmed bowls, and serve immediately with spoons. The secret of this dish is to eat it while it is still hot, and the eggs are soft.

CHICKEN AND MISO PORRIDGE
TORI MISO-ZŌSUI

This dish has a plenty of flavor from the chicken and miso—think of it as a Japanese chicken risotto.

SERVES 4

4¾ cups cooked rice
7 ounces chicken thigh fillets
4 tablespoons sake
5 cups dashi of your choice (see pages 29 to 31)
2 tablespoons soy sauce
½ cup medium-colored miso
4 scallions, finely chopped diagonally

If you are using leftover rice, put it in a large strainer and rinse under hot running water to wash off the starch, and drain. Cut the chicken into thin bite-size pieces, and mix in a bowl with the sake. Put the dashi and soy in a saucepan, and bring to a boil over medium heat, then add the chicken mixture. Reduce the heat to a simmer, skimming off any scum that floats to the surface, and cook for 5 to 7 minutes.

Put the miso in a small bowl, and add a ladleful of the broth to soften, then pour the mixture into the pan. Add the rice, then let it return to a simmer, and cook for an additional 3 to 5 minutes. Scatter the scallions over, and remove from the heat. Divide between four warmed bowls, and serve immediately.

SUSHI

A high-ranking Japanese diplomat once joked that a piece of sushi in his hand, probably did more to raise Japan's profile, and made more friends around the world, than his official efforts. His comment has an element of truth, and many would have no hesitation in nominating sushi as their favorite Japanese food.

Sushi is defined as "fish fermented in rice and salt," but is more commonly understood as "vinegar-seasoned cooked rice served with fish, seafood, or vegetables." It began in Asia as a way to preserve fish by fermentation, and shares the same origin as Thailand's famous fish sauce, *nam pla*. It is not known when it was introduced to Japan, but seventh century records show it was already an important source of protein, and was brought to the land-bound ancient capital of Nara from coastal regions as a tax payment in kind. It was called *nare-zushi*, where fish was salted and pickled in beds of rice and salt, to naturally ferment for up to a year or longer. Airborne bacteria converts the rice starch into lactic acid, and together with salt, preserves the fish. Many varieties of *nare-zushi* are still made as regional delicacies around Japan. The most famous, *funa-zushi*, a highly pungent strong-tasting fermented carp, is made around the largest freshwater lake Biwa near Kyoto.

Nare-zushi, relying on slow natural fermentation, continued to be the only sushi making method until the beginning of the seventeenth century, when the *Tokugawa* clan finally unified the country. One of the major benefits of the new peaceful era, was the increase in food production, especially rice. More rice meant rice-based products, such as sake and rice vinegar, became more readily available, and it was around this time that vinegar began being added to flavor the rice instead of relying on the slow process of airborne bacteria. To distinguish it from *nare-zushi*, the newly invented vinegar-flavored sushi, was named *haya-zushi*, literally "quick-sushi." The addition of vinegar also freed the rice from having to be shaped in molds or boxes, and other styles of sushi, including *maki-zushi* (nori-rolled sushi), were developed.

But the most important development was the invention of *nigiri-zushi*, hand-squeezed sushi, also known as *Edomae-zushi* or Tokyo-style sushi, where a handful of vinegar-flavored rice is shaped into an oblong ball, and served with a topping of sliced fish or shellfish. *Nigiri-zushi* takes only a few minutes to make, and became an instant hit, but only in Tokyo. At the end of the Second World War, in order to get around difficulties posed by post-war food rationing on the restaurant industry, SCAP (the Supreme Commander for the Allied Powers) permitted sushi bars to exchange a cup of uncooked rice for 10 pieces of *nigiri-zushi* and a roll. This guidance led, almost overnight, to the nationwide domination of Tokyo-style sushi, and to the evolution of sushi as a universally recognizable fresh fast-food.

Although *nigiri-zushi* is the most popular style of sushi, it is almost never made at home, as it is an art that requires years of dedicated training. But there's no need to be disheartened, because there are many styles of sushi that can be made at home without undergoing years of apprenticeship.

SUSHI RICE SUSHI-MESHI

Good sushi, whatever the style, always begins with good sushi rice, which is a little harder and chewier than plain boiled rice because it is cooked with less water, to allow for the addition of sushi vinegar. Once cooked, it is quickly cooled, while being tossed with the vinegar in a specially designed shallow wooden tub called *hangiri*, made of Japanese cypress and hooped with copper. *Hangiri* are expensive, even in Japan, so use any wide, shallow, non-metallic tub instead. Always choose short-grain Japanese-style rice and avoid newly harvested rice, as it is too soft, and contains too much moisture.

HOW TO PREPARE SUSHI RICE

MAKES 3½ TO 3¾ CUPS
heaping 2⅛ cups short-grain sushi rice
1 postcard-size piece of dried kelp
⅓ cup sushi vinegar (see opposite)

Wash the rice under cold running water, drain, and set aside for 30 to 60 minutes to let it absorb moisture.

Put the washed rice and a scant 1 cup water in a heavy-bottomed saucepan with a tight-fitting lid. Make some slashes in the kelp to release more flavor, and place it on top of the rice, then wait for 10 to 15 minutes before turning on the heat. Cover, bring to a boil over high heat, and when it just begins to boil, remove and discard the kelp. Reduce the heat to medium and continue cooking for 6 to 7 minutes, then reduce the heat to low and simmer for 12 to 15 minutes, or until steam stops escaping. Turn off the heat, and let steam, with a dishtowel wrapped around the lid to stop condensation dripping down on the rice, for 10 to 15 minutes.

Moisten a *hangiri* (see page opposite) or a wide, shallow wooden or plastic tub to stop the rice from sticking. Spread the hot rice in a thin layer in the tub. Sprinkle sushi vinegar over the rice, then, with a moistened rice paddle or a flat spatula, toss the rice using cut-and-turn strokes (the lateral motion separates and coats the grains without bruising or mashing) and at the same time, cool it quickly by fanning. This is a bit tricky to do by yourself, so either get someone else to fan the rice or, if you are on your own, alternate tossing and fanning, rather than juggling both.

Sushi rice is ready when it has cooled to room temperature, and the grains are fluffy and glisteningly shiny. Try not to overdo this, as the rice will become sticky and heavy. To keep sushi rice from drying out, cover it with a clean damp cloth until needed, but use it up on the day it is prepared.

SUSHI VINEGAR
SUSHI-SU

Sushi vinegar is a blend of rice vinegar with sugar and salt. It is an all-important integral part of sushi making, and gives otherwise plain cooked rice a subtle depth of flavor and sheen. There is no set-in-stone recipe, and the ratio differs according to different types of toppings; for strong flavored ingredients such as broiled eel or cured mackerel, a sweeter vinegar mix goes better, while raw fish and shellfish calls for less sugar, and slightly more salt. There is a huge range of different formulas, and each sushi bar jealously guards their secret recipe. But the most general guide is, using the dry weight of rice as the base measure, 10 percent of vinegar, 5 percent of sugar and 1 percent of salt as shown below.

Rice	Water	Rice vinegar	Sugar	Salt
7 ounces (scant 1⅛ cups)	scant 1 cup	4 teaspoons	2½ teaspoons	½ teaspoon
10½ ounces (1⅓ cups)	1⅓ cups	2 tablespoons	1 tablespoon	½ to 1 teaspoon
14 ounces (heaping 2⅛ cups)	scant 2 cups	3 tablespoons	5 teaspoons	½ to 1 teaspoon
18 ounces (2⅔ cups)	2⅓ cups	scant ¼ cup	2¼ tablespoons	1 teaspoon

(Adjust the amount of sugar or salt as preferred)

It is easier to make up the vinegar in large quantities and have it ready. It keeps very well, refrigerated, for up to 3 months. The table below shows approximately the amount needed to season cooked rice.

Rice	Cooked rice	Sushi vinegar
7 ounces (scant 1⅛ cups)	2⅛ to 2¼ cups	3⅓ tablespoons
10½ ounces (1⅔ cups)	3¼ to 3⅓ cups	5 tablespoons
14 ounces (heaping 2⅛ cups)	4¼ to 4½ cups	6 tablespoons plus 1 teaspoon
18 ounces (2⅔ cups)	5½ to 5¾ cups	8½ tablespoons

ASPARAGUS AND SCRAMBLED EGG SCATTERED SUSHI

I like to serve this sushi in late spring when asparagus is in season and at its best.

SERVES 4

18 ounces asparagus, trimmed

2 eggs, beaten

2 teaspoons sugar

2 tablespoons light soy sauce

½ teaspoon salt

1 to 2 tablespoons vegetable oil for cooking

4¼ to 4½ cups prepared sushi rice (see page 107)

1 tablespoon toasted white sesame seeds

1 sheet of nori, crumbled

Steam the asparagus for 3 to 4 minutes, and rinse under cold running water to refresh, then drain. Reserve the tips for the garnish, and chop the spears into small pieces on the diagonal.

Mix the eggs with the sugar, soy sauce, and salt in a small mixing bowl. Heat the oil in a nonstick omelet pan over medium heat. Pour the egg mixture into the pan, and cook, stirring all the time with either an egg whisk, or 2 pairs of chopsticks. When the egg begins to set, remove from the heat, but continue to stir to get a fluffy consistency.

Mix the sushi rice with the chopped asparagus and half of the scrambled eggs. Transfer to a large serving dish, or divide between four individual bowls. Spread the rest of the eggs over, sprinkle the sesame seeds on top, and arrange the reserved asparagus tips in the center. Scatter over the crumbled nori and serve.

SMOKED SALMON SCATTERED SUSHI

Here is an ultra easy sushi recipe—the only cooking involved is the preparation of sushi rice, and the rest is an assembly job. You can even use cheaper off-cuts of smoked salmon. If you are using salted capers, rinse them thoroughly to rid of saltiness.

SERVES 4

4¼ to 4½ cups prepared sushi rice (see page 107)

2 tablespoons yuzu or lime juice

4 tablespoons capers, rinsed

7 ounces smoked salmon

2 teaspoons sake

4 tablespoons salmon roe

Put the sushi rice in a large mixing bowl, and sprinkle with the yuzu juice. Mix well.

Roughly chop the capers, and mix into the rice. Then transfer the rice mix to a large serving dish, or divide between four individual dishes.

Cut the salmon into large bite-size pieces, and arrange on top of the rice.

In a bowl, mix the sake into the salmon roe to loosen it, and remove the fishy smell. Using a teaspoon, spread the roe over the rice a few drops at a time, and serve.

HOW TO MAKE
THIN OMELETS

It is helpful if you have a rectangular Japanese omelet pan, but a regular pan (about 7-inch diameter) can be used instead. Just cut off the round edges once you have finished cooking.

MAKES 8 OMELETS

4 eggs
4 egg yolks
2 teaspoons sugar
1 teaspoon salt
4 teaspoons cornstarch mixed with 4 teaspoons water
vegetable oil, for cooking

Mix all the ingredients, except the oil, in a bowl and strain through a strainer.

Heat a 7-inch omelet pan over medium heat, and oil lightly. Wipe away any excess oil with paper towels. Pour in just enough egg mixture to thinly cover the surface of the pan. When the omelet surface begins to set, pick it up and turn it over with a chopstick, or a fork, to cook the other side. Don't let the omelet crisp or brown—it should remain golden yellow.

Repeat to make seven more omelets. Keep the round shape if you are making *chakin-zushi* (see opposite), or cut off the round edges to make it a square if you are making *fukusa-zushi* (see opposite).

OMELET PURSE SUSHI CHAKIN-ZUSHI | FUKUSA-ZUSHI

Thin omelets make a colorful edible wrapping material. *Chakin* is a small linen hand towel, and *fukusa* is a large silk handkerchief; both are used in the traditional tea ceremony. However, in the context of sushi, *chakin-zushi* uses a round omelet, which is gathered and tied on the top, while for *fukusa-zushi* a square sheet of omelet is used.

FOR CHAKIN-ZUSHI

MAKES 8 PURSES

4¼ to 4½ cups prepared sushi rice (see page 107)
8 thin omelets (see left)
8 long sprigs of flat-leaf parsley or cilantro

Place about 2 tablespoons of sushi rice in the middle of a round omelet. Bring up the edges, gathering them on the top and tie with a sprig of flat-leaf parsley or cilantro. Repeat with the remaining omelets.

FOR FUKUSA-ZUSHI

MAKES 8 PURSES

4¼ to 4½ cups prepared sushi rice (see page 107)
8 thin omelets (see left), round edges cut off
   to make a square
8 long sprigs of flat-leaf parsley or cilantro

Position 2 tablespoons of sushi rice slightly off-center on an omelet square. Bring up the lower edge over the filling, then fold in the sides to meet at the center, making a neat rectangular parcel. Tie the parcel with a sprig of flat-leaf parsley or cilantro. Repeat with the remaining omelet squares.

STUFFED SUSHI INARI-ZUSHI

This style of sushi uses cooked ingredients such as deep-fried tofu (as here), thin omelets, or cabbage leaves as a wrapper for sushi rice. Because it comes in wrapped form, it is portable, and easy to eat, and ideal for packed lunches and picnics.

MAKES 12 POUCHES

6 *aburaage*, deep-fried tofu
2⅛ cups dashi of your choice (see pages 29 to 31)
4 tablespoons sugar
4 tablespoons soy sauce
6½ to 6⅔ cups prepared sushi rice (see page 107)
2 tablespoons toasted white sesame seeds

SUGGESTED FILLINGS: Minced sushi ginger (gari) with poppy seeds, chopped ham with diced cucumber, chopped cooked shrimp, or seasoned shiitake mushrooms and carrot.

Start by preparing the deep-fried tofu pouches, preferably the night before. To make the pouches easier to open, put the tofu on a cutting board, and roll out with a chopstick until no "squish" noise comes out. Place the tofu on a flat bamboo basket, or in a strainer, and pour boiling hot water on both sides to remove excess oil. Cut in half and carefully prise open, taking care not to tear. Put all the pouches in a single layer in a shallow wide saucepan, or a large skillet, then add the dashi and sugar, and gently bring to a boil over medium heat. Simmer for 5 to 6 minutes. Add the soy sauce, and continue to simmer until the cooking juice has reduced to about one-third. Turn off the heat, and leave in the saucepan to cool down overnight.

The next day, cook and prepare the sushi rice as described on page 107.

Put the sesame seeds on a cutting board and roughly chop—this enhances their nutty flavor.

Mix the rice with the sesame seeds and fillings, if using. Put a tofu pouch between your hands and squeeze gently to drain. Using a tablespoon, make a small egg-size ball of the rice and fill the tofu pouch two-thirds of the way to the top. Fold the sides over the filling and serve.

PRESSED SUSHI OSHI-ZUSHI

Before the beginning of the 17th century, when the addition of rice vinegar became widespread, sushi making relied on long natural fermentation using wooden molds or barrels. Today, *oshi-zushi*, pressed sushi or *hako-zushi*, boxed sushi of many kinds, are still made as regional delicacies all around Japan. Opposite is an example of modern adaptation of *oshi-zushi*, using an ordinary pastry cutter or a cooking ring.

PRESSED SUSHI OF SMOKED SALMON

An *oshi-bako*, a press mold, is a specialist piece of equipment, available on the internet, but you may not want to invest in one unless you are going to make sushi regularly. Alternatively, use an ordinary pastry cutter or a cooking ring.

SERVES 4

4¼ to 4½ cups prepared sushi rice (see page 107)
7 ounces smoked salmon
2 teaspoons wasabi paste
4 teaspoons salmon roe
2 teaspoons sake

Divide the rice into four equal portions. Using a cooking ring or a pastry cutter (about 3¼ inch diameter), stamp out four circles of smoked salmon. Do not worry about offcuts, because they will be used to make edible decorations later. Wet the cooking ring (to stop the rice from sticking) and place it in the center of an individual plate.

Add a portion of sushi rice and press down firmly with the back of a tablespoon, so that the rice is compact and smooth over the top. Spread the wasabi paste evenly on top, and gently lift up the ring. Place a smoked salmon circle on top.

Cut the salmon offcuts into large rose petal shapes, then lay 3 to 5 pieces on the cutting board, overlapping and roll up. Place the salmon rose on the top. Mix the salmon roe and sake together in a small bowl. Spoon a teaspoon of the roe mixture, slightly off-center, over each rose and serve.

THIN-ROLL SUSHI
HOSO-MAKI

A thin roll has just a single filling such as tuna, salmon, or cucumber, cut into long thin strips, and uses a half nori sheet. Each roll is cut into six bite-size pieces.

MAKES 4 ROLLS (24 PIECES)
2 sheets of nori
3¼ to 3¾ cups prepared sushi rice (see page 107)
2 teaspoons wasabi paste
5½ ounces fresh tuna, cut into pencil-size strips
pickled ginger and soy sauce, to serve
a bowl of mild vinegar water, to dip your hands in

WASABI IN SUSHI

Wasabi, a native Japanese perennial semi-aquatic plant, is one of the strongest seasoning ingredients. Indeed, in sushi language, wasabi is otherwise called *namida*, tears. Its root is grated to produce a pungent fragrant pale green paste, and is widely used in sushi and sashimi. When a wasabi root is grated, an organic compound called allyl isothiocyanate is produced, which is responsible for the characteristic pungent taste, and is a natural disinfectant. Wasabi has natural sterilizing antibacterial effects when used with raw fish, and so stops it from getting spoilt. Used correctly, wasabi helps to stimulate appetite, eliminate fishy smells, and enhance sushi's delicate flavor and taste.

The key to successful sushi-making is to have a clean organized worktop. So, before you start, have all the ingredients and equipment ready.

Fold the sheets of nori in half across the grain, pinch along the folded edge, and pull them apart in halves—you should have 4 rectangular nori sheets. Then put a half nori sheet horizontally shiny-side down on a bamboo rolling mat. Wet your hands with the vinegar water, to keep the rice from sticking to your hands as you work. Take a handful of the rice weighing about 2½ to 3 ounces, and roughly shape it into a log.

Place the rice in the center of the nori, then use your fingertips to spread it evenly over the nori, leaving a ⅜ to ⅝–inch border along the edge furthest from you.

With your fingertips, press, and make a groove along the center of the rice, and smear about a half teaspoon of wasabi paste along. Place a tuna strip in the wasabi groove.

To roll, lift up the edge of the mat closest to you with your thumbs and index fingers, while keeping the filling in place with your middle and third fingers, and roll the mat over the tuna filling, so that the top edge of the nori meets the edge of the rice. You should be able to see the uncovered nori strip. Lift the edge of the mat slightly, and push the roll away from you, so that the uncovered strip of nori seals the roll. Gently, but firmly press the mat along the length of the roll, using both hands to evenly shape it.

Push in any stray grains of rice to tidy the ends. Set it aside in a cool place (but not in the refrigerator), while you make the remaining rolls.

To cut, moisten a sharp kitchen knife with vinegar water, to prevent it from sticking. Cut each roll in the middle. Put the two halves next to each other, and cut them twice to make 6 equal bite-size pieces.

To serve, transfer onto a large platter or individual serving plates, and serve with sushi-pickled ginger and soy sauce on the side for dipping.

ROLLED SUSHI
MAKI-ZUSHI

Maki-zushi, rolled sushi, is the generic name for all sushi formed into cylindrical shapes wrapped in nori or other materials. Under this broad category, there are several different types. The easiest, *temaki,* hand-rolls, are cone-shaped containing a single or multiple fillings, and as the name implies, it is made with your hands, and requires no rolling mat. *Hoso-maki,* thin roll, uses a half sheet of nori, and contains a single filling, while *futo-maki,* thick roll, is more substantial typically with four to five fillings, and a whole sheet of nori. *Ura-maki,* inside-out roll, is the most modern type, and has nori-lined rice on the outside, with two to three core fillings. All rolled sushi except hand-roll uses a bamboo rolling mat to make.

HAND-ROLLED SUSHI
TEMAKI-ZUSHI

Hand-rolls are quick and easy to make, and do not require any specialist equipment.

MAKES 8 HAND-ROLLS
4 sheets of nori, halved
4¼ to 4½ cups prepared sushi rice (see page 107)
4 teaspoons wasabi paste
7 ounces fish of your choice, cut into 2½ to 2¾-inch long, pencil-size strips
7 ounces vegetables such as cucumber, avocado, blanched carrot, green beans, cut into 2½ to 2¾-inch long thin strips, arugula, or peppercress

Hold a piece of halved rectangular nori in your left hand. Put a generous tablespoonful of rice on the top left corner of the nori and flatten it slightly. Dab a little amount of wasabi paste on the rice. Arrange your choice of fillings on top of the rice so that they point diagonally to the top left corner of the nori. Then bring the bottom left hand corner of the nori towards the top side center, wrapping it around the rice and fillings forming a cone. Repeat to make 8 rolls in total.

THICK-ROLL SUSHI
FUTO-MAKI

Also called *date-maki*, literally "dandy" roll, because of its colorful fillings, a thick roll typically contains four to five cooked ingredients. The rolling technique is the same as in thin rolls.

MAKES 2 ROLLS (16 SLICES)

2 sheets of nori
4¼ to 4½ cups prepared sushi rice (see page 107)
1 carrot, pared, cut into thick strips, and steamed
¾ ounce fresh green beans (about 8 to 12), trimmed
    and lightly steamed
8 prepared dried shiitake mushroom slices (see below)
½ prepared Dashi-rolled Omelet, cut into
    ⅜ by 8-inch long strips (see page 170)
¾ ounce prepared *kampyō*, dried gourd, cut into
    8-inch lengths (see below)
sushi pickled ginger, to garnish
a bowl of mild vinegar water, to dip your hands in

Place a sheet of nori shiny-side down along the edge of your rolling mat. Moisten your hands with the vinegar water, form two log shapes with half the rice, and put them in the center of the nori. Spread the rice evenly across the whole width of the nori, leaving a 1½ inch border of the sheet furthest from you uncovered.

Lay half the carrot strips across the center of the rice, followed by half the beans, and half the mushrooms on either side. Arrange half the omelet strips, and half the *kampyō* on either side of the beans and mushrooms.

To roll, lift up the edge of the mat closest to you with your thumbs and index fingers, keeping the filling in place with your middle and third fingers, and roll the mat over, so that the top edge of the nori meets the edge of the rice. Lift the edge of the mat slightly, and push the roll away from you so that the uncovered strip of nori seals the roll. Gently but firmly, press along the length of the roll, using both hands to evenly shape it.

Moisten a sharp knife with the vinegar water, and cut each roll in half, then each half into four equal slices, cleaning and moistening the knife before each cut. Arrange on a platter, cut-side up to show off the center, with the sushi pickled ginger as a garnish.

HOW TO PREPARE DRIED GOURD STRIPS

Wash ¾ ounce *kampyō* in cold water with a scrubbing action. Add 2 tablespoons of salt, and continue to rub in the water until soft. Rinse and soak in fresh water for 2 to 3 hours. Drain, and put in a saucepan with enough water to cover and simmer for 10 to 15 minutes. Add 2 generous cups dashi with 2 tablespoons sugar and 2 tablespoons soy sauce, and bring to a boil, then simmer for 10 minutes or until the strips turn golden yellow. Allow to cool in the stock before cutting to desired lengths.

HOW TO PREPARE DRIED SHIITAKE MUSHROOMS

Soak 8 dried shiitake mushrooms in just enough warm water to cover for 10 minutes. Drain, reserving the liquid, and cut off and discard the stems. Put the liquid, mushrooms, 2 tablespoons mirin, 3 tablespoons sugar, and 2 tablespoons soy sauce in a saucepan. Bring to a boil over medium heat, reduce the heat, and simmer for 20 to 30 minutes, or until the liquid has almost disappeared. Let the mushrooms cool in the saucepan, then squeeze to drain, and cut into thin slices.

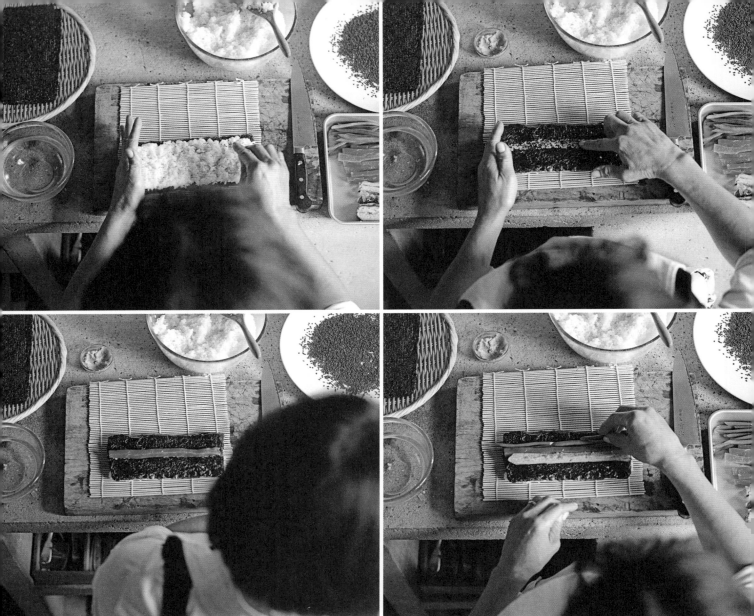

INSIDE-OUT ROLL SUSHI
URA-MAKI

Ura-maki is also sometimes known as California rolls. They were first created by an American-born Japanese chef in the early 1970s to accommodate squeamish American diners, who were unsure about raw fish. *Ura-maki* is deceptively easier to make than the traditional nori rolls. It is also more suited to advance preparations, because the crispness of the nori is not the key element, as in the case of thin and thick rolls.

MAKES 4 ROLLS (24 PIECES)

2 sheets of nori, halved
4¼ to 5¼ cups prepared sushi rice (see page 107)
2 teaspoons wasabi paste
5½ ounces fresh tuna, cut into four pencil-size strips
¾ ounce fresh green beans (about 8 to 12), trimmed and lightly steamed
½ prepared Dashi-rolled Omelet, cut into four 8-inch long strips (see page 170)
4 tablespoons toasted white or black sesame seeds
sushi pickled ginger and soy sauce, to serve
a bowl of mild vinegar water, to dip your hands in

SUGGESTED FILLINGS: White crabmeat with avocado and cucumber strips, salmon with cucumber strips and finely chopped scallion, cooked shrimp with peppercress and omelet strips.

Start by lining your bamboo rolling mat with plastic wrap, so that the rice will not stick to the mat.

Place a half sheet of nori on the mat. Dip your hands in the vinegar water to keep the rice from sticking, then take a large handful of the rice, about ½ cup, and place it in the middle of the nori. Wet your fingers again, and spread the rice evenly to cover the entire surface of nori, and pat it down slightly. Pick up the rice-covered nori, and turn it over on the mat.

Mix the mayonnaise and wasabi paste together in a small bowl.

Lay one strip of tuna, a line of green beans and a strip of omelet along the center of the nori on top of the wasabi. (Don't worry if some fillings stick out of the edges, as it looks attractive when served.) To roll, lift up the nearest edge of the mat to you with your thumbs and index fingers, while holding the fillings in place with the rest of your fingers. Then start rolling to join the two edges of rice-nori together. Lift up the front edge of the mat and push the roll away from you. Re-cover the roll with the mat, and gently squeeze to shape into a round or square shape.

On a large flat plate, spread 1 tablespoon of sesame seeds as evenly as possible, then roll the sushi roll in the seeds to coat all over. Set aside while you make the remaining rolls.

To cut, place a sushi roll on a cutting board, moisten a sharp kitchen knife with the vinegar water, and cut the roll in half. Place the 2 halves next to each other, clean and moisten the knife, and cut them twice to give six equal bite-size pieces.

To serve, transfer the cut pieces onto a platter or individual plates, and arrange the pieces showing the cut-side up. Serve with a mound of sushi pickled ginger, and soy dipping sauce.

HANDBALL-SUSHI
TEMARI-ZUSHI

Nigiri-zushi, hand-squeezed sushi is the most difficult to master—it is not just a case of making small rice nuggets and putting slices of raw fish on top. It is an art that takes years of apprenticeship, and out of respect, in Japan people tend not make this type of sushi at home, but go to sushi bars. But do not be disappointed, because there is a quick and easy version of *nigiri-zushi* called *temari-zushi*, literally handball-sushi. It is the nearest thing to nigiri-zushi without undergoing years of training, and all you need is a plain cotton handkerchief or plastic wrap.

MAKES 20 BALLS

6½ to 6⅔ cups prepared sushi rice (see page 107)
1 ounce smoked salmon, cut into ten
    1½-inch square pieces
10 cooked shelled shrimp
2 to 3 Thin Omelets (see page 110), cut into ten
    1½-inch square pieces
a tube of wasabi paste
2 tablespoons of salmon roe, mixed with
    2 teaspoons of sake
1 to 2 tablespoons peppercress
sushi pickled ginger and soy sauce, to serve
a bowl of mild vinegar water, to dip your hands in

Divide the sushi rice into 3 equal portions—about 2⅛ cups each for the smoked salmon balls, for the shrimp balls, and for the omelet balls.

Moisten a clean cotton handkerchief or a six inch square of plastic wrap with the vinegar water, and hold it open on your left hand. Place a piece of smoked salmon in the middle. Wet a tablespoon in the vinegar water and take out a generous spoonful of the rice (about ⅛ cup), then put on top of the salmon. Bring the corners of the handkerchief toward the middle over the rice, gather and twist to shape, and compact the rice into a small ball.

Unwrap the ball and place it on a cutting board, and cover with another clean damp cloth while you make nine more salmon balls. Next, repeat to make ten shrimp balls and ten omelet balls.

Squeeze a pinhead of wasabi paste in the center of the salmon squares and shrimp crescents, and put a few salmon roe on top. For the omelet balls, garnish with a pinch of peppercress.

To serve, arrange the balls either on a large platter or on four individual serving plates with a mound of sushi pickled ginger and soy dipping sauce on the side.

If you are making this in advance (up to 3 hours), keep the balls covered with a clean damp cloth, or plastic wrap until ready to serve.

MAIN COURSES

MAIN COURSES SHUSAI

A typical Japanese family meal is *ichi-jū san-sai*, 一汁三菜, "one soup three dishes." That is, a soup, which is usually miso soup, and then three dishes normally consisting of sashimi, a broiled dish, and a simmered dish. These "three dishes" are the equivalent of the Western main course dishes, which give character to the whole meal, as well as—in terms of nutrition—providing protein. These soup and three dishes are always served with rice and pickles.

For more elaborate meals, other dishes such as steamed or deep-fried dishes may be added to the table. This basic format of three dishes is not dissimilar to that of a typical Western main course —fish or meat with potatoes and vegetables. The only difference, is that in the West all three are served on the same large plate, instead of in small separate dishes or bowls as they are in Japan. No Japanese, however humble, would dream of serving food on just any old dish, without giving some thought to presentation and composition. Adapting the Japanese way of serving food in separate dishes, to the Western way of presenting a main course, may that be a piece of meat or fish with two or three vegetables on the same plate, is not as outrageously un-Japanese as it may sound. As long as you follow the three basic principles of presentation: present food in three dimensional forms, as if you are creating a landscape, try emulating the natural beauty of asymmetry, and add a touch of seasonality on the plate, then the main points have been taken into account.

SALT-BROILED HORSE MACKEREL
AJI NO SHIO-YAKI

Japanese like seeing a whole fish on a plate. This is because fish, especially small-size ones, cook better on the bone.

SERVES 4

3½ tablespoons salt
4 (9 to 10-ounce) whole horse mackerel
8 teaspoons sea salt
vegetable oil, for greasing
1¾ cups *daikon*, giant white radish, grated, to serve
4 lemon wedges, to serve

In a large bowl, mix 8½ cups of cold water with 3½ tablespoons of salt—this is for washing the fish.

Start by removing the fish's prickly thorn-like scale along its sides, then remove the rest of the scales and gut—you may ask your fish market to do this. Wash off any traces of blood in the salt water, then pat dry with paper towels.

Make 2 to 3 shallow diagonal incisions on both sides. Sprinkle a teaspoonful of sea salt evenly all over each fish, use another teaspoonful to coat the fins for cosmetic effect, and set aside for about 10 minutes.

Meanwhile preheat the broiler to the highest setting. Lightly oil the broiler rack, and return to the broiler to heat.

Place the fish on the rack with the head facing left, and broil for 8 to 10 minutes. Carefully turn the fish over, and continue broiling for an additional 4 to 5 minutes.

Serve the fish with the head facing left on individual plates, with a small mound of grated radish and a lemon wedge on the bottom right hand corner of the plate.

COOK'S TIP
Try this with other smaller-sized fish such as sardines, small porgies or goatfish.

SALT-BROILED BASS SUZUKI NO SHIO-YAKI,

Shio-yaki, is literally salt-broiling where a sprinkling of salt is applied to extract moisture before broiling. The amount of salt depends on the thickness of the flesh and skin type, but the general rule is about two percent of the weight of the fish. Ever-conscious of how food should look on a plate, for the Japanese, the side of the food that faces up, is cooked first in a pan, or second if it is broiled. The fish should not be turned more than once during cooking.

SERVES 4

4 (7-ounce) bass fillets
4 teaspoons sea salt
vegetable oil, for greasing
1 lemon, cut into four wedges, to serve

To prepare the fish, make 2 to 3 shallow diagonal slits on the skin side of each fillet—these incisions are decorative, as well as to help the salt penetrate. Place the fillets on a cutting board, then holding your hand about 12 inches above the fish, sprinkle salt evenly on both sides. Set aside for 15 to 20 minutes.

Meanwhile, preheat the broiler to the highest setting. Lightly oil the broiler rack, then return to the broiler to heat.

Pat the fish dry with paper towels, and place on the rack, skin-side down, and broil for about 5 minutes—the flesh will begin to bead with pinkish sweat. Turn over, and continue broiling for another 2 to 3 minutes, or until the skin becomes crisp and golden brown.

Remove from the broiler. Cut each fillet into two halves, arrange the two pieces skin-side up, and slightly overlapping each other, and serve with a lemon wedge on the side.

COOK'S TIP
Salt-broiling is one of the most basic ways to cook fish, and almost any type can be cooked in this way. Because of its simplicity, there is no disguising the fish's own taste and flavor, so make sure that the fish you are cooking is very, very fresh.

YELLOWTAIL AMBERJACK TERIYAKI
BURI NO TERIYAKI

Teriyaki literally means shiny broil, and it is a tasty and attractive way to cook fish. It's particularly suitable for meaty oily fish such as salmon, tuna, yellowtail amberjack, swordfish, or bonito.

SERVES 4

FOR THE TERIYAKI SAUCE

4 tablespoons soy sauce
4 tablespoons mirin
1 tablespoon sugar
2 tablespoons sake

FOR THE FISH AND VEGETABLES

8 radishes
4 yellowtail amberjack fillets (5 to 7-ounces each)
3 teaspoons vegetable oil
2 yellow or orange bell peppers, seeded, and cut
    into 8 strips
2 green bell peppers, seeded, and cut into eight strips
salt and freshly ground black pepper

Mix all the sauce ingredients together in a shallow dish. Add the fish, and set aside to marinate for 30 minutes, turning occasionally.

Prepare the radishes. With a small knife, make three to four shallow incisions, as if you are peeling the radishes. Transfer to soak in a bowl of cold water—the cuts will open like flower buds.

Remove the fish from its marinade and pat dry, reserving the sauce. Heat 2 teaspoons of the oil in a large skillet over medium heat, and quickly sear both sides of the fish, then remove as much oil as possible using scrunched paper towels. Reduce the heat to low, pour in the reserved sauce, and continue to cook until the sauce has reduced to about a tablespoonful, while turning the fish over a few times.

Meanwhile, in a separate skillet, heat the remaining oil and cook the peppers for 2 to 3 minutes, then season with salt and pepper. Drain the radishes.

To serve, arrange the peppers on the top left hand side of four individual plates, and add two radish buds on the top right side. Place the fish below the vegetables, drizzle a few drops of the sauce over, and serve.

VARIATION

You can also add grated fresh ginger, garlic purée, or red pepper flakes to the teriyaki sauce.

PLAICE IN A PARCEL
HIRAME NO HOIRU-YAKI

Cooking fish wrapped in foil is a gentle, forgiving method, and no washing dishes! All the flavors are enveloped until the diner opens the parcel. This is a particularly suitable way of cooking delicately flavored fish.

SERVES 4

4 (7-ounce) plaice, flounder, or petrale sole fillets
2 teaspoons sea salt
butter, for greasing
4 bok choy, halved lengthwise
4 shiitake mushrooms, stems discarded
4 thick lemon slices
4 tablespoons sake

Start by salting the fish, and leaving it to stand for 20 to 30 minutes.

Meanwhile, preheat the oven to 400°F. Butter the center of four 12-inch foil squares.

Pat the fish dry with paper towels, and place on the buttered part of the foil square. Put the bok choy and shiitake next to the fish, lemon on top, and drizzle sake over the arrangement. Fold the foil into a parcel, allowing as much head room as possible and ensure that you seal the ends tightly. Place the parcels on a large baking sheet, and cook in the oven for 12 to 15 minutes.

Put the parcels on individual plates, bring to the table, and let each diner open their parcel.

COOK'S TIP
This method can be adapted for almost any white fleshed fish, or scallops.

TUNA STEAK WITH BUTTER SOY
MAGURO NO SUTĒKI

This must be one of the fastest fish recipes. Tuna should not be overcooked, but still be pink in the center.

SERVES 4

4 tuna steaks, weighing 5 to 6 ounces each
4 tablespoons all-purpose flour
2 tablespoons vegetable oil
2 garlic cloves, thinly sliced
3½ tablespoons unsalted butter
scant 1 cup sake
2 tablespoons soy sauce
12 snow peas
8 baby corn
salt

Lightly brush the fish with the flour using a pastry brush.

Heat the oil in a large skillet over medium heat, and fry the garlic to flavor the oil. When the garlic has turned crisp and golden brown, remove it with a slotted spoon, and set aside on a sheet of paper towel to drain.

Increase the heat to almost smoking hot, and quickly sear both sides of the fish (do not overcook), then remove from the pan and keep warm. Reduce the heat, and soak up all the oil with scrunched paper towels and discard. Melt the butter in the pan, add the sake and soy sauce and allow to bubble and reduce slightly.

Meanwhile, steam the vegetables for 2 to 3 minutes, and sprinkle salt over to keep the color fresh.

Put the fish on warmed individual plates, arrange the vegetables on the side, spoon a generous amount of the sauce over the fish, add the garlic chips on top, and serve immediately.

PAN-SEARED SALMON NANBAN-STYLE
SAKE NO NANBAN-YAKI

Nanban, translates as southern barbarians and applies to the Portuguese and Spanish or things they brought via Indochina. In the Japanese cooking context, it refers to newly introduced cooking methods of using oil and butter, and ingredients such as onion and chile.

SERVES 4

4 teaspoons sea salt
4 (3½-ounce) salmon fillets
2 baby turnips, trimmed
8 baby leeks
2 teaspoons vegetable oil
2 tablespoons unsalted butter
2 tablespoons rice vinegar
1 tablespoon mirin
2 tablespoons soy sauce
1 onion, minced
1 large red chile, seeded and minced
1 lemon, cut into 4 wedges, to serve

First sprinkle 2 teaspoons of salt evenly over a cutting board, place the fish, skin side down, then sprinkle the rest of the salt on the flesh side, and leave to stand for 20 to 30 minutes.

Meanwhile, quarter the turnips into wedges, and trim the leeks to 2½ to 3¼-inch lengths. Steam the vegetables, and keep warm.

Pat the fish dry with paper towels. Heat the oil in a large skillet, and fry the fish skin-side down for 5 to 6 minutes, flip, and fry the other side for an additional 3 to 4 minutes. Soak up any oil in the pan with scrunched paper towels and discard, then add the butter to the pan, and coat the salmon with the melted butter. Remove the fish to individual plates, and keep warm.

Add all the remaining ingredients, except the lemon, to the pan, and stir over high heat for 2 to 3 minutes. Spoon the sauce generously over the salmon, arrange the turnip wedges at the bottom right corner of the salmon, place the leeks diagonally over the fish, and garnish with the lemon quarters. Serve immediately.

BROILED TUNA IN RED MISO
MAGURO NO AKA-MISO YAKI

Miso paste comes in a variety of colors, ranging from light cream like *Saikyō* miso used in black cod (see opposite) to milk-chocolate brown and dark reddish brown. The color is a good indication of flavor and texture—the darker the color, the saltier and stronger the taste and flavor, and the harder and dryer the texture. Red miso is a generic term for darker colored paste, and *Hacchō* miso from Nagoya is the most famous. Red miso, with its robust stronger flavor, is particularly suitable for marinating strong tasting dark colored fish such as tuna, salmon, bonito, or mackerel.

SERVES 4

FOR THE FISH AND VEGETABLES
4 tuna steaks, weighing 5 to 6 ounces each
2 teaspoons sea salt
vegetable oil, for greasing
scant 2 cups grated *daikon*, giant white radish
2 tablespoons grated red onion
2 teaspoons grated fresh ginger
4 teaspoons finely chopped chives
4 cherry vine tomatoes, cut in half

FOR THE MISO MARINADE
heaping 2 cups red or dark-colored miso
6 tablespoons sake
3 tablespoons mirin

Start by salting the fish, and leave to stand for 20 to 30 minutes.

Meanwhile, mix all the marinade ingredients together.

Rinse the fish, and pat dry with paper towels. Put half the miso mixture in a flat-bottomed ceramic or glass container, and lay the fish steaks in a single layer on top, then spread the rest of the miso over. Cover the container, and refrigerate for 6 to 8 hours, or overnight.

Preheat the oven to 375°F and oil the broiler rack. Take the fish out of the marinade and carefully scrape off all the miso with your fingers or a chopstick.

Put the fish on the lightly oiled rack, rest over a baking pan, and place in the center of the oven to cook for 5 to 6 minutes on each side, taking care to not to let it burn—cover the edges with aluminum foil if necessary.

Meanwhile, lightly drain the grated radish, and combine in a bowl with the onion, ginger, and chives.

To serve, place the tuna steaks in the center of four individual serving plates, and put a portion of the radish mixture in a small mound at the side of the fish with two tomato halves.

BLACK COD
TARA NO SAIKYŌ-MISO YAKI

Saikyō-miso is a famous white miso from Kyoto, which has a delicate mellow sweetness and creamy texture. This marinade is best suited to white-fleshed fish such as cod, porgy, or bass. The name, "black cod" is rather confusing, because it is also a common name for *Anoplopoma fimbria* (sablefish)—which, despite the name, does not belong to the cod family but is a good substitute for black cod.

SERVES 4

FOR THE FISH AND VEGETABLES
4 teaspoons sea salt
4 (5 to 6-ounce) black cod or sablefish fillets, skin on
vegetable oil, for greasing
3½ ounces broccolini, trimmed
½ teaspoon salt
2 tablespoons red or pink pickled ginger, drained

FOR THE MISO MARINADE
heaping 2 cups *Saikyō* miso or white miso
6 tablespoons sake
1½ tablespoons mirin

Start by sprinkling the sea salt all over the fish, and set aside for 20 to 30 minutes—this draws out liquid from the fish, making it easier for the miso marinade to be absorbed.

Meanwhile, mix all the marinade ingredients in a bowl, and put half in a large flat-bottomed ceramic or glass container. Pat the fish dry, and arrange in a single layer on the marinade. Cover with the rest of the miso mix, and refrigerate for 6 to 8 hours, or overnight.

Preheat the oven to 375°F, and oil the broiler rack. Take the fish out of the marinade, and carefully scrape off all the miso with your fingers or a chopstick. The fish should feel a little firmer.

Put the fish, skin-side down, on the oiled rack, and rest over a baking pan. Place in the center of the oven for 6 to 8 minutes, then turn over and cook for an additional 2 to 3 minutes, taking care not to let it burn—cover with a piece of aluminum foil if necessary.

Meanwhile, lightly steam the broccolini for 2 to 3 minutes, and sprinkle the salt over to keep the color fresh.

Remove the fish fillets from the oven and place in the center of four individual serving plates, arrange a portion of broccolini at the top left corner, put ½ tablespoon of the ginger on the top of the fish, and serve.

COOK'S TIPS

The miso marinade can be reused 2 to 3 times. Soak up any excess liquid which comes out of the fish with paper towels before another use.

If you cannot find white miso, use a lighter color variety, but use an equal amount of mirin to sake, or add some sugar to make the marinade sweeter.

PAN-FRIED SCALLOPS WITH BROCCOLINI
HOTATE TO BUROKKORÍ NO ITAME-MONO

Itame-mono is difficult to translate—pan-frying, shallow-frying, sautéing, or even stir-frying—the method is never listed separately in Japanese cookbooks. This is because in reality, *itame-mono* dishes are more like a Japanese version of a Chinese stir-fry. It is arguably the easiest and quickest cooking method.

SERVES 4

14 ounces scallops, without roe
½ teaspoon salt
3 tablespoons vegetable oil
14 ounces broccolini, trimmed
2 eggs, lightly beaten
2 tablespoons all-purpose flour
4 tablespoons sake
2 tablespoons light soy sauce
salt and freshly ground black pepper

Slice the scallops in half horizontally, and sprinkle the salt over; leave to stand for 10 to 15 minutes.

Meanwhile, heat 1 tablespoon of the oil in a large skillet or wok over high heat, add the broccolini, and toss, then add 1¾ cups water. Bring to a boil for 1 to 2 minutes, drain, and keep the broccolini warm.

Wipe the pan clean with paper towels. Heat another tablespoon of oil over medium heat, and add the eggs. Use chopsticks to stir constantly for 3 to 5 minutes to make scrambled eggs. Remove, and keep warm.

Spread the scallops over paper towels and pat dry. Dust with the flour. Heat the remaining oil in the same pan over high heat, and quickly sear the scallops on both sides. Add the broccolini and scrambled eggs to the scallops, and toss to mix. Pour in the sake and soy sauce, stir, and bring to a boil for a minute, then adjust the seasoning with salt and pepper. Divide between four dishes and serve.

COOK'S TIP
Try this recipe with shelled tiger shrimp in place of the scallops.

SIMMERING
NI-MONO

Prehistoric Japanese hunter-gatherers first discovered how to cook by simply putting raw food on a fire. Then some 15,000 years ago, they expanded their cooking repertoire to simmering. By putting food in a vessel with water or some liquid, and letting this bubble away on the fire, simmering is a simple technique, suitable for almost every kind of food, and therefore, has been universally practiced ever since.

In the context of Japanese cooking, simmering, *ni-mono*, has developed into an important category. In a large Japanese restaurant, the chef in charge of the *ni-mono* section is second in command after the head chef, as this requires a multitude of skills and judgement: choosing ingredients and putting them together, cutting, timing, seasoning, and presentation. Yet, fear not, *ni-mono* is also the most home-friendly type of cooking, and you can make delicious, satisfying dishes so long as you follow four basic rules:

I. DO NOT SKIMP ON PREPARATION Parboil harder root vegetables. Green vegetables need to be blanched and refreshed in cold water to retain their color. Fish needs to be carefully filleted and salted prior to cooking.

2. CHOOSE YOUR POTS CAREFULLY Use heavy-bottomed pans that distribute heat gently and evenly. The size is determined by the nature and amount of food: use a deep saucepan which holds an ample amount of liquid for ingredients that need long cooking, but use a shallow pan or skillet for ingredients that only take a few minutes in a little cooking liquid. A shallow pan is also better suited for fragile ingredients such as delicate fish that can crumble easily.

3. FOLLOW THE CORRECT ORDER OF SEASONING Generally speaking, sweetness is applied before saltiness. The most commonly used seasonings in the order of which they are added into the cooking stock are sake, mirin (or sugar), salt, soy sauce, and miso. Sake tenderizes and helps get rid of unwanted odor. Mirin is preferred over sugar to add sweetness, though it is about half as

sweet. In the context of simmering, soy sauce is used for its aroma and taste, rather than the saltiness. Use all-purpose dark soy sauce, except when it is important to keep the natural coloring of solid ingredients, such as white-colored fish, or green vegetables. Miso is almost always added last because its aroma is lost if heated for too long.

4. WATCHFUL HEAT ADJUSTMENT Normally, in *ni-mono*, things are cooked over high heat until the cooking liquid comes to a boil, then the heat is reduced to a low simmer. However, white-fleshed fish is cooked quickly over high heat in a subtly flavored cooking liquid to bring out its natural flavor. In contrast, strong flavored dark-fleshed fish require slow, longer cooking in strongly seasoned liquid.

One indispensable piece of equipment for *ni-mono* is *otoshi-buta*, literally "drop-lid." It is made of cypress or cedar wood, with an edge beveled from the bottom, and a single shallow fin-like strip across the top that acts as a handle. Usually an *otoshi-buta* is about ⅝-inch smaller than the diameter of the saucepan in which it is used. It floats on the surface, acting not only to keep solids submerged in the cooking liquid, thereby ensuring even cooking, but also to stop ingredients from rolling and tumbling around while cooking, so that they keep their shape. In addition, the drop-lid increases the penetration of seasonings into the solid, and reduces heat loss from the liquid surface, hence speeding up the cooking time. It is an invaluable tool, but finding them outside Japan may be problematic as they are inexpensive, giving merchants little incentive to stock and sell them. My suggestion is to look around Asian stores, impose on friends who are visiting Japan or search the internet—by typing in "pig cooking lid" and you will find a cheerful silicone lid with a piggy face (a word-play on "buta," a homonym of both a lid and a pig). Alternatively, use an appropriately-sized flat metal lid, or make a circle with vent holes in the middle with aluminum foil or baking parchment.

SIMMERED COD
TARA NO ASSARI-NI

In a culinary context, the Japanese word *assari*, plain or bland, does not translate well. Perhaps because the Japanese prefer each ingredient's simple, natural flavor over labored complex tastes. This is an elegant, yet satisfying dish in which each ingredient's natural flavor is brought together in a simple broth. The key to the dish is prior salting and parboiling, and only brief simmering. Try this recipe with any fresh white-flesh fish such as porgy, bass, or goatfish.

SERVES 4

4 teaspoons fine sea salt
4 cod fillets, weighing 4½ to 5-ounces each
8 baby leeks, cut into 1½-inch lengths
12 fine green beans, trimmed
4 shiitake mushrooms, stems removed
1 postcard-size piece of dried kelp
7 ounces firm tofu, cut into 4 blocks
⅓ cup sake
⅓ cup light soy sauce
a few sprigs of watercress, to garnish

Start by sprinkling the salt all over the fish. Leave to stand for 20 to 30 minutes.

Meanwhile, bring a saucepan of water to a boil, add the vegetables, and parboil for 1 minute. Remove with a slotted spoon, and set aside.

Using the same water, submerge the fish fillets, one at a time, until they turn white. Drain, and immediately transfer to a bowl of ice water, then drain again.

Lay the kelp at the bottom of a large saucepan and gently place the fish, vegetables and tofu on top without overlapping each other. Add 5¼ cups of water, the sake, and soy sauce, bring to a boil over high heat, then immediately reduce the heat to simmer for 1 to 2 minutes.

To serve, carefully arrange each fillet in the center of four individual dishes, place the tofu on the left, and the vegetables next to them. Garnish with a sprig of watercress, and pour a tablespoon of the broth on top.

NOTE ON SAKE

Sake is Japan's national alcoholic beverage and arguably the best drink to accompany Japanese food. It also ranks among the "big four" seasoning ingredients along with dashi, soy sauce, and miso. These ingredients feature in nearly every Japanese dish, either singularly, or in a combination.

In cooking, sake works as a food tenderizer, due to its amino acid content. It also suppresses saltiness, and helps to remove any overwhelming fishy taste or odor. Small amounts of sake are often added to delicate flavored dishes to give them more rounded depths.

Although there are some "cooking sakes" available in Japanese stores, I use inexpensive drinking sake.

In a strict sense, sake's alcohol should be burned off before use—just pour a few cups of sake into a saucepan and heat very gently then ignite. But if you are in a hurry, just use directly from the bottle.

Sake keeps for a few months after opening. Store in a cool dark place away from sunlight.

SIMMERED SQUID WITH SPINACH
IKA TO HŌRENSŌ NO NI-MONO

Here is a quick and easy recipe for squid, which is best suited to fast cooking.

SERVES 4

14 ounces squid, cleaned
18 ounces baby spinach leaves
2 tablespoons toasted white sesame seeds

FOR THE SIMMERING BROTH

3 tablespoons fresh ginger, peeled and julienned
1 red chile, finely chopped
4 tablespoons sake
4 tablespoons mirin
1 tablespoon sugar
4 tablespoons soy sauce

Cut the body part of the squid into ⅜-inch thick rings and the tentacles into 2 to 2½-inch lengths.

Put all ingredients for the simmering broth into a saucepan, and bring to a boil over medium heat. Add the squid, cook for 1 to 2 minutes only, then immediately remove with a slotted spoon to a bowl. Add the spinach to the same pan, quickly stir, and allow to simmer for 3 to 4 minutes. Return the squid to the pan, stir, and immediately turn off the heat.

Spread the sesame seeds on a dry cutting board and roughly chop—chopping draws out flavor without drawing out oil, as in the case of grinding.

To serve, divide the squid mixture between four individual dishes, and sprinkle the chopped sesame seeds on top.

SIMMERED SHRIMP BALLS AND TURNIPS
EBI TO KABU NO NI-MONO

This is a comforting dish, yet full of taste and flavor from both shrimp and turnips.

SERVES 4

2 small-size turnips, weighing about 10 ounces in total

3⅓ cups dashi of your choice (see page 29)

4 tablespoons sake

2 tablespoons mirin

2 teaspoons light soy sauce

18 ounces fresh shrimp, shells removed

½ teaspoon salt

2 teaspoons grated fresh ginger

6 teaspoons cornstarch

1 egg white

a generous pinch of peppercress, to garnish

Peel and cut the turnips into eighths, then soak in a bowl of cold water for 10 to 15 minutes. Put the turnips in a saucepan with the dashi, and bring to a boil over medium heat. Add 2 tablespoons of sake, the mirin, and soy sauce. Cover the turnips with a drop-lid (see page 134), reduce the heat to low, and simmer for 10 to 12 minutes.

Meanwhile, roughly chop the shrimp. Place in a bowl with the remaining sake, the salt, ginger, 4 teaspoons of cornstarch, and the egg white. Stir well to combine. Form the mixture into about 20 ping-pong size balls. Set aside.

Take the turnips out of the dashi using a slotted spoon and keep warm. Add the shrimp balls to the simmering dashi, increase the heat to medium and cook for 5 to 6 minutes. In a small bowl, mix the remaining cornstarch with 1 tablespoon water. Gently stir the cornstarch mixture into the broth, and simmer for 1 minute to thicken before turning off the heat.

Serve 4 turnip pieces and 5 shrimp balls per person in individual dishes with the simmering sauce and garnish with the peppercress.

SARDINES IN GINGER-VINEGAR
IWASHI NO SHŌGA-NI

This is a clever use of vinegar and ginger—together they take away sardine's fishy odor, tenderize the flesh, and add delicious depth of flavor. Vinegar also softens fish bones, so you can eat the whole thing.

SERVES 4

FOR THE FISH AND VEGETABLES

8 fresh sardines, gutted, and heads removed
scant ½ cup peeled and julienned fresh ginger
2 fresh or dried red chiles
4 tablespoons dried wakame seaweed
2 scallions, finely chopped on the diagonal

FOR THE SIMMERING BROTH

scant 1 cup rice vinegar
¼ cup sake
4 tablespoons mirin
4 tablespoons sugar
½ cup soy sauce

Start by washing the fish in cold water. Use your fingers or a toothbrush to clean them thoroughly of all traces of blood inside and out, then pat dry with paper towels.

Put all the broth ingredients into a large saucepan, and bring to a boil over high heat. Add the fish to the saucepan in a single layer, scatter the ginger strips on top, and place the chiles among them. Place a moistened drop-lid (see page 134) on top, reduce the heat to medium, and simmer for 30 minutes.

While cooking, tilt the pan and ladle the broth all over the fish as if you were basting. Repeat this 2 to 3 times to ensure the fish is covered with the broth.

About 10 minutes before the fish is done, put the seaweed in a bowl, and cover with cold water. Leave for 10 minutes to soften, then drain.

To serve, carefully lift out two sardines with a slotted spoon onto each individual dish. Put a portion of drained seaweed at the side, and garnish with the finely chopped scallion on top.

COOK'S TIP

As sardines are such healthy and sustainable fish, and this recipe keeps for a few days, refrigerated, I often make a large pot of this, and serve it at room temperature with a green salad.

YELLOWTAIL WITH DAIKON
BURI-DAIKON

This is a home-cooking classic for winter, when both yellowtail and *daikon*, giant white radish, are in season. Choose *daikon* with smooth unblemished skin that feels dense and heavy.

SERVES 4

4 teaspoons sea salt

4 yellowtail amberjack steaks, about
   4½ to 5 ounces each

21 ounces *daikon*, giant white radish

¼ cup sake

scant ½ cup peeled and julienned fresh ginger

a few sprigs of watercress or arugula, to garnish

½ lemon peel, thinly sliced, to garnish

FOR THE SIMMERING BROTH

1 tablespoon mirin

2 tablespoons sugar

scant ½ cup soy sauce

Start by sprinkling the fish all over with salt. Leave to stand for 20 to 30 minutes.

Meanwhile, peel and cut the radish into ¾-inch thick cylinder chunks, or if large, cut into half-moon pieces. With a small knife, cut around the sharp angle edge of each radish piece—this is a traditional vegetable preparation cut, which helps to keep the shape during cooking (see page 225).

Bring a large saucepan of water to a boil over high heat. Add the radish, and simmer over medium heat for 15 to 20 minutes, then drain.

Bring another saucepan of water to a boil, then add the fish, and let the water return to a boil again for 1 to 2 minutes. Drain, plunge the fish into a bowl of ice water, and wash off all traces of blood. Drain again.

Put the fish and radish in a large saucepan with 1¼ cups water, the sake, and half the ginger, and bring to a boil over high heat, skimming off any scum that floats to the surface. Reduce the heat to low, place a drop-lid (see page 134) on top and simmer for 7 to 8 minutes.

Add all the broth ingredients and continue to simmer for 15 to 18 minutes, or until the broth has been reduced by one-third.

To serve, transfer the fish and radish into shallow individual dishes, spoon on some broth, then add a portion of the remaining ginger and garnish with a sprig or two of watercress and lemon peel slices.

MACKEREL IN MISO
SABA NO MISO-NI

Here, a combination of mackerel and miso results in a robust hearty dish. I recommend serving this with a refreshing salad of watercress or arugula leaves.

SERVES 4

4 mackerel fillets
4 teaspoons fine sea salt
1 postcard-size piece of dried kelp
2 white or red onions, peeled and finely sliced
thumb-size piece of fresh ginger
1 tablespoon rice vinegar

FOR THE SWEET MISO BLEND

¼ cup medium-colored miso
2 tablespoons sugar
4 tablespoons sake

Cut each fillet into three or four easy-to-eat pieces, and make shallow criss-cross incisions on the skin side of each piece. Salt the fish, and leave to stand for 20 to 30 minutes.

Meanwhile, soak the kelp in a scant cupful of water for 30 minutes, to make water dashi.

At the same time, soak the onion slices in a bowl of cold water for 20 minutes—this removes the strong oniony odor.

Bring a saucepan of water to a boil, blanch the fish for 1 to 2 minutes, and drain.

Peel the ginger, and thinly slice half, and julienne the other half. Mix the miso, sugar, and sake together in a bowl.

Remove the kelp from the water. Heat the water dashi in a large saucepan over medium heat to just boiling, and add the fish, skin-side up. Spread the miso blend, scatter the ginger slices on top of the fish, and cover with a moistened drop-lid (see page 134), then return to a boil. Reduce the heat to low, simmer for 10 minutes, and add the rice vinegar just before turning off the heat.

Drain the onion slices, then spread them over paper towels to dry.

To serve, spread a portion of onion slices on an individual serving plate or dish, arrange the fish pieces on the onion bed, spoon the cooking sauce over the fish, and put a small mound of julienned ginger on top of the fish.

SAKE-STEAMED BASS
SUZUKI NO SAKE-MUSHI

Steaming is a clean and healthy way of cooking delicate fish. You can use any white-flesh fish for this recipe.

SERVES 4

4 teaspoons salt
8 (2 to 3-ounce) bass fillets
4 baby corn
dinner plate-size dried kelp
4 tablespoons sake
8 shiitake mushrooms, stems removed, large caps halved
1 cup broccolini, cut into 1½-inch pieces
4 tablespoons soy sauce
1 lemon, cut into 4 wedges, to serve

Sprinkle the salt on both sides of the fish and leave to stand for 15 minutes.

Meanwhile, trim and blanch the baby corn in a pan of boiling water for 1 to 2 minutes. Drain and immediately plunge into cold water. Drain again, and set aside.

Pat the fish dry with paper towels and fold into loose rolls by tucking both ends under—this is to save space in your steamer. Wipe the kelp with a clean damp cloth, and use it to line a heatproof dish that is large enough to hold the fish. Place the fish rolls on top of the kelp, and pour over the sake. Place the dish in a steamer with about 2¼ cups of water at the bottom, and steam for 10 to 12 minutes over high heat. (If you don't have a large steamer, use a wok with a lid, standing the dish on top of a heatproof bowl.)

Add the baby corn, mushrooms, and broccoli on top of the fish, and steam for an additional 3 to 4 minutes.

Place 2 fish rolls on four individual serving dishes, and arrange the vegetables on the side. Drizzle the cooking juices and the soy sauce on the bottom of each dish, and serve with lemon wedges.

SAKE-STEAMED CLAMS
ASARI NO SAKE-MUSHI

The advantage of steaming clams in sake, is that the sake vaporizes at a lower temperature than water. This way, the sake works to cook the clams faster, as well as erasing any fishy smell.

SERVES 4

2¾ pounds clams
scant 1 cup sake
2 teaspoons light soy sauce
14 ounces dried soba noodles
2 scallions, julienned or minced
salt

Combine 1 teaspoon of salt with 8½ cups of cold water in a large, flat-bottomed container. Add the clams, cover tightly with foil, and stand for 2 hours at room temperature—this will help them spit out any grit and sand.

Wash the clams by gently rubbing them together under cold running water, and drain. Discard any clams with damaged shells. Put the clams in a large saucepan or skillet with a tight-fitting lid over medium heat. When hot, pour in a scant ½ cup water, the sake, and soy sauce, and steam with the lid on for 3 to 5 minutes, until the cooking juices have been slightly reduced. Discard any clams that are not open.

Meanwhile, cook and drain the soba noodles (see page 77), then divide between four serving dishes.

Spoon the clams over the noodles, scatter with julienned or minced scallions, and serve.

DEEP-FRYING
AGE-MONO

The technique of deep-frying is thought to have been introduced by the Chinese as a part of the Buddhism vegetarian cuisine in the seventh century, but it remained relatively unknown outside the temple confines. In the late sixteenth century, the Portuguese and Spanish Catholic missionaries introduced the original form of tempura. Thereafter, deep-frying in Japan underwent centuries of adaptations and innovations to suit local tastes and ingredients, until it was elevated to the very pinnacle of refinement, and became a major category of Japanese cooking. Although tempura is the best known form, there are three types of deep-frying.

Su-age, or naked frying, is, as the name suggests, when food is deep-fried without any coating. This method is best suited to food such as small freshwater fish, *shiso* leaves, or sliced lotus, where retaining the color and shape is important.

Kara-age originally meant Chinese frying, but *kara* also means "empty" (without batter), i.e., dry-frying. Food is often marinated or seasoned before being thinly dusted with flour or cornstarch, which works to seal in the taste and flavor. Typical food for *kara-age* are flatfish such as sole and flounder, or chicken and tofu.

Koromo-age, is where foods are coated with batter and cooked in hot oil—325°F for vegetables, and 350°F for fish. Tempura and katsu (food coated with bread crumbs) are typical examples.

OIL
Always use highly refined pure vegetable oils such as corn, peanut, sunflower, or rapeseed oil, but never animal fats or olive oil.

TEMPERATURE
Different ingredients call for different temperatures, but, generally speaking, vegetables are fried at a low heat, while meat and fish are cooked fast at a high heat to keep juicy tenderness. For home cooks without a thermometer, the temperature of oil can be judged by dropping in a few drops of batter:

325°F The batter drops gradually sink to the bottom and slowly rise to the top.

340°F The batter drops create gentle bubbles around them, sink to the bottom and quickly rise to the top.

350°F The batter drops quickly sink to the bottom and immediately rise to the top.

375°F+ The batter drops skittle around noisily and remain at the surface

If the oil is not hot enough, the food will absorb oil, and become heavy and greasy. If the oil is too hot, the outside will burn, while the inside remains uncooked.

Maintaining the oil temperature at a constant level is equally important. Use a thick, deep, flat-bottomed iron, stainless steel, or copper saucepan for even heat distribution, and better heat retention. The amount of oil needed varies but always use plenty—around 4½ to 5 cups. The general rule is that the depth of oil in the pan should be at least twice or more than double the thickness of the food items being deep-fried, and the pan should not be any more than 70 percent full. Always deep-fry foods in small quantities, so that the pan is never overcrowded—no more than enough to cover one-third of the oil surface at one time. Food should be at room temperature before cooking, and never straight from the fridge. The preferred source of heat is gas, as it responds quickly.

REUSING OIL
After cooking, and once all the food has been removed, heat the oil, and stir lightly, so that any moisture in the oil from food evaporates. Then, while the oil is still warm, but not too hot, pass it through a paper filter into a container with an airtight lid. Seal and store in a dark, cool place. You may top up the used oil with fresh oil (half and half) but such refreshed oil should not be used for deep-frying more than twice. By that time the oil will be darker in color and lose luster and taste. The older the oil is, the more likely it is to froth and foam, which makes it impossible to fry light, crisp food, and it should be discarded.

DEEP-FRIED PLAICE
KAREI NO KARA-AGE

I have already mentioned that Japanese people love seeing a whole fish at the table, and deep-frying is no exception. Don't be intimidated by the idea of cooking a whole fish—it is surprisingly simple, but make sure you have plenty of oil, and use a large pan.

SERVES 4

FOR THE FISH AND VEGETABLES

4 plaice (or any small flatfish), about 7 to 9 ounces each

4 tablespoons sake

1 teaspoon salt

6 tablespoons all-purpose flour

½ cup cornstarch

6 to 8½ cups vegetable oil, for deep-frying

2 green bell peppers, cut into quarter strips, and seeded

3½ ounces *daikon*, giant white radish

2 scallions, minced

½ teaspoon chili powder

FOR THE DIPPING SAUCE

6 tablespoons soy sauce

3 tablespoons rice vinegar

2 tablespoons mirin

3 tablespoons lemon or lime juice

Preheat the oven to 225°F; this is to keep the fish warm after cooking.

Wash and clean the fish, then make a large cross-shaped incision on both sides. Place the fish in a large flat dish. Mix the sake and salt together, drizzle 1 tablespoon over each fish, and set aside.

Mix the dipping sauce ingredients together in a bowl, and set aside until needed. Combine the all-purpose flour and cornstarch.

Pat the fish dry with paper towels, dust with the flour mix, and brush off any excess. In a large heavy-bottomed pan, heat the oil to 340°F to deep-fry the fish one at a time. Hold a fish by its tail and gently submerge it into the oil, darker skin side first. The oil will bubble vigorously at first, but then quiet down, and the size of bubbles will become smaller after about 5 to 6 minutes. Turn the fish over to deep-fry the other side for 4 to 5 minutes, or until golden and crisp. Take the fish out, and put on a wire rack placed over a baking pan, and place the whole thing in the oven to keep warm while you cook the remaining fish. Leave the oven door slightly open, so that moisture from the hot fish can escape, and does not make the fish soggy.

Deep-fry the peppers for 1 to 2 minutes and drain.

Peel and grate the radish, and drain slightly. Mix with the scallions and chili powder in a bowl.

To serve, place a fish with its head facing left on individual plates. Put the peppers and a small mound of grated radish mix on the bottom right corner, and offer a small dish of the dipping sauce on the side. Encourage your guests to eat the crunchy fins and tail.

COOK'S TIP

If the idea of cooking a whole fish seems too daunting, but you still wish to enjoy eating crunchy fins, then use any flatfish steak cuts on the bone.

SPICY DEEP-FRIED SARDINES
IWASHI NO NANBAN-ZUKE

Nanban-zuke is a cooking technique where seafood is deep-fried without any coating, and then seasoned in a spicy vinegar marinade. It is particularly suitable for any small oily fish.

SERVES 4

FOR THE FISH

1 to 2 tablespoons salt
8 to 12 sardines, gutted, and heads removed
1 cup cornstarch
4½ to 6 cups vegetable oil

FOR THE MARINADE

4 tablespoons sake
2 tablespoons sugar
2 tablespoons mirin
4 tablespoons rice vinegar
6 tablespoons soy sauce

FOR THE SPICY MIX

1 medium-size red onion, peeled and minced
1 red bell pepper, seeded and diced
1 green bell pepper, seeded and diced
1 large red chile, seeded and finely chopped
2 tablespoons grated fresh ginger

Start by sprinkling the fish with the salt, paying particular attention to the insides. Leave to stand for 10 minutes.

Put all the marinade ingredients with a scant ½ cup of water in a saucepan, and bring to a boil over medium heat. Reduce the heat, and simmer for 2 to 3 minutes. Turn off the heat, and pour into a large flat dish, and add the onion, peppers, chile, and ginger. Set aside.

Wash the fish in cold water, and dry thoroughly with paper towels. Dust with cornstarch, and brush off any excess.

In a large, heavy-bottomed pan, heat the oil to 330 to 340°F and gently deep-fry two or three fish at a time, for 8 to 10 minutes to cook through to the bone, turning them occasionally. As the oil temperature is low, the fish will sink to the bottom, before rising to the top, and the oil will bubble vigorously at first, then quiet down when the fish are nearly done.

Take the fish out, and immediately transfer into the spicy marinade mix. Repeat to cook the remaining sardines.

Submerging the deep-fried fish straight into the sauce while they are very hot is the key to success. Let them absorb the flavors for 45 to 60 minutes, before serving at room temperature with a tablespoon of the sauce for each sardine.

COOK'S TIP
You can also try this recipe with mackerel or herring. Allow 2 fillets per person and reduce the deep-frying time slightly to about 5 to 8 minutes.

DEEP-FRIED MARINATED MACKEREL
SABA NO TATSUTA-AGE

It is said that the term "Tatsuta-age" comes from the River Tatsuta in Nara, which is a well-known beauty spot for autumn maple leaves, because deep-fried morsels in oil look like red leaves floating down the river. It is a nice story, and typical of the Japanese to find a seasonal depiction even in a deep-fried food. Red maple leaves or not, food cooked in this style is not only visual, but also delicious, due to the marinade even when it is served at room temperature—good news for busy home cooks.

SERVES 4

FOR THE FISH AND VEGETABLES
8 (3½ to 4-ounce) mackerel fillets
2 red bell peppers
2 yellow bell peppers
1 cup cornstarch
4½ to 6¼ cups vegetable oil
1 lemon, cut into 4 wedges, to serve
salt

FOR THE MARINADE
2 tablespoons sake
2 tablespoons mirin
6 tablespoons soy sauce
4 teaspoons grated fresh ginger and juice

Cut the fillets into angular, large bite-size pieces. In a bowl, mix all the marinade ingredients and add the fish. Leave to marinate for 15 to 20 minutes, turning them occasionally.

Meanwhile, cut the peppers, seed, and cut into diamond-shaped pieces (or into maple leaves if you have a maple leaf shaped food cutter).

Spread the fish on layers of paper towels to dry thoroughly, then dust with cornstarch.

Heat the oil to 330°F in a large, deep skillet, and deep-fry the peppers in small batches for no more than 1 to 2 minutes. With a slotted spoon, remove, and drain the peppers over a wire rack or on paper towels. Sprinkle a pinch of salt over them while still hot, to preserve the bright color.

Now deep-fry the fish, again in small batches, for 5 to 8 minutes. They will sink to the bottom first, and float in the middle, before rising to the top. Remove from the oil, and drain well over a wire rack.

To serve, divide the fish and peppers into four portions, make a small mound of fish on an individual plate, scatter peppers on top, and offer a wedge of lemon on the side.

COOK'S TIP
For a spicier flavor, add ½ teaspoon of *shichimi-tōgarashi*, seven-spice chili powder to the marinade.

DEEP-FRIED SCALLOPS IN RICE CRACKERS
HOTATE NO ARARE-TATSUTA-AGE

In *Tatsuta-age*, food is usually marinated first then coated with cornstarch or all-purpose flour, but in this version, rice crackers do both jobs of seasoning and coating. You can use any soy-flavored rice crackers, but my favorite choice is *kaki-no-tane*, small peppery ones, which look like seeds.

SERVES 4

8 sweet chestnuts
3½ ounces *kaki-no-tane*, rice crackers
7 ounces scallops
2 tablespoons all-purpose flour
2 egg whites, lightly beaten
4½ to 6¼ cups vegetable oil

Start by blanching the chestnuts in boiling water, for 10 to 15 minutes, to soften the skins, then peel both the outer skin and bitter pellicle.

Put the rice crackers in a plastic bag, and lightly crush them with a rolling pin to crumble (do not overdo this as what you want is crunchy broken pieces not powdered crackers). Transfer the cracker crumble to a dish.

Lightly dust the scallops with flour. Dip in the egg white to moisten, then roll in the cracker crumbs to coat.

Heat the oil to 320°F in a large deep skillet and deep-fry the chestnuts for 5 to 8 minutes; they will sink to the bottom initially, and slowly rise to the top. Turn them a few times. Remove, and drain on a wire rack or paper towels.

Heat the oil to 340°F and deep-fry the scallops in small batches for 3 to 5 minutes; they will sink to the middle of the oil and rise to the surface. Turn them once. Take one out to test—it should be slightly undercooked in the middle. Remove and drain on a wire rack.

Divide into four equal portions. and put on individual serving plates, place two chestnuts on each, and serve.

TEMPURA

Crisp, airy, light tempura made by a professional and eaten immediately, is almost impossible to re-create at home, and Japanese people go to specialist restaurants. You can, however, produce very good results, if you follow key rules at each stage of preparation. The rules are simple and logical, but must be followed without skimping. The points on oil and its temperatures explained on page 146 also apply to tempura, but where tempura is distinct from the other two deep-frying styles lies in the *koromo*, batter.

HOW TO MAKE TEMPURA BATTER

To achieve feathery light tempura batter you do exactly the opposite of making pancake batter:

Keep the ingredients chilled until needed.

Sift the flour before mixing.

Prepare the batter in small batches just before you are ready to deep-fry and once made, do not let it stand.

In a mixing bowl, lightly beat the egg yolks, pour in the ice cold water, mix, then add the flour all at once, loosely folding it in using the handles of two wooden spoons. The marks of good tempura batter are a powdery ring of flour on the sides of the mixing bowl, and some dry flour lumps floating at the top. Do not over-mix as the batter will become sticky, and the coating will turn out oily and heavy. Keep the mixing bowl away from the heat while cooking.

GETTING THE CORRECT CONSISTENCY

In the professional kitchen, they mix more than one type of the batter for different ingredients—watery batter for mild-tasting vegetables and delicate sashimi-fresh fish, and thicker batter for strong-tasting fish such as conger eel. For home cooks, it is better to use *shita-ko*, literally under-flour (sifted all-purpose flour). Use a soft pastry brush to lightly dust flour over the vegetables and delicate fish and dust a thicker coating over for more robust-tasting ingredients.

HOW TO DEEP-FRY

Before you start, organize your cooking area; the hot oil pan at the center, a plate of dusting flour, a bowl of batter, and a tray of food to be fried on your left, a draining rack with long cooking chopsticks and a slotted spoon, or a mesh scoop on your right. Also, it is useful to have the oven on the lowest setting, with the door slightly open, to keep food warm while you cook.

Start by deep-frying vegetables, then increase the oil temperature for fish and seafood. To keep the oil at the desired temperature, fry the food in small batches— no more than half of the oil surface area should be covered by frying food (see page 146). Turn over food only once, and do not disturb it while frying. Damaged batter coating will result in the food becoming heavy and oily.

TEMPURA DIPPING SAUCE TEN-TSUYU

The key point of *ten-tsuyu*, dipping sauce, is its temperature; if it is hot, the batter coating will absorb too much liquid, and it will become soggy. It should be served just warm to enhance the lightness of the tempura batter.

MAKES 1¼ CUPS
3½ tablespoons mirin
scant 1 cup Dashi (see page 29)
generous 1½ tablespoons light soy sauce
generous 1½ tablespoons soy sauce
3 to 5 tablespoons *katsuobushi*, dried bonito flakes

In a saucepan, bring the mirin just to a boil to burn off the alcohol, then add the dashi and soy sauces. Return to a boil, add the bonito flakes, and turn off the heat. Leave to stand for 5 minutes to infuse. Then filter through a fine mesh strainer, and keep warm until needed.

Tempura dipping sauce is usually served with loosely drained grated *daikon*, giant white radish.

MIXED TEMPURA
KAKI-AGE

Kaki-age is mixed tempura where small bits of seafood and vegetables are bound together with batter. While tempura is a food for special occasions, *kaki-age* is unceremonious and casual, and it is also a great tasty way of cleaning up your fridge of leftover bits. The key to success is ensuring all ingredients are chopped to a uniform size, so that they cook at the same speed, and do not use too much batter.

SERVES 4

½ medium-size onion

1 carrot

4 shiitake mushrooms

4 scallions, chopped on the diagonal

heaping ½ cup canned corn, drained

7 ounces shelled shrimp, roughly chopped

4 tablespoons all-purpose flour, for dusting

4½ to 6¼ cups vegetable oil, for deep-frying

7 ounces *daikon*, giant white radish

2 tablespoons soy sauce

FOR THE TEMPURA BATTER

1 egg yolk

scant 1⅛ cups ice cold water

heaping 1 cup all-purpose flour

Peel and cut the onion and carrot into 1¼-inch long matchsticks. Remove and discard the mushroom stems, and slice the caps. Put all the vegetables and shrimp in a large bowl, and sprinkle with 4 tablespoons of flour. Mix to ensure each piece is well coated.

Grate the radish, and drain slightly. Set aside.

Fill a 6 to 7-inch diameter saucepan, or a deep skillet with the oil to about 1¼ to 1½ inches deep. Heat to 340°F. Meanwhile, preheat the oven to the lowest setting.

In a large bowl, prepare the batter (see page 152), and then add the vegetable and shrimp mixture. Stir with a large serving spoon in a cut-and-turn motion. Although each ingredient should be coated with the batter, do not over-mix, and try to keep as many air pockets in the batter as possible. Divide the batter into four portions.

To test the oil temperature, drop a tiny drip of batter at the tip of wooden spoon handle—it should sink to the bottom before quickly floating up to the top surrounded by tiny bubbles.

Using the same spoon, gently slide a portion of the mixture along the side of the pan, and spread it evenly, just smaller than the diameter of the pan. Deep-fry for 4 to 6 minutes, or until lightly golden and crisp, then turn over to cook the other side for an additional 3 to 5 minutes. Remove from the oil using a slotted spoon, drain, and place on a wire rack set over a baking pan. Keep warm in the oven while you repeat the process three more times to cook the rest of the mixture.

To serve, put each *kaki-age* disc on individual serving plates, with a small mound of the drained grated radish on top, and with soy sauce drizzled over the mound.

COOK'S TIP
You can use almost any combination of chopped vegetables and seafood, but the important point is cutting them into similar size pieces and keeping the batter coating even.

SEAFOOD TEMPURA WITH VEGETABLES
TEMPURA MORIAWASE

Although tempura should be eaten immediately and does not suit home-cooking, you can get good results if you follow these rules: use the freshest ingredients, and dry them thoroughly, keep oil at a constant temperature, and use chilled and lumpy batter.

SERVES 4

8 large tiger shrimp
7 ounces squid, body part only
4 flounder fillets, weighing 4 to 5 ounces each
1 large Western-size eggplant
1 medium sweet potato, weighing about 10 ounces
2 medium white onions
1 green bell pepper, seeded and cut into four pieces
1 red bell pepper, seeded and cut into four pieces
4 shiitake mushrooms, stems removed
¾ cup sifted all-purpose flour, for dusting
7 ounces *daikon*, giant white radish,
    peeled and grated
thumb-size piece of fresh ginger, peeled and grated
4½ to 6¼ cups vegetable oil, for deep-frying

FOR THE BATTER MIX (DIVIDED INTO TWO BATCHES)
2 egg yolks
scant 1¾ cups ice cold water
1½ cups all-purpose flour, sifted

FOR THE DIPPING SAUCE
3½ tablespoons mirin
scant 1 cup Dashi (see page 29)
generous 1½ tablespoons light soy sauce
generous 1½ tablespoons soy sauce
2–3g *katsuobushi*, dried bonito flakes

Shell and devein the shrimp, but leave the tails on. Trim the shrimp tails into a feathered shape, and gently press out any moisture with the flat of a knife. To stop the shrimp curling, make 3 to 4 deep incisions along the belly, and hold each belly side up, then bend over to stretch the tendon.

Cut the squid into 1½ to 2-inch squares, and cross-score the outer sides, taking care not to cut through. Cut the fish fillets into 1½ to 2-inch diamond shapes.

Next prepare the vegetables. Cut the eggplant into eight ⅜-inch thick round slices, lay them flat, and place between paper towels to stop discoloration. Peel the sweet potato, trim off the ends and cut into four ⅜-inch thick round slices. Peel the onions, cut in half vertically, then into ½-inch thick half-moons.

Lay all the seafood and vegetables on a large baking pan lined with paper towels.

Prepare the dipping sauce as shown on page 152. Grate the radish and ginger into a strainer placed over a bowl to lightly drain.

Fill a large saucepan or deep skillet with oil to about 1¼ to 1½ inch deep. Heat to 340°F. Meanwhile, preheat the oven to the lowest setting.

Prepare the batter in two batches (see page 152)—the first for the vegetables, and the second for the seafood. Mix each batch just before you are ready to start cooking. To test the oil temperature, drop in a tiny drip of batter—it should sink to the bottom before quickly floating up to the top surrounded by tiny bubbles.

Dust the eggplant slices with flour, shaking off any excess, then dip in the batter and slide into the hot oil. Deep-fry for 3 to 4 minutes on each side, or until lightly golden and crisp. Remove with a slotted spoon, and drain briefly before transferring onto a wire rack placed over a baking pan. Keep warm in the oven while you repeat for all the vegetables. Occasionally skim off any bits of batter on the surface of the oil.

Increase the oil temperature to 355°F and mix the second batch of batter. With a pastry brush, lightly dust the shrimp, and while holding the tails, dip into the batter. Deep-fry for 2 to 4 minutes, or until golden and crisp, turning over for even cooking. Remove from the oil with a slotted spoon, and transfer to another wire rack. Keep warm in the oven while you repeat for the rest of the seafood.

To serve, either arrange all the food on a large platter or divide between four individual plates lined with folded paper napkins. Provide each guest with a small bowl of dipping sauce mixed with grated radish and ginger.

TOFU

Tofu is a wonderful food, made from soybeans, and is also known as "field meat." It is healthy, and high in protein and calcium, while low in calories and cost.

Tofu originated in China over two thousand years ago, and spread throughout Asia. Although the date of its first arrival in Japan is not entirely clear, it was most probably introduced around the same time as Buddhism in the sixth century.

In Japan, tofu comes in various forms, ranging from regular fresh tofu, or deep-fried, to prized delicacy *yuba*, soy-milk skin, and the store-cupboard staple of *kōyadōfu*, a freeze-dried version. In this book, however, only regular fresh firm and soft types and *aburaage*, deep-fried tofu, are used.

In Japan, fresh tofu comes in a standard block size of 3½ × 7 × 1-inch and weighs about 9 to 10½ ounces. One block of tofu provides about 20g high-quality protein, which is about a third of an adult's daily requirement. Furthermore, while animal protein is high in saturated fat, and raises cholesterol, tofu's soy protein contains non-saturated fat, and actually helps to lower cholesterol. It is also rich in calcium—eating about 3½ ounces of tofu, provides the equivalent of a glass of milk, or twice as much spinach. Isoflavone found in the soy embryo is known to work similarly to estrogen and hence eating about 3½ ounces of tofu a day helps to stave off osteoporosis.

Health benefits of eating tofu regularly cannot be overstated, yet some people are put off by its veggie image, and complain it is bland. This is because nearly 90 percent of tofu is water, and it needs to be drained before use.

HOW TO DRAIN TOFU

NATURAL METHOD Leave to stand on a slightly angled cutting board, or a flat bamboo tray for 15 to 20 minutes.

BOILING METHOD Boil a whole block for 5 to 10 minutes, or for 2 to 3 minutes in smaller pieces.

MICROWAVE Wrap in paper towels and microwave on medium to high for 3 minutes.

SQUEEZING METHOD Wrap the tofu in a clean damp cloth and squeeze.

PRESSING METHOD Sandwich the tofu between two boards, slightly angled, with or without a weight, and leave.

Tofu is essentially a fresh food, and should be used up within a day or two. A tofu peddler going around our neighborhood, on a bicycle with a heavy wooden tub filled with water and tofu inside, precariously strapped at the back, was a familiar daily scene when I was growing up in Japan. Outside Japan, tofu is usually sold in sealed packages date stamped, like dairy products, to give the consumer some idea of freshness. Use tofu within 5 to 7 days of manufacture. Deep-fried tofu keeps for 7 to 10 days, or it freezes well. Tofu must be kept refrigerated. To help keep it fresh, once opened, transfer it into a larger container, cover with water, and change the water daily.

TERIYAKI TOFU STEAKS

A mild taste of tofu is like having a blank canvas for a cook to create any culinary painting.

SERVES 4

21 ounces firm tofu, cut into 4 equal rectangles
2 tablespoons all-purpose flour, for dusting
1 tablespoon vegetable oil
4 tablespoons sake
6 tablespoons mirin
2 tablespoons soy sauce
7 ounces *daikon*, giant white radish
½ teaspoon *shichimi-tōgarashi*, seven-spice chili powder or regular chili powder
a handful of peppercress, to garnish

Drain the tofu by following one of the methods on page 156. Dust the tofu with flour.

Heat the oil in a skillet over medium heat, and add the tofu. Cook for 3 to 5 minutes, until light brown and crisp on one side, then turn over to cook the other side for an additional 3 minutes. Pour in the sake, mirin, and soy sauce, and simmer for 5 to 7 minutes, uncovered.

Meanwhile, peel and grate the radish and drain slightly with a strainer—it should yield about 4 to 5 heaping tablespoons. Add the grated radish to the pan, stir, and then let the cooking juice return to just boiling.

Place the tofu on individual dishes, spoon over the teriyaki sauce mix, and sprinkle over the chili powder. Garnish with the peppercress and serve.

DEEP-FRIED TOFU IN BROTH
AGEDASHIDŌFU

This is probably the best-loved tofu dish—the key is draining the tofu well.

SERVES 4

21 ounces firm tofu

4 scallions

8½ cups vegetable oil

¾ cup all-purpose flour, for dusting

4 tablespoons *momiji-oroshi*, red maple radish sauce (see below)

FOR THE DASHI BROTH

scant 1 cup Dashi (see page 29)

2 tablespoons light soy sauce

2 tablespoons mirin

2 tablespoons cornstarch mixed with 2 tablespoons water

Cut the tofu into four blocks, and leave to drain on a slightly angled board for 15 to 20 minutes, or if you are short of time, sandwich the tofu between two cutting boards, angled slightly on a chopstick, with a can of tomatoes as a weight on top.

Cut the scallions into about 2-inch lengths, then with the tip of a knife, cut into very fine strips lengthwise, and soak in a bowl of water. Once the strips have curled, drain, and set aside.

Heat the dashi in a saucepan to a gentle simmer, and add the soy and mirin. Stir in the cornstarch mixture, to thicken, then keep warm while you deep-fry the tofu.

Heat the oil to 350°F in a heavy-bottomed saucepan. Dust the tofu with flour, and shake off any excess, then immediately deep-fry, one to two pieces at a time, for about 6 to 8 minutes, or until lightly golden. Briefly drain on a wire rack. Repeat to cook the remaining tofu.

Put the tofu in individual serving dishes, pour the dashi broth over, spoon on the red maple radish sauce (see below) and garnish with the scallion curls. Serve immediately.

HOW TO MAKE RED MAPLE RADISH SAUCE

Momiji-oroshi is grated radish with a kick of dried red chiles, and makes an excellent condiment for deep-fried dishes. You can buy it ready-made, but homemade is not difficult. Cut the stems of dried chiles, and without puncturing, remove the seeds from the inside, then soak in warm water for 5 to 8 minutes, to soften. Peel and cut a *daikon*, giant white radish, into 2 to 2½-inch length pieces, then make 3 to 5 holes in one end with a chopstick, and plug the chiles into the holes, using the chopstick to push them in. Grate the whole radish—it should yield about a cupful of very watery red mixture. Drain through a strainer. Fresh *momiji-oroshi* doesn't keep well, so make it as needed.

TOFU BURGER
GANMODOKI

Ganmodoki literally means pseudo wild goose as it is supposed to "look and taste" like goose meat, and originates from the Buddhist vegetarian cuisine.

SERVES 4

14 ounces firm tofu
7 ounces shrimp
⅓ cup edamame beans, cooked
2 ounces Japanese yam, peeled
1 egg white
1 teaspoon salt
1 carrot, pared and finely chopped
2 tablespoons toasted white sesame seeds
4½ cups vegetable oil, for deep-frying
4 tablespoons all-purpose flour, for dusting
Citrus Soy Vinegar, *ponzu* (see page 51), to serve

Wrap the tofu in a clean damp cloth and wring to drain thoroughly, to yield wet pulp.

Put the tofu, shrimp, edamame, yam, egg white, and salt into a food processor, and purée until very smooth.

Transfer to a bowl, mix in the carrot and sesame seeds, then divide into four portions. Rub your hands with a little vegetable oil—this is to make your hands nonstick—and shape into four oval patties about 1¼ inches thick. Chill for 1 hour.

Dust each patty lightly with flour and shake off the excess.

Heat the vegetable oil in a deep, heavy-bottomed skillet over medium heat. Add the patties, and deep-fry on one side, until golden brown, for about 3 to 5 minutes, then turn over to cook on the other side for 2 to 3 minutes, or until golden brown, and then drain.

Serve hot with Citrus Soy Vinegar, *ponzu*.

TOFU STEAKS WITH MUSHROOMS

This is for those people who complain of the mild taste of tofu. Here mushroom sauce gives plenty of woody, meaty flavor.

SERVES 4

21 ounces firm tofu, cut into 4 equal rectangles
5½ ounces shiitake mushrooms
4¼ ounces shimeji mushrooms
4¼ ounces enoki mushrooms
2 tablespoons all-purpose flour, for dusting
1 tablespoon vegetable oil
2 tablespoons unsalted butter
2 tablespoons soy sauce
2 scallions, finely chopped on the diagonal
salt and freshly ground black pepper

Sandwich the tofu steaks between 2 equal-size boards with a small weight (a 14-ounce can is ideal) on top, and leave to drain for 15 to 20 minutes, or use any of the other draining methods described on page 156.

Meanwhile, cut and discard the shiitake stems, and slice the caps. Remove the base of the shimeji and enoki mushrooms where they are joined, then separate.

Dust the tofu with flour and let it stand for a few minutes.

Heat the oil in a large nonstick skillet over high heat, and add the tofu. Fry for 3 to 5 minutes until lightly brown and crisp on one side, turn over, cover with a lid, and reduce to medium–low heat while you cook the mushrooms.

Melt the butter in a separate pan over medium heat, and sauté the mushrooms until soft. Add the soy sauce and stir, then adjust the seasoning with salt and pepper if needed, and scatter over the scallions.

To serve, place the tofu steaks in the middle of individual plates, and spoon one quarter of the mushroom mixture over each steak.

OVEN-BAKED MISO AND TOFU GRATIN

This recipe is full of umami from the dashi broth, miso, and Parmesan cheese. So try it on someone who complains that tofu doesn't taste of anything.

SERVES 4

butter, for greasing
18 ounces firm tofu
7 ounces skinless chicken thigh fillets, cut into bite-size chunks
2 tablespoons all-purpose flour, for dusting
1 tablespoon vegetable oil
1 parsnip, pared and cut into bite-size chunks
1 carrot, pared and cut into bite-size chunks
1 leek, trimmed and cut into thick slices
8 chestnut mushrooms, halved or quartered
12 fine green beans, halved
scant 1 cup Dashi (see page 29)
2 to 3 tablespoons medium-colored miso
2 ounces Parmesan cheese, grated
crusty bread or baguette, to serve

Preheat the oven to 400°F. Grease a large gratin dish with the butter.

Break up the tofu into rough chunks with your hands, and set aside to drain on a flat bamboo tray (or a slightly angled cutting board), or in a strainer.

Cut the chicken into bite-size pieces, and dust with the flour.

Heat the oil in a heavy-bottomed pan over medium heat, and cook the chicken for 3 to 5 minutes, until lightly browned. Add the parsnip and carrot, and cook for 3 minutes. Add the leek, mushrooms, and beans with the dashi, and simmer over medium heat for 6 to 8 minutes, or until all the vegetables are cooked through.

Put the miso in a small bowl, and add a ladleful of the dashi from the pan, stirring to soften. Add the tofu and miso to the vegetables, and mix well.

Transfer the mixture into the prepared gratin dish. Sprinkle with the Parmesan cheese, and bake for 12 to 15 minutes, or until the cheese is melted and light brown.

Divide between four individual dishes, and serve with some crusty bread.

JAPANESE-STYLE MAPO TOFU

Mapo tofu is a famous Sichuan dish that is also very popular in Japan. Like many foods with Chinese origins such as *rāmen* and *gyōza* dumplings, mapo tofu eaten in Japan has been long adapted to suit Japanese tastes. Traditionally mapo tofu is served with plain boiled rice.

SERVES 4

FOR THE TOFU

18 ounces soft silken tofu

1 to 2 teaspoons sesame oil

7 ounces ground raw chicken

7 ounces ground raw pork

1 clove garlic, crushed and finely chopped

1 red chile, seeded and minced

2 leeks, trimmed and minced

salt

½ teaspoon sansho pepper or Sichuan pepper, to serve

FOR THE COOKING SAUCE

4 tablespoons sake

2 tablespoons sugar

4 tablespoons soy sauce

2 teaspoons cornstarch

4 tablespoons red or dark-colored miso

Bring a large saucepan of lightly salted water to just below a boil over high heat. Cut the tofu into ¾-inch cubes, then add to the saucepan. When the tofu begins to sway a little in the water, reduce the heat to low to stop the water from boiling, and simmer for 2 to 3 minutes and drain. A gentle simmering drains the tofu, while stopping it from developing tiny pinholes.

Meanwhile, heat the oil in a large skillet or wok over high heat. Add the chicken and pork, and stir-fry for about 5 minutes. When oil begins to seep out, and the color of the meat is lighter, reduce the heat to medium and stir in the garlic, chile, and leeks, then continue to cook for 3 to 5 minutes.

Mix all the sauce ingredients in a bowl with 1¾ cups of water, then pour into the pan and stir to mix. Let the meat mixture return to a boil. Add the tofu to the pan, and stir the whole mixture carefully, taking care not to break the tofu, and simmer for about 5 minutes.

Divide between four individual serving dishes, sprinkle over the sansho pepper, and serve.

VARIATIONS

I chose to use the soft silken variety of tofu for its smooth slippery texture. But there is nothing to stop you using the firm cotton variety if you prefer.

If you only have regular, medium-colored miso paste (which is milder than the darker type) adjust the seasoning by adding 1 to 2 tablespoons of soy sauce.

VEGETARIAN MAPO TOFU

This recipe is full of flavor. Doubanjiang is a spicy Chinese bean sauce sold in Asian stores or larger supermarkets. As an alternative, use medium-colored Japanese miso paste mixed with chili sauce.

SERVES 4

4 dried shiitake mushrooms
1 eggplant, weighing about 10 ounces, finely diced
18 ounces soft or firm tofu, cut into ¾-inch cubes
2 tablespoons toasted sesame oil
1 garlic clove, crushed and minced
thumb-size piece fresh ginger, peeled and minced
2 leeks, trimmed and minced
2 tablespoons Doubanjiang, Sichuan fermented chili bean sauce

FOR THE COOKING SAUCE

2 tablespoons sake
2 tablespoons soy sauce
1 tablespoon sugar
2 teaspoons cornstarch
½ teaspoon *sansho* pepper or Sichuan pepper, to serve

Soak the shiitake mushrooms in a bowl with 1¾ cups warm water for 10 minutes, or until they are soft. When soft, cut and discard the stems, and mince the caps, reserving the soaking water for later.

At the same time, soak the diced eggplant in a bowl of cold water, to remove bitterness. Change the water two to three times and drain.

Meanwhile, bring a saucepan of water to just below a boil over medium–high heat. Add the tofu cubes, and when the tofu begins to sway in the water, reduce the heat to medium–low, and simmer for 2 to 3 minutes, and drain. A gentle simmering drains the tofu while stopping it from developing tiny pinholes.

Heat the sesame oil in a large skillet or wok over high heat. Add the garlic, ginger, and leeks with the shiitake, eggplant, and Doubanjiang, and stir-fry for about 3 minutes.

Mix all the cooking sauce ingredients with the reserved shiitake water, and add to the pan. Let the mixture come to a boil. Immediately reduce the heat to medium, add the tofu, and carefully stir, taking care not to break the tofu. Simmer for about 5 minutes, then turn off the heat.

Divide between four individual serving dishes, sprinkle over the sansho pepper, and serve.

POULTRY AND EGGS

The Japanese people's relationship with chicken and eggs goes back a long way. Ancient mythology recounts that when *Amaterasuoomikami*, the Sun goddess, revered mother of Japan, had an argument with her brother, and hid herself in a cave, it resulted in the whole country descending into total darkness. A flock of roosters were sent to cock-a-doodle to entice her out. Ancient farmers relied on roosters to tell them when to get up and start working. Chickens were revered as messengers from God, and their eggs were used as holy offerings.

In 675 A.D. an imperial decree was passed prohibiting the killing of cattle, horses, dogs, monkeys, and chickens for eating, in accordance with the Buddhist belief. But interestingly, the banning order did not extend to what were then more common wild birds and animals such as pheasants, ducks, deer, and wild boars. Although Japanese people "officially" did not eat meat and poultry for over twelve hundred years, until the Meiji Restoration in 1868, it is largely thought that people were eating meat inconspicuously, or even quite openly in the case of the samurai who loved hunting and falconry.

The Japanese are rice farmers, and there was no livestock or chicken farming until the late nineteenth century. Both chicken and eggs were more popular than meat, for their mild tastes, but remained relatively expensive until as late as the 1950s when American-style chicken farming was introduced. During the economic boom of the 1970s a buzzword listing the three most popular items was 巨人、大鵬、卵焼き *Kyojin*—a title-winning professional baseball team, *Taihō*—a long-reigning sumo grand champion, and *tamagoyaki*—an egg omelet.

SAVORY THICK OMELET
DATEMAKI TAMAGO

This thick rolled omelet is an essential component on New Year menus. It is made of ground whitefish or shrimp and eggs and has sweet-savory flavors. Although the traditional version calls for a rectangular Japanese omelet pan, and a bamboo rolling mat, this recipe has been adapted using an ordinary round omelet pan.

SERVES 4

7 ounces cooked shrimp
2 tablespoons all-purpose flour
1 teaspoon salt
6 eggs, lightly beaten
4 tablespoons clear honey
1 tablespoon light soy sauce
½ tablespoon vegetable oil
7 ounces *daikon*, giant white radish, grated and slightly drained, to serve

Put the shrimp, flour, and salt in a food processor and blitz, then add a small amount of egg and blitz again. Keep processing the shrimp mixture while adding the eggs gradually, until it is all used up, and the mixture becomes very smooth and elastic. Finally, add the honey and soy sauce.

Heat the oil in a large nonstick skillet over low heat. Wipe away any excess oil in the pan, and pour in the egg mixture. Cover with a lid, and cook for 20 minutes, or until the bottom is light brown, and the top soft set, but not runny. Turn over and cook, uncovered, for an additional 12 to 15 minutes, and if the center begins to rise, gently push down with a spatula.

Cut the omelet into 8 wedges, and serve with a small mound of drained radish on each plate.

HOT SPRING EGGS ON ASPARAGUS
ONSEN-TAMAGO TO ASUPARA

There are countless numbers of hot springs in Japan, and many people enjoy these natural resources, even for cooking. *Onsen-tamago*, hot spring eggs, as the name implies, is where the eggs are cooked by sitting in warm water. This is a perfect healthy vegetarian dish.

SERVES 4

4 very fresh eggs
20 asparagus spears, trimmed
½ teaspoon salt
4 teaspoons soy sauce
2 teaspoons toasted white sesame seeds

If the eggs are kept in the fridge, take them out 20 to 30 minutes before you begin cooking.

Place 4½ cups of water in a saucepan, bring to a boil, and remove from the heat. Add a scant cup of cold water, and stir.

Put the eggs in the pan, cover with a lid, and leave for 12 minutes.

Meanwhile, steam the asparagus for 3 to 5 minutes, and sprinkle with the salt. Divide the asparagus between four plates, sprinkle with the soy sauce and sesame seeds, and loosely cover with aluminum foil to keep warm.

Remove the eggs from the pan, and wait for 3 minutes before cracking open over the asparagus, and serve.

SAVORY STEAMED EGG CUSTARD
CHAWAN-MUSHI

Chawan-mushi, "steamed in rice bowl," is usually served as a side dish, or instead of soup, but this recipe is for a main course. The key formula is the ratio between the eggs and dashi broth, which is 1:3.

SERVES 4

7 ounces mini chicken fillets, cut into bite-size pieces
2 tablespoons sake
½ teaspoon salt
4 shiitake mushrooms
4 large tiger shrimp
4 ounces broccoli, cut into small bite-size pieces

FOR THE EGG MIX

4 eggs, lightly beaten
2½ cups Dashi (see page 29)
4 teaspoons light soy sauce

Season the chicken with half the sake and the salt. Discard the stems of the mushrooms, and slice the caps into quarters. Slit along the back of the shrimp, remove the black veins, and season with the remaining sake.

Combine the egg mix ingredients, and pass through a strainer to make a completely smooth mixture.

Put the chicken, broccoli, and mushrooms in a microwave-proof bowl (I use a 7-inch round dish 3½ inches deep), pour in the egg mix, and stir to ensure the chicken is not lumped together. Pop any air bubbles.

Loosely cover with a lid or plastic wrap, and place in a microwave. It is difficult to be precise on timing, but as a rough guide, cook for 5 to 8 minutes on low to medium. Carefully remove the cover. The custard should be beginning to set around the edges, with a white skin forming on the surface. If it is still runny, cover and cook for an additional minute. Add the shrimp, cover and microwave for 10 to 12 minutes. Divide between four individual warmed soup dishes, and serve.

JAPANESE-STYLE DUCK A L'ORANGE

The famous French dish has been adapted with the addition of classic Japanese ingredients, *yuzu* juice, and refreshing giant white radish.

SERVES 4

14 ounces *daikon*, giant white radish
3½ ounces *mizuna*, mustard greens or arugula
4 (5 to 5½-ounce) duck breasts, skin on
4 teaspoons salt
vegetable oil, to grease

FOR THE CITRUS DRESSING
4 tablespoons sake
2 tablespoons clear honey
2 tablespoons light soy sauce
2 tablespoons *yuzu*, or lime or satsuma juice

Peel the radish and cut it in half lengthwise, then slice very thinly into half-moons with a Japanese mandoline (or use a very steady hand and a sharp knife). Soak in cold water for 10 minutes, then drain. Put the radish, along with the mizuna, in the fridge to chill.

For the dressing, put the sake in a small saucepan over high heat to burn off the alcohol, then mix with the remaining dressing ingredients, and set aside to cool.

Trim off any excess fat from the duck breasts, then with a very sharp knife, lightly score through the skin, taking care not to cut into the flesh. Rub the salt into the skin.

Heat a large heavy-bottomed skillet over medium heat, and brush with a scant amount of oil. Place the duck in the pan, skin-side down, and cook for 6 to 8 minutes to render the fat while spooning the fat over the flesh. Then turn over to cook the other side for 3 to 5 minutes.

Remove the duck from the pan, then pour boiling water over to wash off the fat and pat dry. Put the duck on a wire rack, skin-side up, and cover loosely with a piece of foil. Leave to rest for about 5 minutes. Do not wrap the duck tightly, otherwise the crispy skin will go limp.

Take the radish and mizuna from the fridge, and divide between four individual serving plates.

Place the duck, skin side down, on a cutting board and cut each breast into ⅛ to ¼-inch thick slices. Arrange the slices on the top of the vegetables, drizzle the citrus dressing over, and serve.

DASHI-ROLLED OMELET
DASHI-MAKI TAMAGO

This soft, succulent, dashi-infused omelet makes a delicious and healthy main dish. It is helpful if you have a square or rectangular Japanese omelet pan, but a regular round pan can be used—simply cut off the round edges after cooking.

MAKES 4 ROLLS

12 eggs
2 cups Primary or Vegetarian Dashi (see page 29)
1 tablespoon mirin
2 tablespoons light soy sauce
½ teaspoon salt
2 tablespoon vegetable oil for cooking
about 7 ounces *daikon*, giant white radish, grated and slightly drained
2 tablespoons soy sauce

In a large bowl mix the dashi, mirin, light soy sauce, and salt until the salt dissolves. In a separate bowl, lightly beat the eggs, and add them to the dashi mixture. Roughly combine, but don't over mix—you should still be able to see some whites. Divide the egg mixture into four portions.

Place the omelet pan over medium heat, and lightly oil the pan with folded paper towels. Heat the pan, then drop a spoonful of the egg mixture to test the temperature—if it sizzles a little, the pan is ready.

Ladle about one-third of the egg mixture (from one portion) into the pan, and quickly spread to thinly cover the surface. Cook over medium heat until the surface begins to set, then fold toward you in quarter sections using either chopsticks or spatula. Don't worry too much if your first folding is not perfect—it won't show. Push the folded omelet to the far end of the pan and re-oil the exposed surface of the pan. Ladle in another third of the egg mixture and gently lift the folded omelet to allow the egg mixture to get under it to cover the entire pan surface. When the egg begins to set, fold it toward you in quarters with the first roll at the center. If you are using a square pan, shape the omelet by gently pressing it against the side of the pan. Repeat the process—re-oil, add the last third of the egg mixture, cook and fold.

Remove the omelet from the pan onto a bamboo rolling mat placed on a cutting board. Wrap the omelet with the rolling mat, and gently press to shape while it is warm—a traditional shape is a rectangular brick, but you may choose round cylindrical. Keep the omelet wrapped in the rolling mat while you repeat the whole process to make 3 more rolls.

Mix the grated radish with the soy sauce.

Cut each omelet into about ⅝-inch thick slices, arrange on individual serving plates, put about a tablespoonful mound of soy/radish on the side, and serve at room temperature.

LEMONY CHICKEN TERIYAKI

Because teriyaki sauce is so versatile, it is tempting to use it on almost everything. So here is a slight variation.

SERVES 4
4 (5½ to 6-ounce) chicken breasts, skin on
4 tablespoons all-purpose flour
1 large green bell pepper
2 tablespoons vegetable oil
zest and juice of 1 lemon
FOR THE TERIYAKI SAUCE
scant 1 cup sake
scant 1 cup mirin
4 tablespoons soy sauce

About 30 minutes before you begin cooking, take the chicken breasts out of the fridge and let them come to room temperature.

Lightly dust the chicken breasts with flour. Cut the pepper into quarters, seed, and remove the white membrane inside, then cut each quarter into three strips.

Heat the oil in a large skillet over high heat. Cook the chicken, skin-side down, for 5 to 7 minutes. or until light brown and well sealed, then turn over, and cook the other side for an additional 5 minutes. Clean around the chicken with scrunched up paper towels to soak up any excess oil.

Add all the sauce ingredients to the pan, let it just come to a boil, and then adjust the heat to maintain the just boil for about 5 minutes. Add the pepper strips when the sauce begins to thicken, while shaking the pan constantly to coat the peppers with the sauce for 2 to 3 minutes. Just before turning off the heat, add the lemon zest and juice, then shake the pan to evenly mix the sauce.

Transfer the chicken and pepper strips to four warmed individual plates, and let the chicken rest for about 5 minutes. Spoon the teriyaki sauce over the chicken, and serve.

SOY-SIMMERED CHICKEN
TORI NO SHŌYUNI

Chicken drumsticks can be tough to eat, so this gentle simmering in soy-based broth is ideal.

SERVES 4

14 ounces *daikon*, giant white radish, or parsnips, pared
8 chicken drumsticks
1 postcard-size piece of dried kelp
1 red chile, slit lengthwise and seeded
8 tablespoons soy sauce
4 tablespoons mirin
4 scallions, green parts only
7 ounces broccoli, cut in large bite-size chunks

Cut the radish in half lengthwise, then into 1 to 1¼-inch thick half-moons. With a small knife, bevel the edges so that they look neat, and don't crumble during cooking.

Bring a large saucepan of water to a rapid boil, then submerge the chicken, and parboil it for 2 to 3 minutes, or until the skin and flesh turn pale. Transfer to a bowl of cold water, drain, and pat dry.

At the same time, put the radish in a saucepan of water over medium heat, simmer for 10 minutes, then drain.

Put the kelp at the bottom of a saucepan and place the chicken, radish, and red chile on top. Add 2¼ cups water, the soy sauce, and mirin, and bring to just boiling over medium heat. Reduce the heat to low, add the scallions, and simmer gently for 25 to 30 minutes, skimming off any scum that floats to the surface.

Meanwhile, steam or boil the broccoli for 3 to 5 minutes. Drain, then sprinkle with a tiny pinch of salt to refresh the color. Keep warm.

Divide and arrange the chicken and radish between four individual serving dishes. Put the broccoli between the chicken and radish, ladle over an ample amount of cooking broth without the scallions, and serve.

RICE VINEGAR SIMMERED CHICKEN
TORINIKU NO SUNI

I often add a few drops of vinegar to simmered dishes at the end of the cooking to sharpen the flavor. Here, vinegar is added from the start, but the finished dish does not taste vinegary, because the cooking transforms it into refreshing clean umami.

SERVES 4

2 teaspoons salt
8 (4½ to 5½-ounce) chicken thigh fillets, skin on
1 red chile, slit lengthwise and seeded
scant 1 cup sake
scant 1 cup rice vinegar
3½ tablespoons mirin
3½ tablespoons soy sauce
2 scallions, green parts only
7 ounces cauliflower, cut into bite-size chunks
20 snow peas

Sprinkle the salt over the chicken, and leave to sweat for 10 to 15 minutes, then pat dry with paper towels.

Place a skillet over medium heat. When hot, add the chicken, skin-side down, pressing to make as much contact with the pan as possible, and cook for 5 to 8 minutes, or until the skin turns golden. Reduce the heat slightly, then cook the other side for an additional 3 to 5 minutes. Remove from the pan, pour boiling water over to wash off any fat, then pat dry with paper towels.

Put the chicken in a large saucepan with the chile, sake, vinegar, mirin, soy sauce, and a scant cup of water, and bring to a boil. As it reaches a boil, add the scallions, then reduce the heat, and simmer for 10 minutes. Turn off the heat, remove the chile and scallions, and leave the chicken in the cooking juice.

Meanwhile, steam or boil the cauliflower and snow peas, and keep warm. Divide the chicken between four dishes, arrange the vegetables on top, spoon on the cooking juices, and serve.

SOY-MARINATED ROAST CHICKEN

Because there are no recipes for roasting a whole chicken or a large piece of meat in traditional Japanese cooking, there is no Japanese name for this dish. This is because Japanese food is always designed and served to be eaten with a pair of chopsticks. Up until recently, most Japanese home kitchens did not even have ovens, unless you count microwave ovens. For this recipe, you will need to start the day before for overnight marinating. But you will be richly rewarded for the little bit of extra preparation.

SERVES 4

FOR THE CHICKEN
4½-pound whole chicken
1 whole garlic bulb, cut in half horizontally
1 teaspoon salt
1 teaspoon soft brown sugar

FOR THE SOY MARINADE
scant ½ cup soy sauce
3½ tablespoons mirin
3½ tablespoons sake
2 tablespoons white miso
2 tablespoons vegetable oil
1 teaspoon sesame oil

Prepare the soy marinade by mixing all the ingredients in a large non-metallic dish or bowl that is roomy enough to easily fit the chicken. Put the chicken in the dish, and turn to coat well in the marinade. Slightly loosen the skin of the breasts, by gently sliding your hand under the breast skin from the neck opening, and spoon the marinade under the skin and inside the cavity. Cover with plastic wrap, and refrigerate overnight, turning over occasionally for even marinating.

Take the chicken out of the fridge 45 to 60 minutes before you intend to cook it, so that it can come to room temperature. Preheat the oven to 375°F. Remove the chicken from the dish, but reserve the marinade for later, and place on a rack set over a roasting pan. Stuff the cavity with the garlic, and pour 2¼ cups of water into the bottom of the pan.

Sprinkle the chicken with the salt and sugar, then place in the oven to roast for 75 to 90 minutes, or until the juices run clear when a skewer is pierced through the thickest part of the thigh. Remove from the oven, and allow to rest for 15 minutes before carving.

Meanwhile, put the reserved marinade with any roasting juices left in the pan in a small saucepan and bring to a rapid boil for 8 to 10 minutes, or until reduced slightly. Carve the chicken, and serve with the sauce on the side.

PORK

It may come as a surprise to many, including Japanese people themselves, but pork is the most eaten meat in the country—nearly as much pork is consumed as chicken and beef combined.

Pork and the Japanese go back a long way, already in the prehistoric *Jōmon* period (12,000 to 400 B.C.), Japanese people were eating wild boar, and early immigrants from the Korean peninsula were farming boar in the early seventh century—the dawn of pig-farming in Japan. However, when Buddhism arrived in the early sixth century and spread, meat eating was banned for the next 1200 years. The first imperial decree was passed in 675 A.D. prohibiting the killing of cattle, horses, dogs, monkeys, and chickens for eating, and several more banning orders were to follow, extending to a wider range of animals and birds. Even fishing was stopped in 752 A.D. when the giant statue of Buddha was erected in *Tōdaiji* temple in Nara. Although pigs were never listed in the prohibition, pig-farming disappeared, except in the remote parts of southern Kyūshū and the island of Okinawa, which were then separate kingdoms. Today, both regions are renowned for high-quality pork and their regional pork dishes.

In 1609, Japan began trading with the Dutch, and pig-farming was re-established to meet small demands from the foreign traders. However, livestock farming, including pig-farming, restarted in earnest in the *Meiji* era (1867 to 1912) when the meat eating prohibition was finally lifted in 1872 and the Emperor *Meiji* set an imperial example to the nation by eating beef at the New Year celebration. The middle-sized Yorkshire and Berkshire pigs were imported from England, as they were thought to be most suited to the farming conditions in Japan. However, pigs were fed on discarded foods from restaurants or household leftovers, rather than corn, and therefore, pig farms were often located near urban areas and

remained relatively small. Pork was mainly eaten in processed forms like bacon, ham, and canned. Then in 1922 an eatery in the downtown Asakusa district of Tokyo introduced *tonkatsu*, deep-fried breaded pork cutlet, which was an instant hit, and the dish was a major contributory factor to pork becoming the most preferred meat of the nation.

During the 1960s, as Japan became more affluent, there was an increased demand for pork, and so larger breeds such as Large White Hampshire and Landrace were introduced from America and Europe, and crossbred with the existing middle-sized Yorkshire and Berkshire. There was also a dramatic change from medium to large-scale pig-farming. However, more recently, the emphasis has shifted from quantity to quality, and older breeds especially *kuro-buta*, the black pig farmed in Kyūshū, is making a comeback.

The main health benefits of pork is in its high content of vitamin B1 (10 times more than beef). Vitamin B1 plays a vital role in helping the body to convert sugar into energy. The lack of the vitamin can result in lost concentration, tiredness, and even mood swings. Cooking pork with garlic, onions, leeks, or chives, all of which are rich in allicin, helps the body to absorb vitamin B1 effectively, and converts sugar into energy.

PAN-FRIED PORK CHOPS WITH GINGER
(FOR THICK CUTS)

When pan-frying thick cuts, it's important to let the meat rest for 10 minutes to allow the juices to evenly distribute before serving.

SERVES 4

FOR THE PORK AND VEGETABLES
1 teaspoon salt
4 (5½-ounce) pork chops, at room temperature
1 tablespoon vegetable oil
2 tablespoons grated fresh ginger
4 ounces snow peas
12 asparagus spears
7 ounces baby potatoes, halved and cooked, kept warm
1 lemon, cut in 4 wedges, to serve

FOR THE SAUCE
6 tablespoons sake
6 tablespoons mirin
6 tablespoons soy sauce

Sprinkle the salt all over the pork and set aside for 15 minutes, then wash off and pat dry with paper towels.

Heat the oil in a heavy-bottomed skillet over high heat. When almost smoking hot, sear the pork for 3 to 5 minutes on each side. Take the pan off the heat and remove any excess oil with paper towels. Pour in the sauce ingredients. When the juice stops bubbling, return the pan to a gentle heat, add the ginger, shake the pan to mix evenly, and cook for an additional 5 to 8 minutes on each side.

Remove from the heat, and let the pork rest in the pan for 10 minutes.

Meanwhile, steam or boil the snow peas for 2 to 3 minutes, and the asparagus for 5 to 8 minutes. To serve, arrange a pork chop with a portion of vegetables on four plates, and spoon over the sauce. Serve with a lemon wedge on the side.

JAPANESE-STYLE RÖSTI WITH SOY PORK

Here is a Swiss classic with a Japanese twist.

SERVES 4
14 ounces pork loin, roughly chopped
4 tablespoons sake
4 tablespoons soy sauce
21 ounces waxy potatoes (such as Yukon Gold or Desiree), peeled
6 tablespoons vegetable oil
2 teaspoons cornstarch
12 French breakfast radishes, cleaned and trimmed
salt

Put the pork in a bowl with the sake and soy sauce. Leave to marinate for 10 to 15 minutes.

Shred the potatoes with a Japanese mandoline or a grater, over a large bowl of cold water, and then rinse away any excess starch. Drain the shreds, and spread over a clean dishtowel, then roll up, and press gently to blot away excess water. Unroll the dishtowel, and put the shreds in a large bowl with 2 tablespoons of the oil, and mix.

Squeeze the pork of any excess marinade, and coat with the cornstarch.

Heat 2 tablespoons of oil in a 9½-inch nonstick skillet over medium heat, and spread over half of the potato shreds. Spread the pork evenly over the first layer, then cover with the rest of the potato, as evenly as possible.

Drizzle the rest of the oil over the rösti, and turn over after 15 to 20 minutes, or when the bottom has become golden and crisp. You can either flip it like a pancake (if you are brave enough) or by placing a similar diameter plate over the pan, turning it over, then carefully sliding the rosti back into the pan to cook the other side for 12 to 15 minutes.

Remove from the pan onto a cutting board. Sprinkle with some salt, cut into four and serve with 3 radishes each.

QUICK-SIMMERED PORK BELLY
BUTA NO KAKUNI

The authentic recipe for this popular pork dish takes practically two days to prepare, which isn't realistic for busy home cooks. So here is a relatively quick version, but the result is nearly as tender as the original. Patient, slow frying and rinsing ensures a rich, but not greasy pork dish.

SERVES 4

21 ounces pork belly, cut into 1½ to 2-inch cubes
½ tablespoon vegetable oil
thumb-size piece fresh ginger, peeled and julienned
1¾ cups Dashi (see page 29)
4 tablespoons sake
3 tablespoons sugar
4 tablespoons mirin
4 tablespoons soy sauce
1 tablespoon cornstarch, mixed with
   2 tablespoons water
4 teaspoons strong mustard

Put the oil a large skillet (large enough for the pork to sit in one layer) and add the pork skin-side down. Turn on the heat to medium–low, and slowly fry for 15 to 20 minutes, or until the fat begins to render, and the pork starts to turn pale brown. Turn over, and continue to cook on each side until pale brown all over.

Transfer the pork to a strainer, and rinse under hot running water to wash off all excess fat, then drain.

Wipe the pan clean with scrunched paper towels, then return the pork to the pan, in one layer, and add the ginger, dashi, sake, sugar, mirin, and soy sauce. Bring to a boil over high heat, then reduce to low, and simmer for 60 to 90 minutes. Cut a sheet of aluminum foil slightly smaller than the diameter of the pan, and place loosely on the surface of the pork while simmering (or use a drop lid, see page 134).

When the cooking juices have reduced to about half, take the pork out with a slotted spoon. Increase the heat to high, and further reduce the cooking juice without the foil lid, until reduced by a quarter. Add the cornstarch mixture to thicken. Then return the pork to coat in the sauce.

Divide the pork between four deep-sided dishes or bowls, and garnish with a dab of mustard on top, and serve.

PAN-FRIED PORK LOIN WITH GINGER (FOR THIN CUTS)

Rules for cooking meat differ depending on the thickness. Firstly, for thin cuts, seasoning with cooking juice should be kept brief, and massaging with your hands is sufficient, because marinating for a long time does not add any more flavor and only toughens the meat. Secondly, cooking juices should be squeezed or patted dry with paper towels before cooking in a hot pan because leaving cooking juice on the meat adds to the cooking time. Thirdly, cooking time should be kept to a minimum at a high temperature.

SERVES 4

FOR THE PORK AND VEGETABLES
21 ounces thinly sliced pork loin or thin steaks
8 baby corn cobs
6 ounces broccoli, cut into bite-size chunks
6 ounces cauliflower, cut into bite-size chunks
½ teaspoon salt
2 teaspoons vegetable oil

FOR THE SAUCE
6 tablespoons sake
6 tablespoons mirin
6 tablespoons soy sauce
1 tablespoon grated fresh ginger

Take the pork out of the fridge to let it come to room temperature at least 30 minutes before you start cooking, because fridge-cold meat takes longer to cook.

Put the pork on a cutting board, and pound with a rolling pin to thin and tenderize it, then cut into about 1¼ × 1½-inch slices.

Put the vegetables in a steaming basket, sprinkle with salt, and steam for 2 to 3 minutes, then keep warm.

Combine the sauce ingredients in a bowl, then add the pork. With your hands, briefly knead the meat as if massaging it. Squeeze out as much of the sauce as possible, then spread the pork over paper towels and pat dry, reserving the sauce for later.

Heat the oil in a large skillet over high heat, and add the pork to quickly brown on one side for 3 to 5 minutes. Turn the pork over, and cook for 2 to 3 minutes, or until it is completely browned, then pour in the reserved sauce, and shake the pan to coat the meat. When the sauce starts to bubble, turn off the heat immediately.

To serve, portion the pork between four individual serving plates, then arrange the vegetables, and spoon the sauce over the pork.

PORK DUMPLINGS
GYŌZA

This is another example of a Chinese-origin food that has been adopted and adapted to become a popular dish on Japanese menus. *Gyōza* skins can be obtained from Japanese or Asian grocery stores; they usually come frozen in packs of twenty-four.

SERVES 4

FOR THE DIPPING SAUCE
⅓ cup soy sauce
¼ cup rice vinegar
few drops of sesame oil
few drops of chili oil

FOR THE DUMPLINGS
1 teaspoon salt
7 ounces spring pointed cabbage (sweetheart lettage), or Savoy cabbage
4 dried shiitake mushrooms
7 ounces lean ground pork
3 garlic cloves, crushed
1 tablespoon finely grated fresh ginger
2 scallions, minced
2 tablespoons soy sauce
2 tablespoons sake
2 teaspoons sesame oil
½ teaspoon ground white pepper
2 tablespoons cornstarch
24 *gyōza* skins
vegetable oil, for cooking

Start by preparing the dipping sauce. Mix all of the ingredients together in a bowl, and set aside.

Cut and discard the hard core of the cabbage and slice into fine shreds. Sprinkle the salt over, then mix and set aside for about 10 minutes, or until the cabbage wilts. Drain and finely chop. Soak the shiitake mushrooms in a bowl of warm water for about 10 minutes, or until soft, reserve the liquid, discard the stems and finely chop the caps.

In a large mixing bowl, place the cabbage, mushrooms, pork, garlic, ginger, and scallions with the soy sauce, sake, sesame oil, pepper, and cornstarch and mix well with your hands.

To form dumplings, hold a *gyōza* skin in your left palm and put about a large teaspoonful of the pork mixture onto the center of the skin. Dip a pastry brush in the reserved mushroom liquid, and moisten the edge of the skin, then fold the skin over the filling into a half-moon shape. Press firmly to seal the edges together by making small pleats. Repeat the process with the remaining skins.

Heat about 1 tablespoon of oil in a large skillet over medium heat. Place the *gyōza* in a circle in the pan, and cook for 5 to 8 minutes, or until lightly browned on one side, then turn over with a spatula. Pour about ½ cup of water over the *gyōza,* and immediately cover with the lid to steam for 2 to 3 minutes. You may do this in 2 to 3 batches, depending on the size of skillet you use. Keep cooked *gyōza* warm in the oven at the lowest setting.

Serve on a large platter or four individual plates, with small dishes of the dipping sauce at the side.

COOK'S TIP

I often make *gyōza* in large quantities and freeze some as they can be cooked directly from frozen. The cooking method is the same as above, just increase the time to 8 to 10 minutes for browning, and 5 to 8 minutes steaming.

PORK AND WHITE RADISH STEW
BUTANIKU TO DAIKON NO KONBUNI

Pork contains ten times more vitamin B1 than beef, which helps to transform carbohydrate into sugar, and convert it into energy. B1 is a vital nutrient to maintain brain health and concentration, and to help fatigue recovery. This slow-cooked stew is great comfort food on dark winter nights. Serve with crusty bread, or plain boiled rice.

SERVES 4

14 ounces *daikon*, giant white radish
21 ounces pork belly
2 postcard-size pieces of dried kelp, pierced a few
    times with a knife to make for better infusion
1 onion, cut into 1¼-inch thick rings
4 tablespoons sake
3 tablespoons light soy sauce
1 tablespoon sugar
strong mustard, to serve

Cut the radish into 1-inch thick rings, then into half-moon pieces and bevel the edges for a neater appearance, as straight edges are likely to crumble during simmering. Cut the pork into 1-inch cubes.

Put the radish pieces in a saucepan, and cover with water. Cook over high heat, and when the water begins to boil, with small bubbles rising to the surface, add the pork, and parboil for about 5 minutes, or until the pork is creamy white.

Drain the pork and radish, and rinse off any scum under hot running water, then drain.

Place the kelp in a casserole, add the radish and pork, and the remaining ingredients, along with 3⅓ cups of water, then cook over medium heat. Do not let it reach a rapid boil, but reduce the heat to low to simmer gently for about 1 hour.

Divide between four individual dishes, without the kelp, and serve with a dab of mustard on the side.

SLOW-ROAST PORK BELLY WITH FUJI APPLE SAUCE

Although roasting a large piece of meat is not typically part of Japanese cooking, pork belly is wonderful for roasting and easy carving. Slow-cooking ensures tender, yet not at all greasy, results. Fuji apples were originally developed in Aomori prefecture, the region renowned for apples in 1936, and introduced to the market in the 1960s. They are sweet, aromatic, and crisp, and hold together well during cooking.

SERVES 4 TO 6

2¼ to 2¾ pounds boneless pork belly, skin on
4 teaspoons vegetable oil
1 tablespoon coarse sea salt or salt flakes
2 carrots, pared and roughly chopped
1 parsnip, pared and roughly chopped
1 leek, trimmed and roughly chopped
4 garlic cloves, bruised
scant 1 cup sake
1 tablespoon cornstarch mixed with
   1 tablespoon water
salt and freshly ground black pepper

FOR THE APPLE SAUCE
2 Fuji or 4 Gala apples, peeled and diced
2 teaspoons grated fresh ginger and its juice
scant ½ cup mirin
2 tablespoons rice vinegar
sugar and salt, to taste

COOK'S TIP
If you can't find Fuji apples, use Gala instead

Preheat the oven to 475°F. Score the pork skin, taking care not to cut into the flesh. Drizzle 2 teaspoons of the oil all over the skin, and rub in the salt.

Grease a roasting pan with the remaining oil, and add all the vegetables. Sit the pork on top, and place on the top shelf of the oven for 15 to 20 minutes. Carefully take the roasting pan out of the oven, and reduce the temperature to 325°F. While you wait for the oven to reach the correct temperature, let the roasting pan stand to cool down a little, before pouring in the sake and a scant 1 cup of water. Return the pan to the middle shelf of the oven, and cook for an additional 3 hours.

Meanwhile, prepare the apple sauce. Put all the ingredients in a saucepan with 3½ tablespoons of water, and cook over low heat, stirring occasionally, for about 20 to 30 minutes, or until the apple pieces are soft, but not mushy—they should still hold their shape. Adjust the seasoning with sugar and salt if needed, and set aside.

When the pork is cooked, remove from the oven and transfer to a carving board. Cover loosely with foil and rest for 10 to 15 minutes before carving.

While the meat is resting, tip the vegetables and juices from the roasting pan into a fine-meshed strainer placed over a bowl. Press down to extract as much flavor and juice as possible, using a wooden spoon. You should have about ⅔ cup of liquid. Allow the liquid to sit for 10 to 15 minutes, so that the fat separates. Spoon off as much fat from the surface as possible, and discard. Transfer into a saucepan, and heat over medium heat, then stir in the cornstarch mixture, and bring to a gentle boil for about 2 minutes to thicken. Adjust the seasoning to taste.

Carve the pork into chunky slices, and serve with the gravy and apple sauce.

DEEP-FRIED PORK
TONKATSU

Tonkatsu, deep-fried breaded pork cutlet, is one of the most popular meat dishes in Japan. Like tempura, another famous deep-fried dish, it was originally imported from the West, but has been modified. In Japan, it is normally served with a generous amount of finely shredded raw cabbage. It is also accompanied by *tonkatsu* sauce, a thick brown sauce, based on Worcestershire sauce, which is available ready-made in bottles, or you can make your own by following the recipe below.

SERVES 4

FOR THE PORK

6 slices white bread, crusts removed
4 (4 to 5-ounce) slices of pork loin or tenderloin, about ¼-inch thick
¾ cup all-purpose flour
2 eggs, lightly beaten
4½ cups vegetable oil, for deep-frying
salt and freshly ground black pepper

FOR THE TONKATSU SAUCE (OPTIONAL)

2 tablespoons white sesame seeds
1 tablespoon superfine sugar
3 tablespoons tomato ketchup
3 tablespoons Worcestershire sauce
1 tablespoon soy sauce

TO SERVE

21 ounces spring pointed cabbage (sweetheart lettage) or flat leaf cabbage, finely shredded
1 lemon, cut into 4 wedges
mustard, optional
plain boiled rice

Start by making bread crumbs (ready-made *panko*, Japanese bread crumbs, are available, but homemade are infinitely better and cheaper) by breaking each slice of bread into smaller pieces. Spread the pieces out on a baking sheet and leave to dry for about 10 to 15 minutes. When they are semi-dry, rub between your palms to crumble. Place the crumbs in a shallow dish.

Meanwhile, prepare the *tonkatsu* sauce. Lightly toast the sesame seeds, transfer to a mortar and grind to form a coarse paste. Put the paste in a mixing bowl, add the rest of the ingredients, mix well, and set aside.

Season the pork with salt and pepper. Make some incisions in the meat between the pink lean part and the white fat—this is tendon, which will tighten when cooked. Lightly dust the pork with flour.

Put the eggs in a shallow dish, pierce the pork on one end with a bamboo skewer or fork, and dip the slices in the egg, coating both sides of each piece. Transfer the pork to the bread crumbs and coat on both sides.

Heat the oil to 340°F in a heavy-bottomed saucepan or a deep-sided skillet over medium heat. You may want to preheat the oven at its lowest setting to keep the cooked pork warm. Carefully submerge one or two breaded pork slices into the oil to deep-fry for 6 to 8 minutes, or until the surface turns golden yellow turning once or twice. Lift the pork out of the oil with cooking chopsticks or a pair of tongs holding it almost vertically while keeping its fat side in the oil for 10 seconds, giving the fat a slightly longer deep-frying, while draining the rest. Place on a wire rack to drain, and keep warm in the oven while you cook the rest.

To serve, divide the cabbage in large mounds between four individual plates. Cut the pork crosswise into bite-size slices if you plan to eat it with chopsticks. If you are using a knife and fork, do not bother to cut it. Arrange the pork, resting against the cabbage, and serve with a wedge of lemon and a dab of mustard on the side if you like. The sauce may be poured over the pork and cabbage, or served in small dishes for dipping.

BEEF

In Japan, beef has been eaten for less than 150 years, yet Japanese beef, *wagyū*, has a worldwide reputation for quality. Native cattle have long been used for labor; with their small bodies it was easy for them to move around the rice fields. When the twelve hundred-year prohibition of eating meat was finally lifted in 1872, larger foreign breeds were imported and cross-bred with the native cattle to produce four official breeds of *wagyū*: Black, which accounts for over 90%, Brown, Shorthorn, and No-horn.

A piece of beef is not genuine *wagyū* unless it comes from one of these four breeds, was born and bred in Japan, and conforms to strict criteria. *Wagyū* is a registered brand name, but only in Japan and is neither recognized, nor protected elsewhere. Most so-called *wagyū* beef sold outside Japan is not pure *wagyū,* but is most likely to be "percentage *wagyū, "* so strictly speaking, should be labeled "*wagyū*-style."

Another commonly misused term is *Kobe*-beef. It is a type of *wagyū,* but *wagyū* beef is not necessarily *Kobe*-beef, which is a registered brand name and comes from the Tajima strain of Japanese black cattle. But bloodline is not the only requirement. In addition to being pure Tajima, it has to come from a heifer or steer that was born, raised, and slaughtered within the Hyōgo prefecture, of which Kobe is the capital city. Furthermore, its marbling has to be above a certain grade and have a gross carcass weight of 1,036 pounds or less. With a mere herd of 3,000 certified beef cattle in existence, all in Japan, it is no wonder this beef is so highly prized.

Wagyū beef is characterized by its intense marbling that melts at low temperatures, giving a melt-in-your-mouth feel. The meat is prized for its smooth velvety texture, juicy flavor, and delicate, yet rich taste. These unique characteristics are created by the large proportion of amino acids (the basis of *umami*), and unsaturated fat. *Wagyū* takes time to grow into beef cattle and as raising them is labor intensive it's not suited for mass industrial scale farming, hence expensively priced.

JAPANESE-STYLE STEAK
WITH ONION-MISO SAUCE

The sauce can be made in advance, will keep for 3 to 4 days and is great as a dip with vegetable sticks.

SERVES 4

FOR THE STEAK

4 (5 to 7-ounce) 1 to 1¼-inch thick rump or sirloin steaks
1 tablespoon vegetable oil
salt and freshly ground black pepper

FOR THE ONION-MISO SAUCE

4 tablespoons medium-colored miso
4 tablespoons sake
1 tablespoon soy sauce
1 marble-size piece fresh ginger, grated
1 small garlic clove, grated
4 to 6 scallions, green parts only, finely chopped

TO SERVE

7 ounces mixed salad of arugula and watercress

Take the meat out of the fridge at least 30 minutes before you intend to cook, and allow it to come to room temperature.

Mix together the ingredients for the onion-miso sauce.

Heat the oil in a large skillet over high heat. Season the steaks with salt and pepper just before putting in the pan, and sear for 2 to 3 minutes on each side. Remove the steaks, and set aside on a cutting board, loosely covered with foil, and rest for about 10 minutes. Meanwhile, reduce the heat to low, and add the onion-miso mixture, then stir and warm through. Cut the steaks into ¼-inch thick slices.

Divide the salad mixture between four individual serving plates. Arrange the steak slices on the salad, spoon the onion-miso sauce over, and serve.

JAPANESE-STYLE BURGERS
WAFŪ HANBĀGA

These burgers are light, yet full of flavor. The key to the lightness is in the mixing technique and the steaming. The red soy sauce makes a tasty change to the usual tomato ketchup.

SERVES 4

4 (⅜-inch thick) onion rings sliced
    from 1 large peeled onion
2 tablespoons vegetable oil
4 ounces broccoli, broken into florets
4 ounces cauliflower, broken into florets

FOR THE BURGERS
14 ounces lean ground beef
1½ slices white bread, crusts removed,
    and finely crumbled
4 shiitake mushrooms, stems removed,
    and finely chopped
2 medium-size onions, peeled and minced
3½ tablespoons grated fresh ginger
2 eggs, lightly beaten
4 tablespoons soy sauce
½ teaspoon ground black pepper
2 tablespoons cornstarch

FOR THE RED SOY SAUCE
¾ cup diced carrot
8 ounces canned chopped tomatoes
3 tablespoons mirin
6 tablespoons soy sauce

Put all the burger ingredients in a large bowl and mix well with your hands—try to be light-handed to incorporate as much air as possible, as if you were making pastry. Divide into four equal portions, and form into ovals.

Prepare the red soy sauce. In a small saucepan of boiling water, cook the carrot until soft, and drain. Put the carrot, along with the remaining sauce ingredients, in a food processor, and blitz until very smooth. Set aside.

Heat the oil in a large skillet over medium heat, and cook the onion rings until they are semi-translucent, about 5 minutes. Remove from the pan and set aside.

Using the same skillet, sear the burgers on both sides over high heat for 2 to 3 minutes on each side. Soak up and remove any excess oil in the pan with paper towels. Place the onion rings on top of the burgers, add 4 tablespoons of water to the pan, then reduce the heat to low. Cover with a lid, and steam cook for 8 to 10 minutes.

While the burgers are cooking, bring a saucepan of water to a boil. Add the broccoli and cauliflower florets and cook for 2 to 3 minutes. Drain and keep warm.

Transfer the burgers and onion rings onto four individual serving plates. Arrange the broccoli and cauliflower on the side, spoon the red soy sauce over the burger, and serve.

COOK'S TIP
Red soy sauce keeps for up to a week refrigerated.

BEEF AND POTATO
NIKU-JAGA

You will not find this dish on restaurant menus, but it is arguably one of the most popular simple dishes in Japan with a little naval history. It is said that a young naval cadet, *Heihachirō Tōgō,* (who later became the most admired Japanese naval officer after defeating nearly the entire Baltic fleet in the Russo-Japanese War, 1904–05, and is often compared with Horatio Nelson), developed a taste for beef stew during his stay in England while training with the Royal Navy in the 1870s. On his return to Japan, Tōgō ordered the head chef in the navy to re-create beef stew to feed his sailors. The chef, who had never eaten authentic beef stew, nor could get the vital ingredient of red wine, but with only the admiral's description to go on, had a little choice but to come up with his own interpretation.

SERVES 4

21 ounces waxy potatoes, peeled (see Cook's tip)
2 onions, peeled
1½ tablespoons vegetable oil
14 ounces rib-eye steak, cut into thin slices
scant 1 cup Dashi (see page 29)
4 tablespoons sake
3 tablespoons sugar
1 tablespoon mirin
4 tablespoons soy sauce
peppercress, to garnish

Cut the potatoes into large bite-size chunks, then rinse in water and drain. Cut the onions in half lengthwise, then into ⅜-inch slices.

Heat the oil in a large saucepan. When hot, remove from the heat, and place on a cold damp cloth. Add the meat when the oil stops sizzling—this will help make the pan nonstick.

Return the pan to medium heat, and sauté the beef for 3 to 5 minutes, or until the color of meat turns lighter brown. Add the potatoes and onions, and sauté while shaking the pan for an additional 3 to 5 minutes.

Pour in the remaining ingredients along with a scant 1 cup of water and bring to a boil over high heat. Reduce the heat to medium–high, and continue to cook for about 5 minutes, skimming off any scum that rises to the top.

Reduce the heat to very low, and place a drop-lid (see page 134) on top, then continue to simmer for 8 to 10 minutes. Remove the lid, increase the heat to medium, and cook for an additional 5 to 7 minutes, or until the liquid has reduced slightly.

Remove from the heat, and divide between four individual serving dishes, garnish with a pinch of peppercress, and serve.

COOK'S TIP

There is no golden rule on the choice of potato, and you may prefer to use a starchy variety such as russet—they will crumble in cooking, and thicken the sauce.

JAPANESE-STYLE BEEF BOURGUIGNON

Based on the traditional French *Boeuf Bourguignon*, this adaptation includes smoky dried shiitake mushrooms, sake, and rich earthy miso.

SERVES 4 TO 6

6 dried shiitake mushrooms
2 tablespoons vegetable oil
2¼ pounds stewing beef, cut into 1½-inch cubes
4 slices bacon, chopped
12 shallots, peeled
1¾ cups sake
3 tablespoons dark-colored or red miso
2 tablespoons light or white miso
2 tablespoons sugar
1 teaspoon *sansho* or Sichuan pepper
1 tablespoon grated fresh ginger
3 tablespoons cornstarch mixed with
    3 tablespoons water
a few scallions, sliced on the diagonal, to garnish

Soak the mushrooms in 2½ cups of warm water for about 10 minutes.

Heat the oil in a large skillet over medium heat, and brown the beef in small batches. Do not overcrowd the pan, otherwise the meat will not brown. While the beef is cooking, bring a large saucepan of water to a boil. Transfer the cooked beef into the saucepan, and boil for 1 minute to remove excess oiliness, and drain.

Squeeze the shiitake mushrooms, and reserve the liquid. Cut and discard the stems, and cut the caps into quarters. Using the same skillet in which the beef was cooked, add the bacon, shallots, and mushrooms, and cook over medium heat for a few minutes, or until the shallots are lightly browned, then remove to a plate and set aside.

Put the beef with the mushroom juices and sake in a large saucepan, then bring to a boil over high heat. Reduce the heat to very low, and simmer for 2 hours, partially covered with a lid slightly askew.

When the beef is cooked and soft, and the cooking liquid has been reduced to about one-third, add both types of miso, the sugar, bacon, shallots, and mushrooms. Increase the heat to medium, bring just to a boil, and continue to cook for about 10 minutes. Add the *sansho* pepper and ginger, and stir well to mix. Test the seasoning, and adjust if necessary. Add the cornstarch mixture, stir and simmer for 2 to 3 minutes to thicken the sauce, and serve, garnished with the scallions.

LAMB

Sheep were not introduced into Japan until relatively recently. Even after the meat-eating ban was lifted in the late nineteenth century, and a large number of domestic animals, including sheep, were imported from abroad during the 1870s to boost the domestic meat production, the lack of knowledge, and Japan's warm and humid climate resulted in a dismal failure of sheep-farming. The main purpose of introducing sheep-farming was to secure a domestic wool supply for military uniforms, however farmers in Hokkaido, who kept a small flock of sheep, began to eat the meat.

For the Japanese palate, lamb is too strongly flavored and fatty. It never caught on, even after concerted efforts by both Australia and New Zealand, who were looking for new export destinations when Britain entered the old Common Market in 1973. Just to put it in context, the average Japanese person eats a mere 14 ounces of lamb per year compared to 17 pounds of beef, 33 pounds of pork and 24 pounds of chicken. The average annual lamb consumption in Australia is 38½ pounds per person and 14 pounds per person in Britain.

Although lamb is not a popular choice in Japanese cooking, as the meat is popular elsewhere, I decided to list the following recipes which all have Japanese twists.

LAMB CHOPS WITH SANSHO PEPPER

Sansho, Japanese pepper, is a small, prickly, deciduous, native plant belonging to the mandarin family. Its seed pods are dried and ground, and used as seasoning for its aroma, rather than peppery heat. Although there is no true alternative, Sichuan pepper can be substituted.

SERVES 4

FOR THE LAMB
8 lamb loin chops or cutlets, weighing
   4 to 5 ounces each
2 teaspoons vegetable oil
½ teaspoon *sansho* pepper, or Sichuan pepper

FOR THE SAUCE
3 tablespoons soy sauce
3 tablespoons mirin
1 tablespoon sake
1 tablespoon sugar
1 tablespoon grated fresh ginger
1 tablespoon cornstarch mixed with
   1 tablespoon water

With a rolling pin or a meat mallet, gently pound the lamb chops to an even thickness.

Heat the oil in a large skillet over high heat, and brown the lamb for 2 minutes on each side. Transfer to a wire rack to let excess oil drip off, and loosely cover with aluminum foil to keep warm.

Discard any oil left in the pan, and scrape off any residue stuck to the base. Pour in all the sauce ingredients, except the cornstarch mixture, and bring just to a boil over medium–high heat for 10 to 15 minutes, until reduced by one-third. Add the cornstarch mixture, stirring to thicken. Return the lamb to the pan, and turn to coat in the sauce. Sprinkle over the *sansho* pepper, and remove from the heat.

Arrange the lamb on individual serving plates, drizzle over the cooking sauce, and serve.

GENGHIS KHAN
JINGISUKAN

This famous regional dish from Hokkaidō is named after the twelfth century Mongol warrior, although the dish holds no resemblance to Mongolian food, and was actually a twentieth century Japanese invention. It all began at the turn of the twentieth 20th century, when the government realized the need for home-grown wool for military uniforms, and encouraged farmers in Hokkaidō to keep sheep, and the farmers gradually began eating the meat. It was traditionally cooked on a concave heavy cast-iron griddle with slits. This was heated at the table, and used to cook the lamb and vegetables, which were then eaten with dipping sauce. This recipe is adapted to be cooked in a skillet instead.

SERVES 4

FOR THE COOKING SAUCE
½ onion, peeled and roughly chopped
½ apple, peeled and roughly chopped
2 to 3 garlic cloves
2 marble-size pieces of fresh ginger, peeled
2 tablespoons clear honey
scant ½ cup soy sauce

FOR THE MEAT AND VEGETABLES
1 tablespoon vegetable oil
1 teaspoon sesame oil
2 onions, peeled, and thinly sliced
7 ounces pointed spring cabbage (sweetheart lettage),
   or Savoy cabbage, cut into large bite-size pieces
7 ounces bean sprouts, trimmed
21 ounces lamb steak, cut into thin slices
1 teaspoon toasted white sesame seeds, to serve
salt and freshly ground black pepper

Prepare the cooking sauce by putting all the ingredients in a food processor, then process until smooth, and set aside.

Mix the two oils together, then heat half in a large skillet over medium heat. Add the onions and cook for 5 to 8 minutes, or until softened, then add the cabbage and bean sprouts and cook for 3 to 5 minutes. Season with salt and pepper. Cover loosely with foil to keep warm.

Add the rest of the oil mixture to a separate skillet, and place over high heat. When the pan is almost smoking hot, add the lamb and cook for 2 to 3 minutes, or until just turning brown. Add about one quarter to one-third of the sauce, and stir to coat.

Divide the vegetables between four individual serving plates. Portion the meat, and arrange on top of the vegetables. Spoon the remaining cooking sauce onto the meat mounds. Sprinkle the sesame seeds over, and serve.

COOK'S TIP
It is awkward, but the thin root ends of bean sprouts should be trimmed off, as they taste dusty, and have a stringy texture.

LAMB STEAKS WITH BROILED EGGPLANT

Here I have matched a traditional Japanese method of preparing and smoking eggplant with lamb, a meat not often seen on the Japanese table. The smoky flavor of the eggplant is perfectly paired with the strong-flavored lamb. The number of eggplants is based on average-size eggplants found in the West, so adjust the amount if you are able to source the smaller, slender ones that are similar to those sold in Japan.

SERVES 4

FOR THE MEAT AND VEGETABLES
2 eggplants
1 tablespoon vegetable oil
½ teaspoon sesame oil
4 (7-ounce) lamb steaks
shichimi-tōgarashi, seven-spice chili powder,
    to season
salt and freshly ground black pepper

FOR THE SOY-GINGER SAUCE
1 tablespoon rice vinegar
2 tablespoons soy sauce
1 teaspoon grated fresh ginger

Preheat the broiler to high. Prick the eggplants with the tip of a knife or a skewer, then place under the broiler and cook for 15 minutes, turning regularly until the skin is blackened and wrinkled, and the flesh feels soft to the touch. Put them in a plastic bag, seal, and leave until cool enough to touch. With a bamboo skewer inserted just beneath the skin, slide along the length of the eggplants to remove all the blackened skin. Cut the eggplant into 1½-inch long pieces, and put in a bowl.

Combine all the ingredients for the soy-ginger sauce, then pour over the eggplants and mix to coat. Cover with foil to keep warm, and set aside.

Heat both oils in a large skillet over medium–high heat. Season the lamb with chili powder, and salt and pepper, then cook on each side for 2 minutes for rare, or a little longer if preferred. Transfer the lamb onto a cutting board and loosely cover with cooking foil to keep warm, then rest for 5 minutes. Cut the steaks into large, diagonal bite-size slices.

Divide and arrange the lamb and eggplant between four individual serving plates. Drizzle over any remaining sauce from the eggplants, and serve.

LAMB SHANK
AND POTATO STEW

This unlikely marriage between a Japanese home cooking of *niku-jaga* (see page 191) and an Irish lamb stew works deliciously well.

SERVES 4

28 ounces waxy potatoes, peeled and cut into
   1½-inch chunks
4 (12 to 14-ounce) lamb shanks
1 tablespoon vegetable oil
1¾ cups sake
scant ½ cup soy sauce
2 tablespoons sugar
7 ounces carrots, pared, and cut into large chunks
2 to 3 leeks, cleaned, trimmed, and cut into
   ⅝-inch thick diagonal slices
1 tablespoon rice vinegar
salt and ground white pepper

Bevel the edges of the potatoes by running a small sharp knife along the sharp edges. This is to stop them getting damaged during the cooking. Soak in cold water briefly, to wash off any excess starch, and drain.

Heat the oil in a large heavy-bottomed saucepan over medium heat, season the shanks with salt and pepper, and brown all over for 10 to 15 minutes.

Cover the shanks with 6¼ cups of water, add the sake, soy sauce, and sugar, then bring to a boil over high heat, skimming off any scum that rises to the top. Add the vegetables, partially cover with a lid slightly askew, reduce the heat, and simmer for 1½ hours.

With a slotted spoon, carefully remove the lamb and vegetables, and keep warm while you reduce the cooking juice by about one-third over high heat. Add the rice vinegar, and adjust the seasoning if required.

To serve, divide the lamb and vegetables between four shallow bowls, with a little of the cooking juice spooned over.

MISO-MARINATED
RACKS OF LAMB

Miso is not just for soups, but has many other uses, including marinating and preserving. It also renders meat very tender and flavorsome, as well as removing lamb's strong smell.

SERVES 4 TO 6
2 6-bone racks of lamb, any excess fat trimmed

FOR THE MISO MARINADE
⅓ cup white miso
⅓ cup medium-colored miso
4 tablespoons sake
2 tablespoons sugar
2 garlic cloves, grated, or 1½ tablespoons
   garlic purée

FOR THE BREAD CRUMB MIX
2⅓ cups *panko*, Japanese breadcrumbs
1 teaspoon finely grated lemon zest
2 tablespoons finely chopped flat-leaf parsley
3½ tablespoons butter, melted
salt and freshly ground black pepper

Prepare the miso marinade by mixing all the ingredients together. Spread the marinade over the meaty part of the racks. Place the meat in a non-metallic dish, cover tightly with plastic wrap, and refrigerate overnight.

Preheat the oven to 400°F. Combine all the bread crumb ingredients in a shallow dish and season.

With a clean damp cloth, wipe the bones of the racks to remove excess miso marinade. Then, holding the racks by the bone with one hand, wipe off any excess miso on the meat with your other hand. Put the racks in the dish of bread crumbs, and press down to evenly coat all over with the crumbs.

Place the racks together so that their bones interlock, then stand the racks upright in a small roasting pan. Roast in the preheated oven for 20 minutes. Remove from the oven, and rest for 10 minutes, loosely covered with foil, before carving each rack in half to serve.

HOT POTS NABEMONO

Warm friendship and conviviality are the keynote of *nabemono*, hot pot meals. *Nabemono*, literally translates as "things-in-a-pot," and refers to one-pot dishes cooked at the table, where diners do their own cooking, choosing what they like from big plates of raw ingredients, and cooking it in a communal pot placed at the center of a table.

If a Japanese person says to another, "Come and have a *nabe* with me," this is the ultimate expression of wanting to become friends. He/she is telling you that they like you enough to dip their chopsticks into the same pot and eat food with you. Japanese are quite hygiene-obsessed, and formality-conscious people, but when they want to make friends, they eat food together that is cooked in the same pot. *Nabemono* is the utmost friendliest way of eating.

It is not difficult to imagine how it began—it probably derived from the soup kettle that used to hang over the central open hearth, *irori*, in old farmhouses where families and friends sat around and ate in the olden days.

Nabemono is popular throughout Japan—each region, prefecture, or even family, has its own favorite recipes using local and seasonal produce. For family dinners, *nabe* is particularly suited to letting children participate in cooking. In fact, men who usually stay well away from the kitchen, suddenly want to take control and become *nabe-bugyō*, hot pot sheriffs, just like some Western men at barbecues.

A FEW RULES WHEN PREPARING HOT POT MEALS:

• Use approximately twice the amount of vegetables to fish and meat. This is for aesthetic, as well as balanced nutrition reasons.

• Select ingredients that harmonize in taste and flavor. For example, for mild-flavored fish such as cod and porgy, use vegetables with a similar lightness like Napa cabbage. For strong flavored or oily fish like tuna and salmon, use leeks and onions, but avoid celery, which completely dominates other foods.

• Resist the temptation of using a whole range of your favorite ingredients, but keep it simple and focus on one key ingredient and its taste, while others should work to complement, not to compete.

• Since each ingredient requires different timing for cooking, cut vegetables and fish or meat into pieces of such a size that the overall cooking time is the same. Root vegetables such as *daikon*, giant white radish, turnips, and potatoes, take relatively long cooking times, and therefore, should be parboiled first.

• Some ingredients, like chicken, exude fats and create scum when simmered. Such ingredients therefore should be parboiled beforehand, so that the cooking broth in the pot does not become foam-ridden.

NABEMONO FOR WESTERN DINERS

I have thought long and hard about how to make this quintessentially Japanese table cooking more accessible to non-Japanese cooks. The *nabemono* setup can look intimidatingly elaborate—a simmering pot at the center of a table, a large platter of prepared ingredients beautifully laid out like a flower arrangement, many dishes of condiments, etc., and although it is fun to cook at the table, diners need to know when to take food out of a communal pot and eat. The timing of cooking is important, and Japanese people know this almost instinctively, as they would have had countless numbers of *nabe* evenings since a young age. After many attempts of *nabe* evenings at my home with non-Japanese friends, I have always ended up doing everything. So, I have therefore adjusted several traditional recipes, and instead of cooking at the table, the following recipes are to be prepared in the kitchen, then taken to the table in a pot for diners to serve themselves, just like a big pot of comforting stew.

CHICKEN HOT POT
TORI NO MIZUDAKI

The best way to describe this dish is as Japanese-style *pot-au-feu*, after the famous French recipe. It is vital to parboil the chicken, in order for the cooking liquid to remain clear.

SERVES 4 TO 6

FOR THE CHICKEN BROTH
1 fresh chicken carcass
1 postcard-size piece of dried kelp
2 tablespoons sake

FOR THE MEAT AND VEGETABLES
21 ounces boneless, skinless chicken thigh or breast, cut into ⅓-inch thick bite-size slices
21 ounces Napa cabbage, cut into large bite-size pieces
14 ounces leeks, cut into ⅝-inch thick diagonal slices
8 shiitake mushrooms, stems removed
7 ounces enoki mushrooms, base removed, and separated
2 scallions, minced, to serve
Citrus Soy Vinegar, *ponzu* (see page 51), for dipping

Start by preparing the broth by washing and rinsing the chicken carcass in water to get rid of any trace of blood, then put in a large saucepan with the kelp, sake, and 8½ cups of water. Bring to a boil over high heat. When boiling, take the kelp out, and reduce the heat to low, then simmer for about 1 hour, while skimming off any scum that floats to the top. Strain the broth, and discard the carcass.

Meanwhile, parboil the chicken slices for 2 to 3 minutes in a pan of boiling water, then transfer to a bowl of cold water, and drain.

Put the chicken and broth in a large casserole or a saucepan, and bring to a boil over medium–high heat. When it begins to boil, reduce the heat to low, and skim off any scum from the surface. Add all the vegetables, apart from the scallions, to the casserole, and return to a gentle simmer for 15 minutes.

At this point, you can either take the hot pot to the table, and let your guests serve themselves, or, using a slotted spoon, divide it between individual serving dishes. Whichever way you choose, sprinkle the minced scallions on top, and offer the Citrus Soy Vinegar for pouring over on the side.

COOK'S TIP
The leftover broth is very tasty and would be a shame to waste. In Japan, it is customary to end hot pot meals by adding cooked rice to the leftover broth to make risotto. There should be about 4½ to 6¼ cups of broth left in the pot. Add about 14 ounces cooked rice, return to a boil for a few minutes while stirring, then pour in 2 beaten eggs, and mix, adjust the seasoning with salt and soy sauce to taste, and serve.

COD HOT POT
TARA-CHIRI-NABE

This is one of the standard hot pot dishes eaten in the winter. In order to enjoy cod's understated taste, keep the other ingredients simple.

SERVES 4

FOR THE COOKING BROTH
2 postcard-size pieces of dried kelp
scant ½ cup sake

FOR THE FISH AND VEGETABLES
1 teaspoon salt
21 ounces cod fillet, cut into large bite-size chunks
14 ounces soft silken tofu
7 ounces leeks, cut into ⅜-inch thick diagonal slices
4 scallions
7 ounces spinach, roughly chopped

TO SERVE
Citrus Soy Vinegar, *ponzu* (see page 51), for dipping
shichimi-tōgarashi, seven-spice chili powder, optional

Prepare the cooking broth by putting 5 cups of water in a casserole pot, or a large saucepan, with the kelp and sake, and leave to infuse for 30 minutes.

Meanwhile, sprinkle the salt over the cod, and set aside for 10 minutes. Blanch the cod in boiling water for 1 to 2 minutes, or until the color begins to turn translucent, then transfer to ice water, and drain.

Cut the tofu into 1¼-inch square pieces, and leave in cold water for about 10 minutes, then drain—this prevents the tofu from clouding the cooking broth.

Heat the broth over medium–high heat, and bring to a boil. When it begins to boil, remove the kelp, add the cod and leeks, return to a boil, and skim off any scum that floats to the surface. Reduce the heat to low, cover with a lid, and simmer for 10 minutes.

Meanwhile, cut the scallions into 2-inch lengths, and very finely slice lengthwise. Soak in a bowl of cold water for about 10 minutes, or until they curl. Drain well.

Add the spinach and tofu to the pot, and let the broth return to a boil for 2 to 3 minutes. Remove from the heat, and using a slotted spoon, divide between four serving bowls, garnish with the scallion curls, and serve with Citrus Soy Vinegar to pour over, and chili powder on the side.

COOK'S TIPS

You may try this recipe with other white-flesh fish such as porgy or turbot. Also, why not finish the dinner by adding cooked udon noodles to the broth instead of cooked rice (see page 201). There should be about 4½ cups of broth left in the pot. Cook 7 ounces dried udon noodles as described on page 77, and add to the pot. Bring the pot to a boil over medium heat, cook for 3 to 5 minutes, and adjust the seasoning with mirin and soy sauce if required.

MIXED HOT POT
YOSE-NABE

Yose means putting things together, and as the name implies, there is no fixed set of ingredients for this popular hot pot.

SERVES 4 TO 6

1 postcard-size piece of dried kelp
1½ teaspoons salt
14 ounces porgy fillet, cut into bite-size pieces
7 ounces boneless, skinless chicken thighs or
    breast fillets, cut into bite-size pieces
3 tablespoons mirin
2 tablespoons soy sauce
8 tiger shrimp, shelled and deveined
2 leeks, cut into ⅜-inch thick diagonal slices
7 ounces Napa cabbage, cut into bite-size pieces
1 carrot, pared and cut into ¼-inch thick slices
8 shiitake mushrooms, stems removed
14 ounces firm tofu, cut into 1¼-inch cubes

Put the kelp and 5 cups of water in a large casserole pot and leave to infuse for 30 minutes.

Sprinkle ½ teaspoon of salt over the fish and leave to stand for 10 minutes. Parboil for 2 to 3 minutes, and transfer into ice water and drain.

Bring another saucepan of water to a boil, and parboil the chicken for 3 to 5 minutes or until the color changes to opaque cream. Plunge into cold water then drain.

Add the mirin, soy sauce, and 1 teaspoon of salt to the pot with the chicken and bring to a boil over medium–high heat. Remove the kelp and discard. Scoop out any scum that floats to the surface. When just boiling, reduce the heat to medium, add the fish, shrimp, vegetables, and tofu, then cover with a lid and simmer for about 10 minutes.

To serve, either bring the pot to the table and let your guests serve themselves or divide between four individual bowls with some cooking broth.

TUNA HOT POT
NEGIMA-NABE

The name of this hot pot is an abbreviation of *negi*, spring onion, and *maguro*, tuna. It is hard to believe but some 250 years ago when tuna was plentiful, fatty belly of tuna was considered a cheap inferior cut while residents of Edo, old Tokyo, prized the lean back part for their favorite sushi. This dish was invented as a cheap food for ordinary people. I use leeks instead of the traditional scallions because Japanese scallions are much larger than their Western counterparts and more similar to leeks.

SERVES 4

14 ounces tuna steak
4 thin leeks
scant ½ cup sake
scant ½ cup soy sauce
4 tablespoons sugar
shichimi-tōgarashi, seven-spice chili powder,
    to serve

Cut the tuna into ⅜-inch thick bite-size slices. Cut the leeks into 1¼-inch long pieces.

Put the leeks, with the remaining ingredients and 1¾ cups of water, in a casserole pot and bring to a boil over medium–low heat. When the broth begins to boil, add the tuna and cook for 3 to 5 minutes.

Divide between four individual serving bowls, and serve with the seven-spice chili powder on the side.

VARIATION
You may also try this recipe with yellowtail.

NOODLE HOT POT
UDON-SUKI

This noodle hot pot is one of the Osaka region's favorites, and where people pride themselves as true gourmets. The key to success is to use thick, robust udon noodles, or I found thick Tuscan pasta called *pici* also makes an excellent substitute.

SERVES 4

1 postcard-size piece of dried kelp
4 dried shiitake mushrooms
14 ounces dried udon noodles
7 ounces chicken breast fillets, cut into
   thin bite-size slices
scant ½ cup soy sauce
scant ½ cup mirin
scant ½ cup sake
4 Napa cabbage leaves, thinly sliced
1 *agedōfu*, deep-fried tofu, thinly sliced
4 tiger shrimp, shelled and deveined
4 scallops without roe
2 scallions, thinly sliced on the diagonal
shichimi-tōgarashi, seven-spice chili powder,
   to serve

Put the kelp and dried shiitake mushrooms with 5 cups of water in a large saucepan, then leave to infuse for 30 minutes.

Bring a saucepan of water to a rapid boil, then add the udon noodles, and stir to separate the strands. When the water begins to rise to the top, add a cup of cold water, and let it return to a boil again. Immediately remove from the heat, drain and rinse under cold running water, and drain again.

Parboil the chicken for 3 to 5 minutes, or until the color changes to opaque cream, rinse in cold water, and drain.

Take the softened shiitake mushrooms out of the broth, and squeeze as much liquid as possible, remove the stems, and cut the caps into thin slices.

Return the mushroom slices to the broth, and add all the remaining ingredients, except the noodles and scallions, then bring to a boil over medium–high heat. When it begins to boil, reduce the heat to medium, add the noodles, then let it return to the boil for 2 to 3 minutes.

Turn off the heat, and sprinkle the scallions over, then divide between four individual bowls, and serve with the chili powder.

SALMON AND MISO HOT POT
ISHIKARI-NABE

This famous regional favorite of Hokkaidō, the northernmost island of Japan, contains local produce such as salmon, onions, and potatoes. The name of the dish derives from the river *Ishikari*, where salmon returns to spawn.

SERVES 4

14 ounces waxy potatoes such as red or new potatoes

1 postcard-size piece of dried kelp

3½ tablespoons sake

3½ tablespoons mirin

2 tablespoons soy sauce

2 onions, peeled, and cut into ¼-inch thick rings

2 carrots, pared, and cut into ¼-inch thick slices

7 ounces Napa cabbage, hard core removed, and cut into bite-size pieces

3 tablespoons white or light-colored miso

heaping ½ cup red or medium-colored miso

3½ tablespoons butter, softened

14 ounces salmon fillets, cut into ¾-inch thick chunks

4 tablespoons salmon roe mixed with 2 teaspoons sake, optional

Peel and cut the potatoes into large chunks, then bevel all the edges and soak in cold water to wash off excess starch, and drain.

Put the kelp, sake, mirin, soy sauce, onions, potatoes, and 5 cups of water in a large casserole pot or saucepan, cover with a lid, and bring to a boil over medium heat. When the broth begins to boil, remove the kelp, and reduce the heat to medium–low, then simmer for 12 to 15 minutes, or until the potatoes are nearly cooked through. Add the carrots and cabbage, and continue to cook for 10 to 12 minutes.

In a small bowl, mix the two types of miso and the butter together with a little broth from the pot to soften, and stir the mixture into the pot. Add the salmon, and let the pot return to a gentle simmer. Cook for 3 to 5 minutes, or until the salmon is just cooked.

To serve, divide between four individual serving bowls and, if using, spoon the salmon roe mixture on top.

SIDE DISHES

SIDE DISHES FUKUSAI

A perfectly balanced meal should consist of three parts—主食, *shushoku*, a staple to provide the main source of energy in the form of carbohydrates like rice, then 主菜, *shusai*, a main dish to provide protein such as fish or meat, accompanied with 副菜, *fukusai*, side dishes. The main purpose of side dishes is to provide vitamins, minerals, and fiber to help the smooth, healthy workings of the body. The main ingredients for side dishes are vegetables, mushrooms, and seaweeds. One important rule in putting a Japanese menu together, is that a side dish should not be cooked using the same method as for the main dish—for example, if the main dish is deep-fried like *tonkatsu* or tempura, then side dishes should ideally be oil-free items like salads or simmered dishes. Although in supporting roles, as well as providing nutrition, side dishes also add taste and flavor, and texture and color to complement main courses.

QUICK CUCUMBER PICKLE

Japanese people love pickles, and there are literally countless types of pickles, using a variety of preserving materials such as salt, rice bran, rice vinegar, or soy sauce. Some pickles take days or even months to make, while others are quicker. Instant pickles, like this, make ideal side dishes.

SERVES 4

2 tablespoons fresh ginger, peeled and julienned
3½ tablespoons soy sauce
3½ tablespoons sake
½ teaspoon chili oil
4 to 6 Lebanese cucumbers, weighing
    about 14 ounces

Mix all the ingredients, except the cucumbers, in a large glass bowl, and set aside.

Cut and discard the ends off each cucumber. With a rolling pin, lightly beat and bruise the cucumbers then break into rough bite-size pieces with your hands.

Bring a saucepan of water to a boil, and place the cucumbers in a heatproof strainer. Lower the strainer into the boiling water and blanch for 2 to 3 minutes in small batches. Drain and shake off excess water, and immediately transfer into the bowl of pickling sauce and mix well.

The cucumbers are ready to eat after 30 minutes, but the flavors will develop if left overnight. The cucumbers, left in the pickling sauce, will keep for up to 5 days refrigerated.

PAN-FRIED ASPARAGUS WITH SOY AND SESAME

Asparagus, although a relative newcomer to Japanese cuisine, is loved for its taste, and prized for its tantalizingly short season.

SERVES 4

12 to 16 asparagus spears
1 tablespoon sesame oil
2 tablespoons sake
2 teaspoons soy sauce
1 teaspoon white toasted sesame seeds, to serve

Asparagus has a natural breaking point below which it is stringy and inedible—hold a spear between your hands, then bend until it breaks, and discard the lower part. Cut each trimmed spear into 1½-inch lengths.

Heat the oil in a skillet over medium heat. Add the thicker lower part pieces of asparagus first, followed by the rest, shaking the pan to toss, and cook for 2 to 3 minutes. Add the sake and soy sauce, and continue to cook while still shaking the pan, until most of the liquid has evaporated.

Turn off the heat, then sprinkle the sesame seeds over and serve.

SALT-SQUEEZED NAPA CABBAGE
HAKUSAI NO SHIO-MOMI

Shio-momi, salt-squeeze, is one of the easiest and quickest method for preparing vegetables. Another bonus is that there is no need for washing-up.

SERVES 4

18 ounces Napa cabbage
2 teaspoons salt

Using your hands, roughly tear off the leafy part of the cabbage from the thick white stem, and keep them separate. Cut the leaves into 1½-inch wide pieces. Cut the stems diagonally into ⅜-inch wide slices.

Put the leaves in a ziplock plastic bag, and add 1 teaspoon of salt. Seal with plenty of air and shake to distribute the salt evenly inside the bag.

Put the stem slices in another ziplock bag, add the remaining teaspoon of salt, reseal and shake. For each bag, open the seal slightly to let all the air out, then reseal, and hold the bag between your hands and squeeze as if you are massaging it for 2 to 3 minutes, or until the cabbage becomes wilted and soft.

Cut a little hole on the bottom corner of each bag, and drain as much of the salty liquid as possible.

Add the leaves into the stem bag, mix, and then divide between four portions to serve.

NEW POTATO TUMBLE
SHINJAGA NO NIKKOROGASHI

In this, one of my grandma's and mother's recipes, the sweetness of new potatoes is enhanced by a soy-caramel sauce.

SERVES 4

1 tablespoon vegetable oil
21 ounces baby new potatoes, skins on, scrubbed clean
2 tablespoons sugar
2 tablespoons sake
2 tablespoons mirin
4 tablespoons soy sauce

In a skillet large enough for the potatoes to sit in a single layer, add the oil. Set over medium heat, add the potatoes, and stir-fry for about 5 minutes while shaking the pan constantly.

Add the sugar and continue to stir-fry for 2 to 3 minutes.

Add the remaining ingredients, and cover with a lid, then continue to cook for 10 to 12 minutes over very gentle heat, while turning the potatoes occasionally to ensure even cooking.

Remove from the heat, and with the lid on, give the pan a shake. Leave for 5 minutes to steam before serving.

SWEET-SIMMERED FAVA BEANS

In Japanese, fava bean is written *soramame*, literally sky bean, because its pod grows upwards. It is eaten simmered or deep-fried as an accompanying dish, or dried, then deep-fried as a snack.

SERVES 4

2¾ pounds fava beans in pods or 14 ounces frozen baby fava beans
½ teaspoon salt
2 tablespoons sake
2 tablespoons mirin
2 tablespoons sugar
1 tablespoon light soy sauce
1 tablespoon cornstarch mixed with
    1 tablespoon water

Fresh fava beans in pods typically yield only a quarter of their weight when shelled. Shell the fava beans and remove their skins—this is awkward, but the result is well worth the extra effort. Or alternatively use frozen baby fava beans.

Bring 2¼ cups of salted water to a boil over medium heat, add the beans, and cook for 3 to 5 minutes. Add the remaining ingredients, except the cornstarch mixture, and let it return to just below a boil. Reduce the heat to low, and simmer for about 3 minutes. Stir in the cornstarch mixture and simmer for 1 to 3 minutes, or until the sauce thickens.

Remove from the heat, divide between four small bowls with some cooking juices, and serve.

OKRA IN SESAME VINEGAR WITH NORI
OKURA NO NORI-GOMASU AE

Okra, *okura*, originates in Africa, and is known to have been cultivated in the ancient Egypt. It became popular in Japan around the 1960s. Its characteristic stickiness derives from pectin, which helps to regulate healthy digestion, as well as lowering cholesterol and blood pressure.

SERVES 4

7 ounces okra
1 teaspoon salt
2 tablespoons Sesame Vinegar (see page 52)
2 teaspoons soy sauce
1 sheet nori, crushed into small pieces

Bring a saucepan of water to a boil. Lay the okra on a cutting board and sprinkle with the salt. Gently roll them around with your hands—this gets rid of fluff, and preserves the color. Blanch in the pan for 2 to 3 minutes, then drain, and immediately plunge in a bowl of ice water and drain. Pat dry thoroughly with paper towels.

Cut and discard the stem ends, then chop into about ¼-inch thick slices. In a medium-size non-metallic bowl, mix the okra with chopsticks or a fork, until it becomes sticky, then add the sesame vinegar and soy sauce, and mix well to combine. Add the crushed nori pieces, and lightly mix just before serving.

SOY-BUTTERED CORN

This simple dish makes a tasty accompaniment for barbecued meats.

SERVES 4

2 corn on the cob, halved
2 tablespoons butter, melted
1 teaspoon superfine sugar
4 teaspoons soy sauce
salt

Preheat the broiler to high. Line a broiler tray with foil.

Put the corn in a large saucepan, and cover with mildly salted water. Bring to a boil over high heat, and cook for 5 to 7 minutes. Drain, and put the corn on the metal rack of the lined broiler tray.

Mix the butter, sugar, and soy sauce together, and brush generously over the corn. Place under the broiler to cook for 5 to 8 minutes while turning and basting regularly, until slightly blistered.

Brush any remaining butter mix over the corn, and serve immediately.

ROAST PUMPKIN GINGER MASH

Kabocha, pumpkin, has a naturally sweet taste, which is further enhanced by roasting. This side dish goes particularly well with rich roasted meats.

SERVES 4

2¾ pounds pumpkin or winter squash,
    quartered and seeded
1 tablespoon vegetable oil, mixed with
    1 teaspoon toasted sesame oil
1 teaspoon sea salt
2 tablespoons unsalted butter, softened
1 tablespoon light soy sauce
1 teaspoon finely grated fresh ginger
salt and ground white pepper

Preheat the oven to 400°F.

Brush the inside of the pumpkin with the oil mixture, then sprinkle the sea salt over. Place the pumpkin, skin side down, in a roasting pan and roast for 50 to 60 minutes, or until very tender.

Scoop the flesh from the skin and put in a bowl. Add the butter, and mash until very smooth. Add the soy sauce and ginger, then season to taste with salt and pepper. Serve warm.

GREEN AND YELLOW PEPPER KINPIRA

Kinpira is the name of a fictional puppet theatre character from the eighteenth century, who was renowned for his mighty strength. But no one knows exactly how the name became synonymous with this shallow-fried dish.

SERVES 4

1 tablespoon sesame oil
2 green bell peppers, quartered, seeded, and cut into strips
1 yellow bell pepper, quartered, seeded, and cut into strips
2 teaspoons sugar
1 tablespoon sake
1 tablespoon soy sauce
a pinch of red pepper flakes or *shichimi-tōgarashi*, seven-spice chili powder

Heat the oil in a skillet or wok over medium–high heat and stir-fry the peppers for 1 to 2 minutes.

Add the sugar and stir, followed by the sake and soy sauce. Reduce to medium–low heat, and continue to cook, stirring, until the juice has been slightly reduced.

Turn off the heat, sprinkle over the red pepper flakes, and serve either hot or at room temperature.

LEEKS IN GINGER MISO

Japanese use several different types of scallions, and this recipe is based on one using *naga-negi*, long-onion or sometimes called *shiro-negi*, white-onion, and as the names suggest it has a longer white part. The nearest equivalent is leeks, which go particularly well with pork or chicken dishes. Pickled ginger is typically served as a digestive condiment.

SERVES 4

2 leeks, cleaned and trimmed
2 tablespoons medium-colored miso
1 teaspoon sugar
1 tablespoon soy sauce
1 tablespoon rice vinegar
1 tablespoon pickled ginger, drained and finely chopped

Cut the leeks diagonally into ¼-inch thick rings. Put the leeks in a saucepan, just cover with water, and bring to a boil over medium heat. Reduce the heat to low, and simmer for 10 to 12 minutes.

Meanwhile, mix the remaining ingredients in a small bowl.

Turn off the heat and drain briefly, so that the leeks are still quite wet, then return to the saucepan. Add the ginger miso and mix well. Divide into four equal portions, and serve warm.

SOY-STEEPED MUSHROOMS

I am delighted to see more and more Japanese mushrooms are sold in supermarkets. And here is a quick and easy way of serving them as a tasty side dish.

SERVES 4

10½ ounces mixed mushrooms such as shimeji, enoki, and shiitake

½ red onion, peeled and thinly sliced

1 tablespoon rice vinegar

2 tablespoons soy sauce

1 teaspoon toasted sesame oil

½ teaspoon toasted white sesame seeds, to garnish

Both shimeji and enoki mushrooms come clustered and joined at the base—cut and discard the bases and separate. Cut and discard the stems of the shiitake mushrooms and split the caps in half, by hand.

Bring a saucepan of water to the boil and blanch the mushrooms and onion slices for about 3 minutes and drain. Transfer the mushrooms to a bowl then add the vinegar, soy sauce, and sesame oil and mix to incorporate evenly. With the back of a spoon, flatten the top surface of the mushroom mixture and leave to stand for 15 to 20 minutes to marinate.

Divide between four individual bowls, garnish with the sesame seeds, and serve at room temperature.

CAULIFLOWER AND BROCCOLI IN MUSTARD MISO

Seasoned miso adds extra taste and flavor to what is otherwise rather bland boiled vegetables.

SERVES 4

7 ounces cauliflower

7 ounces broccoli

salt

FOR THE MUSTARD MISO

2 teaspoons wholegrain mustard

4 tablespoons white or light-colored miso

1 teaspoon sugar

2 tablespoons rice vinegar

Cut the broccoli and cauliflower into large bite-size chunks.

Bring a saucepan of mild salted water to a boil over high heat and add the cauliflower. Wait for the water to return to a boil before adding the broccoli to blanch for 1 minute. Drain.

In a large bowl, mix all the miso ingredients together. Add the vegetables and mix to coat evenly.

Divide into four portions and serve warm, or at room temperature.

ASPARAGUS WITH WHITE SESAME DRESSING

Dutch traders first introduced asparagus to Japan as an ornamental plant nearly two hundred years ago. Asparagus contains a lot of asparagine, a kind of amino acid that aids fatigue recovery and boosts stamina.

SERVES 4

12 asparagus spears
1 teaspoon salt
2 tablespoons White Sesame Dressing (see page 50)

Hold one asparagus spear at a time between your hands, bend until it snaps, and discard the lower end. Repeat the process for the remainder of the asparagus. Cut each spear into 1½ to 2-inch long pieces. Put the asparagus pieces in a medium-size mixing bowl, sprinkle salt over, and gently rub them together with your hands.

Bring a saucepan of water to a boil, add the asparagus to blanch for 2 to 3 minutes, and drain. Then plunge them into a bowl of ice water and drain again. Pat them dry with paper towels.

Put the asparagus in a mixing bowl, add the sesame dressing, and toss. Divide into four portions and serve.

COOK'S TIP

If you are storing fresh asparagus for a few days, wrap in damp newspaper, and stand upright in the refrigerator.

ROLLED NAPA CABBAGE AND SPINACH WITH SESAME SOY

For a side dish, this recipe calls for a little extra effort of rolling, but the result is very elegant, and guaranteed to impress your guests. This goes well with broiled fish or chicken dishes.

SERVES 4

4 leaves Napa cabbage
½ teaspoon salt
7 ounces spinach
3 tablespoons toasted white sesame seeds
1 tablespoon sugar
2 tablespoons soy sauce
1 teaspoon red pickled ginger, to garnish, optional

Bring a saucepan of water to a boil, and holding the cabbage leaves together with your hand, submerge from the lower end first, for 2 minutes, then remove and drain, reserving the water. Sprinkle with the salt, and leave to cool. Use the same water to blanch the spinach for 1 minute. Transfer to a bowl of ice water to cool. Drain.

On a bamboo rolling mat, place the cabbage leaves overlapping, while alternating the top and bottom sides. Put the drained spinach in a cylindrical shape on top of the cabbage and roll tightly, then set aside in the mat.

Put the sesame seeds in a *suribachi*, a ribbed Japanese mortar, and finely grind. Add the sugar and soy sauce and mix well. If you do not have a *suribachi*, use a normal mortar and pestle.

Unroll the mat, and cut the cabbage roll into eight pieces (see page 245). Place on the side of four individual serving plates. Drizzle the sesame soy sauce over each piece, top with the pickled ginger to garnish, and serve.

SIMMERED RADISH WITH EGG MISO
FUROFUKI-DAIKON TO TAMAMISO

This is one of the most popular home-cooked winter dishes.

SERVES 4

21 ounces *daikon*, giant white radish
1 postcard-size piece of dried kelp
shichimi-tōgarashi, seven-spice chili powder,
   or red pepper flakes, to garnish

FOR THE EGG MISO
heaping ¾ cup red miso
½ cup sugar
1 egg yolk
2 tablespoons mirin
2 tablespoons sake

Peel and slice the radish into eight round ¾ to 1¼-inch thick pieces, and bevel the edges. Beveling the edges is both for a neater appearance, and to prevent crumbling during cooking. Put in a saucepan, cover with plenty of water and bring to a boil over high heat, reduce the heat to medium, and cook for 10 to 15 minutes, or until the radish is cooked through, but still firm. Remove from the water and drain.

Make a few incisions in the kelp to help it infuse, and place in a saucepan that is large enough to sit all the radish pieces in a single layer. Put the radish on the kelp, and add just enough water to cover. Cover with a drop-lid (see page 134) or circle of baking parchment with a vent on top. Bring to a boil over medium heat, then reduce the heat to low, and continue to simmer for 30 to 40 minutes, or until it softens and becomes slightly translucent.

Meanwhile, put all the egg miso ingredients in a saucepan, and cook over gentle heat, while constantly stirring with a rubber spatula, for 4 to 5 minutes. Remove from the heat, and let it cool down to room temperature.

Divide the radish between four individual serving dishes. Top with a generous teaspoonful of egg miso, and a sprinkle of chili powder, then serve hot.

COOKS TIP
The egg miso keeps in an airtight container in the refrigerator for up to a month.

DESSERTS

DESSERTS

In Japan, there is no tradition of serving sweet food as the last course. Instead, seasonal fruits (which are listed as *mizu-gashi*, literally "water-sweets") may be served, or on more formal occasions, traditional Japanese confectionery with *matcha*, powdered green tea. However, these sweets are not considered part of the meal. In Japan, the classic meal ends on a savory note, with a bowl of miso soup, and rice with a few slices of pickles at the side. There is no direct equivalent of dessert in the Japanese cuisine.

Yet the Japanese adore *kashi*, confectionery, of all sorts, both Japanese and Western-style. Traditionally, *kashi* are enjoyed between meals and otherwise called *o-yatsu*, (the old-fashioned clock reading referring to between 2 and 4pm). They are nearly always accompanied with normal drinking tea like *bancha* or *sencha* (see pages 241 and 242).

Before Chinese characters were introduced, Japan had no written language. The Japanese ate two meals a day, and in between, either fresh or dried fruit. So, when writing was brought over, they used the word for confectionery 菓子 *kashi*, which derives from the word for fruit ,果実 *kajitsu*. Notice how similar the two first characters are 菓／果. This is because originally the two characters were the same, and the term, *kashi* meant fruit. The distinction between fruit and confectionery was made when Chinese confections known as Chinese fruit were introduced. These *tōgashi*, Chinese fruit, were made of ground grains or soybeans, salted, kneaded, and deep-fried in oil, and were the precursors of Japanese sweets, *wagashi*. Although sugar was introduced in 754 A.D. the Buddhist monk Ganjin, for centuries it remained a luxury, used only occasionally by the aristocracy and high priests for medicinal purposes. It was not until the middle of the sixteenth century that sugar was used by more than a fraction of the population, and not until the nineteenth that its use spread among the ordinary people.

The capital moved from Nara to Kyoto in 794 A.D. and the Chinese confections came to be served at both Shinto and Buddhist ceremonies and feasts, as offerings to gods and deities. To this day, in the vicinity of many temples and shrines, one can find local specialty confections made the same way for centuries.

A Zen Buddhist monk, Eizai (1141 to 1215 A.D.) is credited for introducing tea and tea ceremonies as a part of the Zen way. And as the tea ceremony developed and flourished, Japanese confections, *wagashi*, most notably *manjū*, sweet bun and *yōkan*, firm sweet adzuki bean paste, began to find their way into the kitchens of the ordinary people.

The next significant development came when Japan began trading with the Portuguese and Dutch in the sixteenth century, and Western confections such as *kasutera*, sponge cake, and *konpeitō*, sugar candy were introduced. Called *nanba n-gashi*, literally southern barbarian sweets, they were distinctively different because of their use of ingredients such as eggs, sugar, butter, and flour, and had a considerable influence on Japanese confectionery thereafter.

In 1603 A.D., Tokugawa Ieyasu established a new government in Edo (present-day Tokyo), and laid the foundations of the powerful shogunate, which lasted about two hundred sixty years. The policy of *sankin-kōtai*, literally "alternate attendance," was designed to strengthen the power of the ruling Tokugawa shogunate by requiring feudal lords to travel every other year between their dominion and Edo. The policy not only reinforced the central power, but also contributed to the development of the domestic transport. At the same time, Japan barred all foreign ships except the Dutch, and became isolated from the rest of the world. The over-two-century-long isolation resulted in the establishment of Japanese culture and identity, and food was no exception. Japanese food as we know it today, was largely established during the Edo period.

Then came the Meiji Restoration in 1868. Japan opened its doors and began eagerly consuming all things from the West, including food. The biggest change in the Japanese food culture was that the nation began eating meat again after 1200 years.

Today, the Japanese distinguish between *yōgashi*, Western confectionery that typically uses dairy products and wheat flour, and *wagashi*, indigenous Japanese sweets made from fruits, tubers, beans, nuts and seeds, seaweeds, and rice flour. Both types of confectionery, along with many hybrid creations, are enjoyed with the accompaniment of green tea (both normal drinking tea and ceremonial *matcha*), Indian tea, or coffee.

Wagashi, Japanese sweets, can be divided into three distinct types:

NAMAGASHI, RAW CONFECTIONS: As the name implies, these sweets are to be eaten within a few days of making. The category includes delicate, fresh jellies and pastes, and doughs made of various starches, or *mochi*, soft rice cakes formed into dumpling shapes, and often containing sweet adzuki bean paste. They may be eaten with normal drinking green tea, or *matcha*, strong powdered green tea.

HAN-NAMAGASHI, HALF-RAW CONFECTIONS: These sweets are made to last longer than the raw ones, and more often than not, are associated with a specific region of Japan, and made with special local ingredients.

HIGASHI, DRY CONFECTIONS: These sweets come closest to what one would call candies and cookies, and the water content must be less than 20 percent. The category also includes *senbei*, rice crackers, which are savory. However, the term most commonly refers to the little confections used in the tea ceremony, which are made from rice flour and sugar, colored and pressed into small decorative molds. The best quality sweets are made with *wasanbon* sugar and those from Kyoto are particularly famous.

Because the notion and the role played by confections in the Japanese cuisine is so very different from the Western food culture, choosing recipes in this chapter was especially challenging. The aim of this book is to get you to start cooking Japanese food in your kitchen, so I decided to adapt Japanese confections and their ingredients into Western-style desserts.

YUZU TOFU CHEESECAKE

Tofu is such a versatile ingredient with the bonus of being low in calories and fat. So here is a cheesecake that you can enjoy, without feeling too guilty.

MAKES ONE 8-INCH CHEESECAKE

FOR THE BASE
14 squares graham crackers
3½ tablespoons unsalted butter, melted, plus extra for greasing
2½ tablespoons soft brown sugar

FOR THE FILLING
7 ounces soft silken tofu
¾ cup cream cheese
¼ cup superfine sugar
2 tablespoons *yuzu* juice
1 tablespoon gelatin powder sprinkled over 2 tablespoons water
blueberries and raspberries, to serve, optional

Line an 8-inch diameter springform cake pan with baking parchment, and grease with butter.

Roughly break up the crackers, put them in a plastic bag, and crush with a rolling pin, to form fine crumbs. Mix the cracker crumbs with the melted butter and sugar. Spoon the crumb mixture into the bottom of the pan. Then using the back of the spoon, evenly spread and press down.

Wrap the tofu in a clean dish towel, and squeeze to drain, until it has the same consistency as soft cream cheese. Put the tofu, cream cheese, sugar, and *yuzu* juice in a bowl, then, with an electric hand blender, mix well until smooth. Heat the soaked gelatin in the microwave on high for 30 seconds and combine with the tofu mixture.

Pour the tofu mixture onto the crumb crust, and spread evenly. Top with some berries, if using, then place in the fridge until ready to serve.

COOK'S TIP
Instead of graham crackers, try 1⅛ cups ginger snap crumbs.

YUZU CRÈME BRÛLÉE

Refreshing *yuzu* juice gives this French classic dessert a wonderful Japanese twist. I am delighted to see *yuzu* juice sold in small bottles in some larger supermarkets.

SERVES 4
1¾ cups heavy cream
4 extra large egg yolks
4 tablespoons superfine sugar, plus extra to top
2 tablespoons *yuzu* juice
berries such as raspberries, strawberries, or blueberries, to serve, optional

Preheat the oven to 300°F.

Bring the cream to a boil in a saucepan over high heat, then remove from the heat as soon as it begins to boil.

Meanwhile mix the eggs, sugar, and *yuzu* juice in a heatproof bowl, and whisk until pale.

Pour the slightly cooled cream into the egg mixture, mix well, and divide between four small ramekin dishes.

Stand the ramekins in a baking pan, and pour in enough water to come halfway up the sides of the ramekins.

Bake in the oven for about 30 to 35 minutes, until softly set. To test, gently sway the ramekins—the surface of the custard should be beginning to set around the edge, but wobble like jelly in the middle. Do not let it set too firm.

Lift the ramekins out of the baking pan, and set aside until cool enough to handle, then place in the fridge to chill for a few hours.

When ready to serve, sprinkle over enough superfine sugar to thinly cover the surface of the créme brûlée. Sprinkle over a little water. Then, with a cook's blow torch, brown the sugar, holding the flame just above the surface and moving it around to brown evenly. Serve with some berries.

MOUNT FUJI

An adaptation of the famous French dessert, Mont Blanc, using meringues and sweet adzuki bean paste.

SERVES 4
FOR THE MERINGUES
2 extra large egg whites
heaping ½ cup superfine sugar

FOR THE TOPPING
7 ounces mascarpone cheese
7 ounces lowfat quark
1 tablespoon superfine sugar
1 teaspoon *matcha*, green tea powder

FOR THE FILLING
4 tablespoons *an*, sweet adzuki bean paste
confectioners' sugar, to serve

Preheat the oven to 300°F. Line a baking sheet with parchment paper.

Put the egg whites in a large stainless steel or copper bowl, and whisk using an electric hand whisk on low speed for 2 to 3 minutes until foamy. Increase the speed to medium and whisk for an additional minute. Increase to high, and continue whisking until the whites are stiff, then begin adding the sugar, a tablespoonful at a time, until the mixture is stiff and glossy.

Divide the meringue mixture into four and spoon onto the baking sheet, spacing them evenly. Then, using the back of a tablespoon, hollow out the centers. Place on the middle shelf of the oven, and bake for 30 minutes. Turn off the oven, and leave the meringues in the oven until they are completely cool.

Put the mascarpone, quark, and sugar in a bowl, and mix until the sugar is completely dissolved. Sift in the green tea powder, then mix until it is evenly combined. To assemble, first spoon the sweet adzuki paste into each meringue, top with the mascarpone mixture, then dust with the confectioners' sugar and serve.

BLACK SESAME ICE CREAM

Black sesame seeds give this ice cream a rich nutty taste, and a dramatic dark appearance. It is made easier if you can source the ready-made sesame paste from Japanese or Asian stores.

SERVES 4 TO 6

1¼ cups 2% reduced fat or whole milk
1¼ cups heavy cream
4 extra large egg yolks
¾ cup superfine sugar
¼ teaspoon salt
2 tablespoons black sesame paste (see below or use ready-made from a Japanese store)
1 teaspoon vanilla extract
black sesame seeds, to garnish

Heat the milk and cream in a medium saucepan over medium heat to just below a boil.

Put the egg yolks, sugar, and salt in a medium heatproof bowl, and beat until pale. Then slowly begin to pour the hot milk mixture into the yolk mixture, while constantly stirring. Do not hurry this process, otherwise the eggs may curdle.

Pour the mixture back into the pan, and place over medium–low heat. Cook for 10 to 12 minutes, stirring the mixture, until it is thick enough to coat the back of a spoon. Add the black sesame paste and vanilla extract, then mix well, and set aside to cool completely.

If you have an ice cream maker, put the mixture in and follow the manufacturer's instructions. But if you are not using an ice cream maker, put the mixture in a plastic container with a lid, place in the freezer, and keep stirring every 30 minutes for 3 to 4 hours.

Serve with a sprinkling of sesame seeds.

BLACK SESAME PASTE

MAKES ABOUT ¾ CUP

¾ cup black sesame seeds
1 tablespoon clear honey

Dry toast the sesame seeds in a nonstick skillet over medium heat until they start to pop. (They may be sold ready toasted, but it is worth refreshing them.) Immediately transfer the seeds into a *suribachi*, a ribbed Japanese mortar, and grind for 30 to 45 minutes or until you have a smooth paste. Add the honey, and continue grinding until evenly mixed. The paste will keep for 3 to 4 weeks refrigerated in a sterilized jam jar.

MATCHA ICE CREAM

With a hint of bitterness from the *matcha*, this ice cream not only looks beautifully green, but also tastes fresh and rather sophisticated. The powder is sold in a small tin, and lasts up to a year, but once opened, store refrigerated.

SERVES 4 TO 6

1¼ cups 2% reduced fat or whole milk
1¼ cups heavy cream
4 extra large egg yolks
¾ cup superfine sugar
¼ teaspoon salt
1 tablespoon *matcha*, green tea powder
a few mint leaves, to garnish

Follow the same process of making a custard mixture as for Black Sesame Ice Cream (opposite), until just before adding the sesame paste.

In a small bowl, mix the *matcha* with 3 tablespoons warm water, and stir well to form a smooth paste.

Add the tea paste to the custard and milk mixture, and stir well until it is completely combined, and the color appears uniformly light green, then set aside to cool.

If you have an ice cream maker, put the mixture in and follow the manufacturer's instructions. But if you are not using an ice cream maker, put the mixture in a plastic container with a lid, place in the freezer, and keep stirring every 30 minutes or so for 3 to 4 hours.

Serve decorated with the mint leaves on top.

YUZU SORBET

Yuzu, a Japanese citron, is used mostly for its zest and juice, which has an unforgettable delicate refreshing aroma and taste. The juice is sold in small bottles and it is expensive, but well justified for its flavor.

SERVES 4 TO 6

heaping ½ cup superfine sugar
3⅓ cups warm water
4 tablespoons *yuzu* juice
thinly sliced strips of lemon zest, to garnish

FOR THE MERINGUE
2 extra large egg whites
3¼ tablespoons superfine sugar

Put the sugar and warm water in a stainless steel mixing bowl, and mix until the sugar is completely dissolved, then add the *yuzu* juice. Set aside to cool. When it has cooled down to room temperature, place in the freezer until it begins to freeze around the edges—this will take 1½ to 2 hours.

Beat the egg whites in a separate stainless steel or copper mixing bowl until soft peaks form, then slowly add the sugar, a scant tablespoonful at a time, and continue to beat until the mixture becomes thick, glossy, and forms stiff peaks when the whisk is lifted.

Stir the meringue into the semi-frozen sugar mixture to incorporate, then return to the freezer for an addditional 2 to 3 hours, stirring every 30 minutes.

Serve decorated with a few strips of lemon zest on top.

BLACK SESAME PANNA COTTA

Panna Cotta is one of my favorite Italian desserts—here I've given it a Japanese twist. You can buy ready-made black sesame paste from Japanese stores, but it is easy to make with a bit of elbow grease.

SERVES 4

2 teaspoons gelatin powder
1⅛ cups whole milk
1⅛ cups heavy cream
1 tablespoon superfine sugar
2 tablespoons Black Sesame Paste (see page 232)

Put 2 teaspoons of cold water in a small bowl and sprinkle over the gelatin. Leave to soak for 5 to 8 minutes.

Meanwhile, put the milk, cream, and sugar in a saucepan, and heat over medium heat, taking care not to let it boil over. Add the sesame paste and soaked gelatin, mix well, then return just to a boil, and simmer for 3 to 5 minutes.

Remove from the heat, and set aside for about 10 minutes to cool slightly, then pour into four heatproof individual glasses. Stand to cool further, before placing in the fridge to chill for 3 to 4 hours, or until set.

VARIATION

Instead of sesame seeds, try this with a tablespoon of *matcha* (green tea powder). Sift a tablespoon of green tea into a bowl with 2 tablespoons of milk and add to the panna cotta mix once slightly cooled. Mix well to ensure it is evenly combined.

KYOTO TIRAMISU

Like many foreign dishes that have been adopted by the Japanese, tiramisu has been remodeled using green tea and sweet adzuki bean paste.

SERVES 8 TO 10

4 eggs, separated
¾ cup superfine sugar
10½ ounces mascarpone cheese
1 tablespoon *matcha*, green tea powder, plus extra for dusting
scant 1 cup warm water
36 small ladyfinger cookies
10½ ounces *an*, sweet *adzuki* bean paste
3 tablespoons sake

Whisk the egg whites in a clean, dry, stainless steel or copper mixing bowl until soft peaks form.

In a separate large bowl, beat the egg yolks with the sugar until the mixture is light and fluffy, and leaves a ribbon trail when dropped from the whisk. Add the mascarpone, and blend until the mixture is smooth. Fold the egg whites into the mascarpone mixture.

Sift the green tea powder into a medium-size bowl, and whisk in the warm water, little by little. Dip half the ladyfingers, enough to cover the base of a 2½-inch deep 10-inch square dish (about 2 quart capacity), into the tea—they should be fairly well-soaked, but not so much that they break up. Arrange in a tightly packed layer in the bottom of the dish.

Mix the bean paste with the sake to soften. Spread half the bean paste mixture over the ladyfinger layer as evenly as possible using the back of a spoon. Then spread half the mascarpone mixture over the adzuki layer. Add another layer of soaked ladyfingers, and then another layer of adzuki and mascarpone, smoothing the top layer neatly. Put about a teaspoon of *matcha* in a small strainer, and dust over the top just before serving. Serve in small portions, as this is a very rich dessert.

TOKYO ROLL

This is a Japanese variation on the jelly roll.

SERVES 6 TO 8

½ cup superfine sugar, plus extra for dusting
¾ cup all-purpose flour, plus extra for dusting
10g *matcha*, green tea powder (about 5 teaspoons)
4 extra large eggs
scant 1 cup heavy cream
3½ ounces *koshi-an*, smooth sweet adzuki bean paste
confectioners' sugar, for dusting

Preheat the oven to 350°F. Grease and line a 15 × 10-inch jelly roll pan with baking parchment. Dust with a half-and-half mixture of sugar and flour.

Mix the flour with the green tea powder and sift two to three times to ensure there are no lumps.

Put the eggs and sugar in a bowl, place over a pan of simmering water, and whisk, using an electric hand whisk, until pale and creamy, and thick enough to leave a trail on the surface when the whisk is lifted.

Remove the egg mixture from the heat, then sift half the green tea-flour mixture over, and gently fold in with a metal spoon. Repeat with the remaining flour mixture, then lightly stir in 1 tablespoon of hot water.

Pour the mixture into the prepared pan, then tilt the pan backwards and forwards to spread the mixture evenly. Bake in the oven for 10 to 12 minutes, until well-risen, and firm to the touch.

Meanwhile, place a large sheet of waxed paper on top of a clean, damp dish towel. Dredge the paper thickly with superfine sugar.

Working quickly, turn out the cake onto the paper, trim off the crusty edges, and let it cool down.

While the cake is cooling down, whisk the cream until soft peaks form. Spread the cream over the cake, and add a line of adzuki bean paste along the long edge nearest to you.

Roll up the cake, starting from the long edge with the bean paste, with the aid of the paper. Make the first turn firmly, so that the whole cake will roll evenly, and have a good shape when finished, but roll more lightly after the first turn.

Place the cake, seam-side down, on a cutting board, dust with the confectioners' sugar, then slice and serve.

KINAKO AND BLACK SESAME CUPCAKES

Kinako, parched soybean flour, is aromatic and has a pleasant nutty flavor. It is used for making traditional Japanese confectionery, and is available in small packs in Japanese stores.

MAKES 12

4 ounces (1 stick) unsalted butter, at room temperature
heaping ½ cup superfine sugar
2 eggs, lightly beaten
8½ tablespoons self-rising flour
heaping ¼ cup *kinako*, soy flour
2 teaspoons baking powder
1 to 2 tablespoons 2% reduced fat or whole milk, as needed
2 tablespoons black sesame seeds

Preheat the oven to 350°. Line a 12-hole muffin pan with paper cupcake cases.

Cream the butter and sugar in a bowl until fluffy and pale. Then beat in the eggs, a little at a time.

Put the flours and baking powder in a fine-meshed strainer and sift over the butter mixture, then fold in with a large metal spoon, adding a little milk until the mixture is of a dropping consistency.

Spoon the mixture into the paper cases, filling them up to about halfway. Sprinkle the sesame seeds on top.

Bake in the oven for 12 to 15 minutes, or until golden brown on top, and a toothpick inserted into one of the cakes comes out clean.

Remove from the oven, and set aside to cool for 10 minutes, then remove from the pan, and cool on a wire rack. Eat within 1 to 2 days of making.

MATCHA JELLY

This is an easy, yet highly sophisticated and visually stunning dessert.

SERVES 4

1 tablespoon *matcha*, green tea powder
2⅛ cups warm water
2 tablespoons granulated sugar
1½ teaspoons agar-agar powder, dissolved in 1 tablespoon cold water

Sift the green tea powder into a medium-sized bowl then add 3½ tablespoons of the warm water, and mix well until there are no lumps.

Add the sugar and the agar-agar mixture to the tea, then add the rest of the warm water and stir to mix. Transfer the tea mixture into a saucepan, and heat over medium heat until it reaches just below a boil, then reduce the heat slightly, and simmer for 2 to 3 minutes.

Remove from the heat, and cool down a little before dividing between four wine glasses. Let it cool down to room temperature before placing in the fridge.

Serve chilled.

THREE JAPANESE-STYLE MERINGUES

If you've made the Yuzu Créme Brûlée (page 230) and are wondering what to do with the leftover egg whites, here is the answer.

MAKES 12

4 extra large egg whites, at room temperature
heaping 1 cup superfine sugar
1 tablespoon *kinako*, soybean flour
1 teaspoon *matcha*, green tea powder, sifted twice
½ tablespoon black sesame seeds
whipped cream and berries, to serve (optional)

Preheat the oven to 300°F. Line three baking sheets with baking parchment.

Put the egg whites in a large clean stainless steel or copper mixing bowl. Beat with an electric hand whisk on low speed for 2 to 3 minutes, until the whites become foamy. Increase the speed to medium, and whisk for an additional minute, before increasing the speed again to high, until the whites form stiff peaks. Divide the mixture into three portions, and put each into a clean mixing bowl. Also divide the superfine sugar into three equal portions.

Next, whisk one portion of the sugar into one portion of egg white, on high speed, about a spoonful at a time, until the mixture becomes stiff and glossy. Set aside while you repeat the process with the second and third portion.

Sift the soybean flour into the second portion of sugar, then mix and sift the whole mixture again. Now whisk this sugar into the second bowl of egg whites, on high speed, as before, and set aside.

Clean and dry the beaters. Mix the green tea powder into the last sugar portion, and sift the whole mixture once more to ensure an even mixture. Whisk this tea and sugar mixture into the third portion of egg whites on high speed as before.

Spoon four scant tablespoons of each meringue mixture onto the prepared baking sheets, spacing them generously apart. Do not worry if they are not evenly shaped. Sprinkle the sesame seeds on top of the plain (first portion) meringues.

Bake in the middle of the oven for about 1 hour, until the meringues sound crisp when tapped underneath. Turn off the oven, and leave the meringues in the oven until completely cooled.

Serve either on their own, or with whipped cream and berries.

COOK'S TIP
The meringues will keep in an airtight container for up to two weeks.

JAPANESE TEA

Tea originated in China several thousand years ago and was introduced to Japan around the eighth century, when the newly established Imperial court in Nara enthusiastically adopted all things Chinese. Originally regarded as a precious medicine and a stimulant, leaves were crushed and compressed into brick-shaped blocks. The brick was scraped, and shavings dropped into water, which was then boiled vigorously to infuse. Early tea cultivation is not thought to have been very successful, and so tea remained exclusively reserved for the aristocracy and high-ranking Buddhist priests.

Tea was re-introduced in its powdered form (*matcha*) in the twelfth century, brought back by Japanese monks after studying Zen Buddhism in China. By this time, agricultural techniques had developed enough to make tea cultivation more successful, and tea flourished at the same rate as Zen Buddhism, becoming an indispensable part of everyday life but also intertwined with the religion—the vehicle of the spiritual discipline of Zen Buddhism's *chadō*, the Way of Tea.

In the late sixteenth century, *sencha*, leaf tea, was imported from China. Just over one hundred years later, a Japanese tea merchant invented a technique of steaming tea leaves to make green leaf tea, which, because it is simpler to prepare, and less expensive than *matcha*, became popular among ordinary people. *Matcha* remained part of Zen spiritual training, and also became increasingly associated with wealthy merchants, the ruling Samurai class, and the aristocracy.

JAPANESE GREEN TEA

Tea bushes, Camellia, wherever they are grown, are all the same. The difference in color is due to the processing—Japanese tea is green because once the leaves are picked, they are immediately steamed. The steaming destroys an enzyme in the leaf, and stops it from fermenting and turning black, like Indian tea.

TYPES OF GREEN TEA

Japanese tea is divided into two major types: leaf and powder. For leaf tea, steamed leaves are rubbed, either by hand (for top-quality tea) or machine (for lesser quality), while still moist, and as they dry, they curl up into shred-like pieces. For powdered tea, steamed leaves are dried flat, and ground into an extremely fine dust. Leaf tea is for everyday drinking and is quick and easy to make. Powdered tea is more expensive, and whisking it into a froth without making it bitter takes some practice, so it is used for tea ceremonies, which involve a complex ritual, and follow strict rules and etiquette. However, it can also be enjoyed just like a shot of espresso coffee, and indeed, this is how Zen monks sustained themselves during their long, hard training.

All leaf tea belongs to one of the following broad grades with prices dependent on quality:

BANCHA 番茶 is the lowest grade green tea. Consumed in great quantities every day, it is made from larger, more mature leaves that are left after those fit for *sencha* are picked. All *bancha* is good to drink with meals, as it tastes mild and has hardly any aroma, so does not interfere with the taste of food. It is also thirst quenching. The poorer grade of *bancha* is often roasted to enhance flavor and made into *hōji-cha* 焙じ茶, literally "roasted-tea", and the leaf is ebony brown, with a characteristic deep smoky aroma and taste. Because of the roasting, it has less caffeine than other green tea, and is often served after dinner in the evening. Another type of *bancha* is *genmai-cha* 玄米茶, sometimes called "rice-tea", as it is made from *bancha* mixed with grains of roasted popped rice. It is brewed in the same way, and has a slightly nutty flavor.

SENCHA 煎茶 literally means infused tea. The leaves are younger, and more tender than those used for *bancha*, and picking is done with great care, so unlike *bancha*, there are no stems or twigs mixed in. *Sencha* is appreciated for its taste and aroma, and is often served in exclusive restaurants or hotels, and in places of work to visitors of note, while at home, it is served to impress guests and relatives.

GYOKURO 玉露 means "jewel dew", and, as the name implies, it is the top grade. When new buds begin to appear on mature bushes, each bush is sheltered in a slatted bamboo blind to shut out the sunlight for about twenty days, which results in an increase in thiamine, giving the tea its characteristic rounded faintly sweet flavor. When leaves are about three quarters of an inch long, only the top two to three are hand-picked. Rare and expensive, *gyokuro* is savored purely for its flavor, and sipped in small quantities, just as if you are tasting precious dew drops. The initial taste is highly aromatic, and might even be a bit strong, but roll it around inside the mouth and it mellows. Dried *gyokuro* leaves are about five eighths of an inch long, with a thin needle-like appearance, and a uniform deep green color.

HOW TO MAKE A PERFECT CUP OF TEA

There is no one-way-fits-all method in making a perfect cup of green tea as each variety requires different water temperature and infusion periods. However, there is one easy principle to remember; the higher the grade tea, the lower the water temperature, and longer the infusion. While using good-quality tea and following an appropriate method of preparation is paramount to making a good cup of tea, the quality of water is equally important. Do not use water straight from the tap, but instead use soft mineral water, or at least filtered tap water.

The other main type of tea is powdered tea, known as *matcha* (抹茶), green powdered tea, which is made from the same tender leaves that have been cultivated for *gyokuro*, the top grade leaf tea. But instead of hand-rubbing carefully hand-picked leaves into tight needle-like pieces, the steamed leaves are dried flat then ground into a fine powder.

To prepare *matcha*, you need a small bamboo hand whisk called a *chasen* (茶筅) and a bowl. Warm the bowl with hot water, empty, and dry with a cloth. At the same time, soak the bamboo whisk in hot water to prevent the tea powder from sticking and staining it. Add a teaspoonful of tea powder (for the best result, though not ceremonial, sift the powder through a tea strainer) in the middle of the bowl, then add two fluid ounces (about a full espresso cupful) of warm water at 140°F. Whisk with the bamboo whisk in a letter M motion for no longer than 15 seconds. Do not over-whisk as this will make the tea taste bitter.

Japanese green teas are sometimes infused in water or even in ice in summer. *Hōji-cha* and *mugi-cha* (麦茶) roasted barley tea is excellent served chilled, and even *gyokuro* may be steeped in water during hot weather.

Both loose tea and powdered tea should be bought a little at a time, and used within two to threee weeks after opening. It should be stored in an airtight container in a cool, dark dry place or even in the fridge, particularly in the case of powdered tea. Loose tea freezes well, and can be kept in the freezer for up to a year. Defrost, and let the leaves come to room temperature before using.

HEALTH BENEFITS

Various studies show that green tea

- Reduces cholesterol
- Reduces blood pressure
- Reduces risk of cancer
- Reduces blood sugar levels, so Reduces risk of type 2 diabetes
- Increases fat burning, and boosts the metabolic rate
- Protects the aging process, and reduces the risk of Alzheimer's and Parkinson's disease

GETTING THE MEASUREMENTS RIGHT

Type of tea	Amount of tea	Amount of water	Water temperature	Infusing time
Bancha	5 teaspoons	1 cup	194 to 212°F	30 seconds
Hōji-cha	5 teaspoons	1 cup	194 to 212°F	30 seconds
Genmai-cha	5 teaspoons	1 cup	194 to 212°F	30 seconds
Sencha	5 teaspoons	scant 1 cup	175°F	60 seconds
Gyokuro	5 teaspoons	5 tablespoons	140°F	90 seconds

INGREDIENTS AND EQUIPMENT

JAPANESE KITCHEN UTENSILS

If you have a reasonably well equipped kitchen, you shouldn't have to buy a great deal of equipment. A few improvisations may be necessary sometimes, but such things are fun, and should pose no discouragement to adventurous cooks. As the aim of this book is to get you started cooking Japanese food, I have taken a minimalist approach, so the following items are bare essentials. Most are available either in specialist shops, or on the internet. In Japanese kitchens, knives are the most important utensil of all, and so a separate section is devoted to them on page 247.

BAMBOO BASKETS ZARU 笊

For draining, rinsing, salting, tossing, and lots of other food preparation, Japanese cooks have traditionally used bamboo baskets of various sizes and shapes. Although metal and vinyl varieties more like Western colanders or strainers are available, there is something rather satisfying in using a traditional tool made of a natural material. And they make an attractive bread basket when not used for Japanese cooking.

BAMBOO ROLLING MAT MAKI-SU 巻きす

Strips of bamboo are woven together into a mat with strong cotton string. It is used most commonly to make sushi rolls, but also to shape soft ingredients, such as omelets, and to press out excess moisture. The mat usually measures ten inches square. After using, carefully wash under lukewarm water, without any detergent, and allow to dry completely before storing. These are widely available, even in supermarkets.

DROP-LID OTOSHI-BUTA 落とし蓋

The drop-lid is an essential tool in preparing simmered dishes. It not only ensures even heat distribution, meaning flavors penetrate better into the ingredients, but also stops the cooking liquid from reaching a rapid boil, so preventing ingredients being tumbled about and damaged. Traditionally made of wood, it should be slightly smaller in diameter than the pan, so that it sits directly on top of the foods being simmered. Soak briefly before use to stop it sticking to foods.

GRATER OROSHIGANE おろし金

Traditional Japanese graters give much finer results than most Western equivalents. The best ones are tin-coated, double-sided copper graters, that are used by professionals, but they are expensive. The average home cook uses graters made of stainless steel, aluminum, or ceramic, which gives just as good results. Available online or from Japanese stores.

MANDOLINE SLICER

This is a recent addition to the Japanese kitchen and hence, there is no traditional Japanese name for it, although it is often known by the manufacturer's name of "benrīna." It is an efficient tool for shredding and slicing large quantities of vegetables. These are available from kitchen shops.

MORTAR SURIBACHI すり鉢
AND PESTLE SURIKOGI すりこぎ

The traditional Japanese mortar is a sturdy, warm brown-colored ceramic bowl. Inside, it is unglazed and textured, with a combed pattern for a better grip. They come in various sizes from 5½ inches in diameter to more than 12 inches across, but for home use, 9 inches across is the most versatile. Hardwood from the Japanese pepper tree makes the best pestles, but other wood, such as paulownia or willow may be used. A pestle is sometimes sold together with a mortar, but if buying separately, choose one that is twice as long as the diameter of the mortar to be used with. To use, place the mortar on top of a damp cloth to stop it sliding while you work. Add the ingredient to be ground, gradually. Assuming you are right-handed, loosely cap the top of the pestle with your left hand, and hold the pestle about halfway down the length with your right hand, then rotate while pressing down at the same time. To clean the mortar, you may need to use a stiff brush, or the tip of a bamboo skewer once in a while, to loosen any material stuck in the grooves. Available on the internet or from Japanese stores.

OMELET PAN TAMAGOYAKIKI 卵焼き器

Although it is possible to make the Japanese rolled omelet with an average Western round omelet pan, having a rectangular pan makes it easy, and reduces wastage. Professionals use heavy copper pans coated with tin, but for home cooks, Teflon-coated nonstick ones are easier to use and maintain. To clean, wipe with oil-soaked paper towels, then a clean cloth, but never use an abrasive material or detergent. Available online or from Japanese stores.

A TRADITIONAL KITCHEN INHERITANCE

Not essential, but the most symbolic kitchen utensil is the small wooden rice paddle, *shamoji*. It represents domestic authority, and when an older woman hands over her *shamoji* to her daughter-in-law, it symbolizes her wish to pass over management of household affairs, and is also an unspoken admission that the younger woman has finally become the mistress of the house.

KNIVES

Japanese chefs jealously guard their knives, and would never allow anyone else to touch them. Japanese knives are in a different league from their Western counterparts. Like Samurai swords, they are forged of carbon steel, and the blades are thicker, and have only one cutting edge on the right. A single-edged blade cuts faster, much more accurately, and cleaner than a double-edged one, and the thickness of the blade helps to separate each slice. There are three basic types of knives:

CLEAVER DEBA-BŌCHŌ 出刃包丁
This sturdy, sharp pointed, carving knife is used to prepare fish, and to a lesser extent, chicken and meat. They come in different lengths, but on average, measure between 7 to 12 inches.

VEGETABLE KNIFE USUBA-BŌCHŌ 薄刃包丁, NAKIRI-BŌCHŌ 菜切り包丁
This single edged knife is used for preparing vegetables. Although names and shapes differ slightly between Tokyo (rectangular) and Osaka (rounded top front), it does the same job of cutting, slicing, chopping, and peeling. Japanese cooking involves a lot more preparation than Western cooking, as the foods are all designed to be eaten with chopsticks. If you are going to invest in just one Japanese knife, a rounded top front vegetable knife is the one to buy.

SASHIMI KNIFE SASHIMI-BŌCHŌ 刺身包丁
This long, slim-bladed knife is only used to slice boned fish fillets. There are two main shapes; in Osaka, the knife is pointed, and called *yanagi-ba bōchō*, willow-leaf blade, while in Tokyo, it has a square end, and is called *tako-biki bōchō*, octopus slicer. Both come in various lengths ranging from 7 inches to an impressive 16 inches. The reason for the long blade, is in the way the entire length of the blade is used to slice sashimi. The Japanese dislike using the word *kiru*, cutting, because in the Samurai tradition, the word implies killing, so instead, *hiku*, drawing, or pulling is used. You hold the knife pointing up at about a 45 degree angle, and touch the fish with the lowest part (nearest to the handle) of the blade, then bring down the blade,

lightly pressing down and letting the weight of the knife itself do the work, while drawing the knife towards you, using the entire length of the blade all in one go. This smooth one-stroke motion, no up-and-down or sawing movement, ensures each sashimi slice is cleanly cut.

CARBON STEEL VS. STAINLESS STEEL
There are two main materials for knives: carbon steel and stainless steel. While carbon steel knives are always the preferred choice among the professionals, stainless steel knives are popular in the domestic kitchen. Most stainless steel knives are softer than carbon steel knives, and are easier to sharpen, but do not stay sharp as long. Carbon steel is harder than most stainless alloys, but it can also be brittle, so pieces of the knife-edge can break off if it is not used correctly. Another disadvantage of carbon steel knives, is that unless they are wiped dry before storing they can rust easily and quickly. Choosing a knife is highly personal; a knife that feels perfect in someone's hand, whether carbon or stainless steel, may not be the right choice for someone else. So if you want to invest in a knife, first assess how and what you mainly cook, and how much maintenance you are prepared to devote to the knife. A good kitchen shop or, better still, a knife specialist, will be able to advise you on choosing a knife and also teach you how to sharpen and maintain the blade.

SOY SAUCE SHŌYU 醤油

One of the most important primary seasoning ingredients, soy sauce is made of fermented soybeans, wheat, salt, and water. Outside Japan you will find dark, light soy sauce, and tamari. Dark is the general all-rounder used for both cooking and dipping, while light is saltier, and used only for cooking. Tamari is thicker and slightly sweeter, and is used for dipping. It contains no wheat, which is thought to enhance the aroma. Although soy sauce keeps for a long time, it is best kept refrigerated, or at least in a cool dark place, and used within a few months of opening.

RICE VINEGAR SU 酢

Rice vinegar is made from fermented rice or sake lees, and is milder and more fragrant compared to wine vinegar (4.2 to 4.5 percent acidity, opposed to 5 to 10 percent acidity). As one of the key seasoning ingredients in Japanese cooking, it is widely used in many categories—most famously in making sushi rice, *sunomono*, Japanese-style salads, pickles, simmering, and some food preparations. It disinfects, preserves, suppresses saltiness, neutralizes strong odors, tenderizes tough meat, and brightens and preserves colors. It also has many health benefits—it prevents arteriosclerosis, reduces blood pressure, aids healthy digestion, helps fatigue recovery, stimulates healthy appetite, and is even known to slow down the aging process. It is widely available in bottles, but can also be substituted with slightly diluted cider vinegar.

MISO 味噌

A protein-rich salty fermented soybean paste, with a distinctive aroma and flavor. It is one of the most important ingredients in Japanese cooking, and is used in a number of different ways. Read notes on miso on page 36.

MIRIN 味醂

A golden-colored syrupy sweetened wine, often described as "sweet cooking sake," used to add sweetness and glaze. It is made from glutinous rice, rice malt, and *shōchū*, Japanese spirits, and has a 40 to 50 percent sugar content with 14 percent alcohol. Although it has become easier to find, do not try adding sugar to sake as an alternative, but instead just use sugar alone—1 teaspoon sugar is equivalent to 1 tablespoon mirin.

SAKE 酒

Read the note on page 135.

INSTANT DASHI STOCK DASHI-NO-MOTO だしの素

Let's be honest—Japanese home cooks use instant *dashi* all the time, so you shouldn't feel guilty about doing so. Available in either dry form in powder or granules, or as a liquid concentrate, it is sold under the name of *dashi-no-moto*, or *hon-dashi*. The granules contains freeze-dried ground bonito flakes and other ingredients used for making dashi, but it is very strong —1 teaspoon instant dashi powder makes 4½ cups. Liquid dashi is normally 4 to 5 times as concentrated.

AGAR-AGAR KANTEN 寒天

Agar-agar is made from a type of red seaweed called *tengusa*, 天草, meaning "heavenly grass," and has long been used for making traditional Japanese confections. In the West, it has been used as the standard culture medium in research laboratories until quite recently, when its marvelous quality as a jelling agent and its health benefits, began to be recognized.

Agar-agar is about seven to eight times more coagulant than gelatin, sets at 102 to 108°F and melts at 185°F, which means it stays set in the mouth, whereas gelatin melts quite quickly. Agar-agar is completely vegetarian, and has no calories, fat, or carbohydrates, but is rich in both water-soluble and non-soluble fiber, and helps to eliminate toxic wastes out of the body. It is for this quality, recently in Japan, that the agar-agar based diet became popular for weight loss. It is available in sticks, sheets, or powdered form.

KELP KONBU 昆布

This seaweed is one of the two key ingredients of making dashi, the stock on which so many Japanese dishes depend for its subtle flavor. There are many varieties of kelp, and nearly all are harvested off the coast of Hokkaidō, dried in the sun, cut, folded, and packaged.

More often than not, it may be speckled with white powder, which is dried salt and a umami element, so it should never be washed or rinsed, but just wiped with a clean, lightly dampened cloth. Keep in an airtight container, placed in a dry, dark cupboard.

NORI 海苔

Used as a wrapping for sushi, nori comes in standard 7 × 9-inch packs of ten sheets. Also shredded, *kizami-nori*, for use as a garnish, or to be ground to a powder, and as *ao-nori*, also used as a garnish.

Two other types of seaweed commonly used in Japan that are also easy to find elsewhere, are *Hijiki*, which is rich in calcium and iron, and used in simmered or stir-fry dishes. It is sold dried, and looks like black long-grain rice. *Wakame* is also sold dried, and is used mainly in soups, and some salads. Keep in airtight containers in a cool, dry, dark cupboard.

BONITO FISH FLAKES KATSUOBUSHI 鰹節

Bonito, skipjack tuna, a member of the mackerel family, has been fished since very early times by the Japanese. Its fillet is steamed, dried, smoked, and mold-cured to hardwood-like form. The shavings, which have an intense smoky aroma, are one of the two essential ingredients of dashi, as well as being extensively used as a seasoning and a topping for chilled tofu, and in salads. Outside Japan, it is usually sold ready-shaved.

SESAME SEEDS GOMA 胡麻

Oil-rich nutty-flavored seeds come in 3 different colors: white, black, and golden. They are used extensively whole or ground for flavoring, in dressings, and as a garnish. The aroma and flavor intensify when heated, crushed or ground.

PICKLED PLUMS UMEBOSHI 梅干し

This intensely salty and sour red pickled plum is Japan's panacea—it is regarded as a tonic, digestive aid, and believed to keep the intestinal tract clear, and therefore, always appears at the traditional Japanese breakfast. It also stops rice from spoiling, and thus is an essential item in *bento*, the Japanese packed-lunch box. It can be soft and large, or firm and small. As well as being consumed on its own, it also provides refreshing tartness in dipping sauces or salad dressings.

DRIED MINIATURE SARDINES CHIRIMEN-JAKO ちりめんじゃこ

Tiny young sardines and anchovies are boiled, then dried. They are used as calcium-rich toppings, or a garnish in salads, also eaten mixed with grated *daikon* (giant white radish).

SEVEN-SPICE CHILI POWDER
SHICHIMI-TŌGARASHI, 七味唐辛子

There is no fixed recipe for the blend, but it is usually a mix of red chile, *tōgarashi*, *sansho*, tangerine peel, black hemp seeds, black and/or white sesame seeds, and green nori seaweed. It is used as a seasoning to add a kick to many dishes especially udon noodles. Outside Japan, small bottles are easy to find.

SANSHO 山椒

The seed pods of the indigenous Japanese prickly ash belonging to the citrus family, are dried and ground and used as pepper. It is highly aromatic, rather than hot and spicy, and has a slightly numbing effect on the tongue, not dissimilar to Sichuan pepper. The tender young leaves, *kinome*, are used as an aromatic condiment for clear soups, simmered dishes, or salad dressings. Its buds, *hana-sansho*, also provide decorative and aromatic edible condiments for the dipping sauces for *sashimi* and other fish dishes. *Sansho* pepper is sprinkled on broiled eel or chicken to counterbalance the flavor and smell of fat. It is sold in small bottles.

WASABI 山葵

Wasabi is a perennial semi-aquatic plant indigenous to Japan, found both in the wild and also extensively cultivated. The name in Japanese translates as "mountain hollyhock" and has attractive leaves. All parts of the plant are eaten—leaves are made into a refreshing vinegar pickle, while its grated root yields an aromatic and pungent paste, which is an essential accompaniment for sashimi and sushi. It is often inaccurately described as Japanese horseradish. Although it is grown on a small scale in Taiwan, New Zealand, US, and UK, fresh roots are expensive even in Japan and reserved for top restaurants. It is usually sold in dry powder form or paste in tubes. Powdered wasabi needs to be mixed with water, and set aside for about ten minutes to develop flavor before use. Wasabi paste in tubes needs to be refrigerated once opened.

NOODLES

Read the notes on pages 76 to 77.

RICE

Read the notes on page 90.

FRESH INGREDIENTS

BAMBOO SHOOTS TAKENOKO 筍

Takenoko, literally "bamboo's child," is one of the most commonly used ingredients in Asian cooking. Although it has no particular nutritious value other than fiber, it is prized for its mild taste, meaning it can be cooked together with many other ingredients in soups and simmered dishes, and for its crisp texture, especially in deep-fried or stir-fry dishes. Fresh bamboo shoots still covered in layers of brown husks, are welcomed as the edible symbol of the arrival of a new season by the Japanese, although both in Japan and abroad, it is available year-round, ready-cooked either in cans, or vacuum packed in water. Once opened, both canned and water-packed bamboo will keep for up to 10 days if stored in fresh water in a covered container placed in the fridge, with the water changed daily.

BURDOCK GOBŌ 牛蒡

It is only in Japan that this long (20 to 40-inch), thin (¾ to 1¼-inches in diameter) root is eaten as a vegetable, although its seeds are used in Chinese medicine. It has a rather bland taste, and no particular nutritious value, but is eaten for its crunchy texture, and its ability to absorb a wide range of flavors during cooking. The most popular way of cooking burdock is *kinpira-gobo¯*. Fresh burdock can be obtained in Japanese shops—most of the flavor lies just under the skin, so it should be scrubbed clean, rather than peeled. Burdock is typically cut into matchsticks, or shaved like a pencil. Once cut, it must be put straight into a bowl of cold water to stop discoloration. Although available in cans, it has no flavor, and the texture is disappointing. Instead, choose the semi-prepared frozen variety.

GIANT WHITE RADISH DAIKON 大根

Daikon or "great root" is the most cultivated vegetable in Japan. It can measure up to two feet long, be as thick as a girl's leg, and weigh as much as 4½ to 6¾ pounds. Indeed, in Japanese "*daikon-ashi*," *daikon*-leg, is a derogatory expression used to describe a woman with thick legs! Almost all parts of a *daikon* are used—the green leaves for stir-fries and pickles, the peppery upper part for grating and salads, the middle part for simmering and hot pots, and the dried peel to make *kiriboshi-daikon*. Even the tapering root is used for pickles and miso soups. Regarded as a natural digestive, especially for oily foods, *daikon* is always served grated in *tempura* dipping sauce, and with broiled fish. Do not let grated *daikon* stand around for long, as it will emit a rather unpleasant odor. Shredded *daikon* is also an essential accompaniment for *sashimi*. *Daikon* flesh is dense, and needs a long cooking time. Choose *daikon* with tight unblemished white skin that feels dense.

DEVIL'S TONGUE KONNYAKU こんにゃく

Konnyaku, is another candidate for the list of strange foods. A gelatinous paste is made from the starchy root of *Amorphophalus konjac*, which originates in Indonesia, and is made into either slabs or strings. It consists of 97 percent water, and has no calories, and thus is a popular diet food. It is eaten for its slippery, jelly-like texture, and is used as a side ingredient in many simmered dishes. A white or sometimes green slab is sliced thinly, and served as a vegetarian sashimi. Thin strings, called *shirataki*, are essential ingredients in *sukiyaki,* and feature in many hot pot dishes. Both slabs and strings must be parboiled before use. It is sold in water-filled vacuum packs, and can often be found sitting next to tofu in Japanese stores.

LOTUS ROOT RENKON 蓮根

This is actually a rhizome, not a lotus root, that has long been associated with Buddhism—the Buddha always sits on a cushion modeled on a lotus flower. In Japan, it was first mentioned in eighth century poems, and the sub-aquatic plant has been cultivated for both ornamental and eating purposes. It has a fine crisp texture, rather than flavor, is used in salads and tempura dishes, and is simmered and stir-fried. It needs to be boiled in mild vinegared water before use. It is available fresh from Asian stores, semi-prepared in water-pack vacuum bags or in cans (not recommended).

PERILLA SHISO 紫蘇

This tender annual is also called beefsteak plant, grows to about 20 inches high, and comes in three distinct types; the purple leaves, *akaziso*, are used as a natural red coloring for pickles, green leaves, *aoziso*, look deceptively similar to stinging nettles, but have a refreshing astringent taste and flavor, and are used as

an edible decoration for sashimi, in sushi, salads, and in tempura, and rare *kataziso*, which is green on one side of the leaf, and purple on the other. Its sprigs of buds are served with sashimi and also made into a strong flavored condiment. There is no close substitute, so omit from a recipe if not available.

TOFU 豆腐

Read about on tofu on page 156.

YUZU 柚

A yuzu looks like a cross between a lemon in color and a tangerine in appearance. It is not eaten for its flesh, but used widely for its refreshing clean zest, peel, and juice. A little sliver of its peel, a pinch of grated zest, or a drop of the juice in clear soups, simmered dishes, salads, or hot pots, gives the most unforgettable, yet delicate aroma and flavor. The juice mixed with soy sauce and rice vinegar makes a refreshing salad dressing, which is also available ready-mixed as *yuzupon*. Outside Japan, the fresh fruit is rarely available, but the juice is available in small bottles from Japanese shops, and even supermarkets. It is expensive, but well worth the money, and a little goes a long way. Its dried peel is available from specialist spice shops. *Yuzu-koshū*, yuzu-pepper paste, is a regional speciality of *Kyūshū,* and is made of grated zest mixed with green chile and salt. It is used as a spicy condiment for hot pots and noodles.

INDEX

ACKNOWLEDGMENTS

My foremost thanks goes to Kyle Cathie and her brilliant team—Judith Hannam, the editor, and her assistant, Hannah Coughlin—and my agent Clare Hulton. My big special thanks to Emma Lee, the photographer, her assistant Lizzie Mayson, prop stylist Lucy Attwater, and, above all, Aya Nishimura, the food stylist, and her assistants Sian Henley, Iona Blackshaw, Charlottle O'Connell—for striving together to make this book happen. I also extend my gratitude to the copy editor Jane Bamforth and designer Miranda Harvey, and Tim Delaney of Legas Delaney and David Green of Carnell Green for helping me to come up with the title.